# LIVES TOGETHER/
# WORLDS APART

# LIVES TOGETHER/ WORLDS APART

## Mothers and Daughters in Popular Culture

SUZANNA DANUTA WALTERS

UNIVERSITY OF CALIFORNIA PRESS
BERKELEY   LOS ANGELES   OXFORD

The quotation on p. xiii is from "The Envelope," from *The Retrieval System* by
Maxine Kumin. Copyright © 1978 by Maxine Kumin. Used by permission of
Viking Penguin, a division of Penguin Books USA Inc.

University of California Press
Berkeley and Los Angeles, California

University of California Press, Ltd.
Oxford, England

© 1992 by
The Regents of the University of California

Library of Congress Cataloging-in-Publication Data

Walters, Suzanna Danuta.
    Lives together/worlds apart : mothers and daughters in
popular culture / Suzanna Danuta Walters.
        p.   cm.
    Includes bibliographical references and index.
    ISBN 0–520–07851–9 (cloth : alk. paper)
        1. Mothers and daughters. 2. Women in popular culture.
    3. Mothers and daughters—United States. I. Title.
    HQ759.W332   1992
    306.874'3—dc20                                    91–32331
                                                       CIP

Printed in the United States of America
9 8 7 6 5 4 3 2 1

The paper used in this publication meets the minimum requirements of American National Standard for Information Sciences—Permanence of Paper for Printed Library Materials,
ANSI Z39.48–1984. ⊚

*To my mother, Marianne Walters—in glorious enmeshment*

# Contents

# Figures

# Acknowledgments

I am deeply grateful to Stanley Aronowitz, Serafina Bathrick, and Stuart Ewen for their continued and substantive support and encouragement. Each has stuck with me from my earliest days of graduate school through the production of this book. Stanley taught me the joys of theoretical pursuit and has provided me with a constant example of an "engaged intellectual." Stuart initiated me into the delights of teaching and forced me to reckon with the turbulent tides of historical analysis. Both have been great teachers, inspired scholars, and dear friends and colleagues. Particular thanks must go to Fina, whose engagement with this project was a moving reminder of just how exhilarating feminist mentoring can be. To her credit, she never let her stubborn commitment to psychoanalysis intrude on my equally stubborn commitment to its critique. Her warmth, humor, and all-around feminist smarts continue to enrich my life.

Thanks also must go to those friends and family members whose unfailing support through these years kept me rooted in the politics of this research, particularly my dearest friend, Annie Gibeau, whose decade-plus of feminist friendship has so enhanced my life and my work. Literally a midwife, she has undoubtedly been a more figurative midwife to this research. Thanks also to Diane Lopez, Ara Wilson (for her always one-step-ahead mind), Lynn Chancer (for the regular "are you finished yet?" phone calls), Dan Poor, Tam Stoner, and my always supportive sisters, Lisa and Pamela Walters. I am also grateful for the encouragement of my colleagues at Colorado College, particularly Molly Andrews, Adrienne Lanier

Seward, and Margi Duncombe. My heated discussions/arguments with film maven Adrienne (particularly on the two versions of *Imitation of Life*) continue to provide much-appreciated energy, pleasure, and insight. Margi's support as the chair of the sociology department has gone beyond the call of duty and exemplified to me the meaning of feminist leadership. And Molly's exemplary collegiality during the final days of this project provided warm and sisterly encouragement.

My year spent at the Centre for Contemporary Cultural Studies in Birmingham, England, was enhanced by the supervision of the faculty: Richard Johnson, Michael Green, and Maureen McNeil. Elaine Tyler May has been very generous with her time, and her comments on early drafts were thorough, insightful, and always responsive to the goal of contextualizing cultural criticism. I would like to thank erstwhile ready-ear Laurie Leitch for nudging me into grad school and thus setting the stage for this project. I must always acknowledge Joan Cocks, feminist professor extraordinaire at Mount Holyoke College, whose early mentoring indelibly marked my own teaching practice.

I would like to also thank the film archivists of the Museum of Modern Art and the librarians at the Film and Television Division of the Library of Congress for their assistance. My editor, Naomi Schneider, has remained supportive and encouraging throughout this process, and her easygoing style was a welcome contrast to my own obsessiveness. My copyeditor, Sylvia Stein Wright, provided invaluable assistance, as did Erika Büky of UC Press.

My book on mothers and daughters would not be complete without acknowledging my own mother. Although the exact memory eludes me, her own interest in this subject has most assuredly been a catalyst for my investigation. Innumerable discussions over the years—on everything from feminist theory to the politics of Madonna—have kept me continuously on my toes, striving to keep up with a mind that seems infinitely expanding.

But for the presence of my mother, Marianne Walters, this book would not exist. Her example of feminist mothering and our eternal collaboration on a relationship and a life continue to provide the sweet and fragrant food for my heart and for my mind.

> It is true, Martin Heidegger, as you have written,
> I fear to cease, even knowing that at the hour

of my death my daughters will absorb me, even
knowing they will carry me about forever inside them . . .
even as I carry the ghost of my mother under my navel,
a nervy little androgynous person, a miracle
folded in lotus position.

Like those old pear-shaped Russian dolls that open
at the middle to reveal another and another, down
to the peasized, irreducible minim,
may we carry our mothers forth in our bellies.
May we, borne onward by our daughters, ride
in the Envelope of Almost-Infinity,
that chain letter good for the next twenty-five
thousand days of their lives.

Maxine Kumin, "The Envelope"

## Chapter One

# The Sacrament of Separation / The Penance of Affiliation

## On the Subject of Mothers and Daughters

In a film called *'night, Mother,* a mother is trying to prevent her thirtyish daughter from shooting herself. During the climactic scene, the mother, clutching her breast and trying to comprehend her daughter's decision, screams in anguish, "I don't know what I did but I know that I did it!" In an otherwise forgettable film, these few words stand out as poignant and resonate with what we take to be the "truth" about relationships between mothers and daughters. Whatever else occurs between these two women during the evening of the daughter's death, we know—like the mother—that somehow, in some way, she *was* responsible.

Personal experience, always the touchstone for the feminist scholar, reiterates this mixing of love, responsibility, and (all too often) blame that seems to characterize the mother/daughter relationship. Over the years, I (like most women) have had innumerable conversations with other women about their mothers and their daughters. One such conversation occurred one sunny weekend, early on in this project, while I still enjoyed the fantasy of beach-time scholarship. I sat looking out at the turbulent Atlantic Ocean, wondering aloud about the curious fascination that the subject of mothers and daughters holds for so many women. I had been conducting an interview of sorts with a friend—a young woman in her early thirties, professional, very successful in the field of social services, married, mother of two young sons. We had been talking about her relationship with her mother, which she described in less than laudatory terms. Throughout the discussion, one thing struck me: Regardless of how hurt or invalidated she felt in relation to her mother, the *relationship itself* elicited a great deal of thought and concern. She felt, in no uncertain terms, that working out her relationship to her mother somehow held the key to her own identity and emotional health. When I asked her why an adult, mature, successful woman would be so concerned with delving into this relationship above all others, her response was quite telling: "because it's about me."

My friend was not alone, for my own entry into this research was by no means accidental, constructed to a great extent by a deep and abiding relationship with my own mother and our mutual bewilderment at this being considered "deviant" or unhealthy. Upon entering graduate school, I wrote down a fairy tale, a bit of conventional folklore mixed with the anxious thoughts of a young woman curious to figure out the sacrament of "separation" and the penance of daughterly affiliation. It was with these thoughts that I embarked on this study:

> Once upon a time, there was a young woman who loved her mother very much. She thought her the most wise, compassionate, powerful person in the whole world. She dreamed of being just like her when she grew up, and would announce that regularly to anyone within hearing range. She felt quite lucky to have such a parent. As a young child, the girl had been rather wild and impetuous and fought often and vigorously with her mother. And her mother had fought back, often and with vigor. They had struggled only as two people do who recognize sameness and thirst to understand what that means for each other. They had fought—and loved—truly for each other.
>
> As the years went by, the relationship grew and grew, and the possibilities seemed limitless. Yet the girl experienced what in contemporary parlance was called a "double message." Although she learned in school that this relationship was to be the most formative one of her life, that her mother was the "primary nurturer," her "socializer," she was also told, at about age seventeen, that it was time to separate. Being a literal and pragmatic girl, the daughter assumed that meant she must move to another state, so she went away to college many miles away.
>
> The relationship between the mother and daughter continued to

*flourish despite this distance, this "separation." They missed each other regularly and with passion. They had very, very large telephone bills. Yet the daughter kept being told that something was wrong. People didn't seem to understand it when she wanted to spend vacations at home—with her mother. A feminist professor suggested that her mother was "clinging" and "dependent," and she had better watch out. The girl giggled at the thought of her mother clinging to her same-size body like a hothouse vine. She knew her mother would laugh too—it had never been one of their favorite metaphors.*

*It seems her mother experienced a similar phenomenon. She was told to allow her daughter to grow up. She was encouraged to cut the old apron strings. She mused on the fact that she had never had an apron—with or without strings. Maybe that was the problem. Friends were angered at the amount of time she spent with her daughter. Her mother declared that she let her daughter run her life. It wasn't natural, they said. It wasn't healthy.*

*The relationship continued to grow despite these difficulties. The mother and daughter continued to share their lives with each other. And they were happy. But they began to wonder—to each other and in their work and study—why this happiness made so many people so angry and nervous. The mother began to wonder why being a mother was so very different from being a father. And the daughter began to wonder why being "her mother's daughter" was so very different.*

The recognition of shared womanhood expressed in both the beachside chat and the fairy tale is indeed a sharing that remains a highly contentious aspect of our culture. Yet the relationship of mothers and daughters is of interest to all women because it is so much about us as well as about our mothers. Most women feel that, in some vital and fundamental way, working out their relationships with their mothers is central to working out their own issues and problems. Because they too will (in most cases) someday be mothers, understanding how they were mothered plays an increasingly important role in women's development.

If the subject is central to women's individual development, it has also emerged as central to the project of a feminist theory and politics. The feminist theorist Adrienne Rich once wrote, the "cathexis between mother and daughter—essential, distorted, misused—is the great unwritten story."[1] Yet this is not quite true; we *do* know the patriarchal mother/daughter stories, always playing cliched melodrama to the epic narrative of mothers and sons. In our culture, mothers and daughters are the slightly tawdry "B" movies to the deMille extravaganzas of mother/son passion and torment. Never achieving the stature of the Oedipal spectacle, the mother/daughter nexus nevertheless wanders through our cultural landscape in a sort of half-light, present and persistent but rarely claiming center stage.

This cultural landscape is increasingly defined by the overwhelming presence of the mass media. We live in a world not only characterized by vast economic and political changes, but increasingly marked by the influence of the mass media. In a world saturated, perhaps even dominated, by the image, it is close to impossible to understand any given interaction without reference to the multitude of mass-produced images that often seem like only so much background noise to the "real" business of "social forces." Mothers and daughters come to understand their relationship not only through the exigencies of family life, economic survival, and social policies, but through the systems of representation and cultural production that help give shape and meaning to that relationship.

In elaborating the social construction of the mother/daughter relationship, the question of representation immediately emerges as central, for the relationship of mother and daughter does not simply materialize onto the social field, nor is it produced only through the machinations of explicit social policies and social theories. Rather, the mother/daughter relationship is formed, at least in part, by the cultural images that give it meaning. Indeed, when we go to the movies, read a novel, see a television sitcom, or open the pages of a women's magazine, we are presented with vivid and often contradictory images that provide us with a variety of messages concerning our behavior and self-image as mothers and daughters. Films like *Terms of Endearment*, television programs like "Maude," and popular books like *My Mother/My Self* furnish us with examples of mother/daughter interactions that contribute to our understanding of our own affiliations. The relationship of mother and daughter is located in *culture* in the most fundamental sense, where issues of gender, genre, and generation intersect and interact.

## A Curious Confluence: Women, Media, and Social Change

The years from 1945 to the present are crucial both for the history of women and for the history of the media; in this period, we witness the development and elaboration of a women's movement that has critically challenged our very sense of what it means to be women and men in the modern world. Arguably, no social movement in recent years has so altered and challenged human arrangements—from personal relationships to public policies. Concurrently, within these last forty-five years, the institutions of the mass media, particularly television and the associated technologies of video and cable, have seemingly come to dominate our public discourse about everything from politics and national elections to fashion and family life.

These postwar years have therefore witnessed a critical intersection of feminism and the mass media. An examination of the changes in the representations of mothers and daughters during this period will reveal the multiple and often contradictory ways the media shape the consciousness of our personal relationships. In addition, analyzing these images will help us understand the activity of the media as a force *mediating* our view of social movements, particularly the women's movement.

This is an especially important historical moment in which to rethink the way our culture represents the mother/daughter relationship. Whatever one calls it—backlash, revision, rerouting— the women's movement is in the midst of an undeniably trying time. In this period of backlash and revisionism, the popular narrative of the history of the contemporary women's movement goes something like this: In the beginning, our newly awakened anger and astonishment at the realities of our own oppression caused us to take positions that were "extreme." One of these extreme positions was the radical rethinking of motherhood as the sole fulfilling role for adult women. But now, as the popular pundits would have it, we have emerged from the dark angry night of early women's liberation into the bright dawn of a "postfeminist" era. The personal history of feminist pioneer Betty Friedan is instructive here. In her first, ground-breaking book, *The Feminine Mystique,* Friedan bemoaned the state of American womanhood, overeducated for the menial and unfulfilling role of "housewife/mother" that was forced upon her with vigor since the end of World War II. She urged women into the work force, into careers, as the only way to develop fully and liberate themselves.[2] She was the model for my mother's generation. Her words spoke to a generation who felt some vague malaise, sensed a grave injustice, but were unable to find a voice or a name for it. That name is sexism.

But by the early 1980s, Friedan was singing another tune, wondering aloud if we hadn't perhaps gone a bit too far, bemoaning now not the state of imprisoned womanhood, but the sorry lack of family life. After all, she seemed to ask, isn't motherhood what women *really* want after all? In *The Second Stage*, Friedan recanted and railed against those feminists who still thought that the family was a central site of women's oppression.[3]

For Friedan and others, we may have come a long way (baby), but we've still got a long way to go (back). This era, we are told, has its own set of problems. We are being punished for "wanting it all": "Superwoman syndrome" and "Cinderella complex" are the watchwords that construct a female identity in crisis, a subjectivity at war with its own history, a woman bereft. As popular wisdom would have it, contemporary women are now caught in the binds their foremothers unwittingly made for them: In renouncing traditional values of mom and apple pie (especially mom), today's woman is a lost soul, a career woman who, in climbing to the top, has lost touch with that essential part of her femaleness: motherhood.

Two popular films of the late 1980s say it all. In one, *Fatal Attraction,* the bad woman is the childless, single, professional woman who seduces the innocent family man and tellingly attempts to blackmail him with a fantasized pregnancy. The good woman is, like old times, the good mother. In the other, Diane Keaton in *Baby Boom* lets us all know the deep dissatisfaction of women at work and lays bare the budding mama lurking behind every gleaming corporate desk. These films are meant to speak to us, the daughters of feminism. They are warnings, pleadings, urgings: Don't become the women your mothers fought for you to be.

Mothers and mothering are central in this new dialogic of female angst. The immensely popular *My Mother/My Self* and the more recent work of Colette Dowling, *The Cinderella Complex* and *Perfect Women,* tellingly point to our relations with our mothers as setting the psychic stage for our tendency to "love too much," as Robin Norwood would have it, or our inability to recognize that we can never "have it all."[4] These and other popular treatises have located unloving/too loving mothers as the ultimate cause of their daughters' neuroses and unhappiness. In this age that has declared itself "postfeminist," we are most assuredly returning to the days of Philip Wylie's infamous "momism," first given voice in the 1940s.

## The Frames of Psychology and the Lessons of History

It is time, therefore, for a reexamination, a rethinking of this relationship that for so long has been relegated to the footnotes of masculine history. It is undoubtedly an important historical period in which to reconsider the subject of mothers and daughters, and there are several outstanding reasons that demand this reexamination. In the first place, as many feminist critics, particularly Adrienne Rich, have noted, the mother/daughter relationship has been either ignored or mystified by mainstream, male-dominant scholarship. If the history of the world has been written largely by men, then sons are going to figure more prominently than daughters and fathers more than mothers. The story of mothers and daughters thus requires reconsideration as a revision or amendment of male-defined scholarship and history.

Second, the mother/daughter relationship is a central nexus between women: If part of the feminist insight has been that women are too often defined and understood solely in terms of their relationship to men, then it is important for us to begin to stress that women's lives are also shaped and impacted by their interaction with other women, particularly other women in the family.

Third, the mother/daughter relationship is a central aspect of family life. Moreover, it could be argued that mothers and daughters are the *bridge* of family life and are responsible for the reproduction and maintenance of family growth and development. One need only glance at the literature of psychotherapy, for example, to prove the point that it is the women in the family who are expected to nurture and "take care." That same literature reveals that it is the women who are turned to in eliciting change and to whom therapeutic interventions are most often directed. Importantly, women travel both backward and forward across this generational bridge. Mothers are responsible for creating mothers out of their daughters, and daughters are responsible for looking after the older generation. All the statistics and social service records tell us daughters predominate in caring for their elderly parents.

Thus the relationship of mothers and daughters is central to the important question of changing the traditional structure of the family. If mothers and daughters are indeed the bridge of family life, then it is precisely this bridge that will need to be rebuilt so both mother and daughter can walk over it in the search for new, nonoppressive family forms. If part of the feminist project, indeed a very central part, has been to challenge the existing structure of the nuclear family, to liberate women from its restrictive hold, then the mother/daughter relationship must be fundamental to that challenge. The dismantling of the male-dominant family—and the construction of alternative family forms—can be accomplished only when both mother and daughter are empowered to struggle and resist.

Most important, we need to reconsider the subject of mothers and daughters if our aim is to enhance and encourage the continuum of women. The historical and public dimension of this continuum—recovering, rewriting, rethinking our history as women— cannot be separated from that personal continuum that links us back over the years to our mothers and their mothers before them. And this takes us back to where we started: "because it is about me." Although individual women can of course feel positive and good about themselves even when they are deeply unhappy with their mothers, the internalization of empowering and complex images of their mothers enables daughters to enjoy a more powerful and realistic self-image.

It is not that the mother's liberation is the "key" to the daughter's liberation, or vice versa for that matter. But the meaning of "woman identification" and "sisterhood" implies a recognition of the shared experience of *all* women, however differently structured by race, class, sexuality, or identity as a mother or a daughter. If most daughters will in turn become mothers—and this remains true— then it must certainly mean that damage will be done if that daughter-to-be-mother must negate *her* mother to reach her own liberation. The liberation of women *cannot* be won as a liberation *from* other women, but only as a reaching *toward* every one of us.

In a culture so infused with mother-blame and so quick to construct women's relationships as inherently conflictual, anything that runs against this overwhelming tide can be seen as "Pollyanna" theorizing. To speak of mothers and daughters outside the familiar constructs of struggle and separation and even question those constructs can be read as claiming a sort of joyous transcendence in mothering and the relationship of mother to daughter. I do not intend to create a naive commentary on the blissful bonding of mothers and daughters. Whether the relationship itself, in all its permutations, is painful or joyous or any combination therein is not the issue here. Rather, the point is to subject *all* these paradigms of mother/daughter relationships to a critical and historical gaze and thus to liberate ourselves from the psychological frames that keep women under male dominance.

Another conceptual problem is that, until quite recently, motherhood and mothering have almost always been talked about generically. Only since the contemporary feminist movement have we gained any sense that it is different to mother sons and daughters and that mothering functions are valued unequally and imbued with dissimilar meanings depending upon the gender of the child. Developmental psychology, in particular, has until very recently examined mothering without any specific reference to the sex of the child, or rather it assumes the male child speaks for all children, an omission that today we would consider problematic.

Connected with this sort of "generic" mothering discussion is an insistent emphasis, still very deeply entrenched today, on the *activeness* of being a mother and the *receptiveness*, even *passivity*, of being a daughter. Our language itself is revealing: "Daughtering" is nonexistent; "mothering" is a fact of life, with various and sundry interpretations. This imbalance is not solely restricted to mothers and daughters. There is no concept of "sonning" either, but neither is there a concept of "fathering" that connotes nurturance and caretaking in the way that "mothering" does. To father is literally to produce a child by virtue of insemination, although "fathering" has recently become more attached to concepts of rearing a child than previously. "To father" usually implies to produce a child; "to mother" usually implies to take care of and nurture a child. So this imbalance is not restricted to the differences in our understanding of parents and children; it also takes on special significance when speaking about mothers and daughters. As long as no concept of "daughtering" remains, "mothering" lives under the extraordinary burden of being the active member in a relationship in which she is semantically overburdened.

One of the most important steps we can take in rethinking the mother/daughter relationship is to remove it from the confines of psychological description and prescription and locate it in the more varied and comprehensive realm of culture and society. The very terms we use to describe the mother/daughter relationship are inextricably linked to a psychological framework: bonding, symbiosis, separation, differentiation, autonomy. These terms are not innocent; they have a history and, most important, are gendered. In other words, part of our work has to be going beneath the seemingly "neutral" categories with which we describe and understand a relationship and uncovering and deciphering its "genderedness."

For example, although the term "separation" has a general meaning in relation to processes of development, it also has a particular resonance when we think of the term "mother," as will become apparent in this book. A recent book by psychologist and therapist Evelyn Bassoff entitled *Mothers and Daughters: Loving and Letting Go* exemplifies this unfortunate resonance: "In order to realize the full possibilities of her individual life . . . the middle-aged mother must not only separate from her adolescent daughter, she must also complete her separation from her aging mother. It is, after all, only as mothers and daughters *grow* apart, that each becomes a full woman."[5] Separation from whom, we need to ask, and for what purpose? Not only do we need to question these concepts for their gender bias, but we need to locate them historically and culturally. For example, autonomy and individuation are highly valued characteristics of a *capitalist* society and as such are naturalized so as to appear as unassailable *truths* about the nature of adulthood and maturity. Not coincidentally, these highly valued attributes of a functioning adult in a capitalist society are found to be lacking or deficient in women.

More simply, the mother/daughter relationship needs to be described, understood, and analyzed in fully social and historical terms. The ways we understand and talk about mothers and daughters are structured by our own unconscious acceptance of certain concepts and paradigms that are not innocent but are, in fact, often destructive to the possibility of mother/daughter intimacy and continuity. Nothing should be taken for granted or assumed about this relationship. Practically, this means that the themes we take to represent psychological truths about the relationship need to be seriously and rigorously questioned; they need to be deconstructed to uncover and reveal the ideological agendas inscribed within many commonsense understandings of this relationship.

Many of these "commonsense" ideas are manifested in popular culture, particularly in the narrative forms of popular culture such as film, literature, and television. How the relationship is represented there will tell us a great deal about how we think about the relationship in our own everyday lives, for there is no greater index of practical knowledge than popular culture. This is not to say that popular images of mothers and daughters are a simple reflection of already existing ideas that come from psychology or sociology. Rather, these popular images both reflect and construct; they both *reproduce* existing mainstream ideologies and help *produce* those very ideologies. And those psychological "truths" are themselves made apparent to the population through the mediation of popular forms: If we live in a Freudian culture, it is not because most people have studied Freud, but because the institutions of cultural production have so absorbed Freudian thinking that it has become part of the foundation of how we tell a story or perceive a character's motivation.

The ideas we have today about mothers and daughters (e.g., that conflict between them is inevitable and in fact essential to the full development of the daughter into an adult; that too much closeness between mother and daughter is unhealthy beyond a certain age and signals "immaturity" in the daughter and "clinging" or "possessiveness" or "overprotectiveness" or "living through" on the part of the mother; that separation from the mother, both literally and developmentally, is the hallmark of mature individuation) were not always with us. Ideas about "good" mother/daughter relationships have changed throughout history, and it is important not only to recognize those changes but to see how those different ideas relate to significant shifts and developments in the society at large.

Feminist historians such as Carroll Smith-Rosenberg have argued, for example, that mother/daughter conflict and opposition was much less evident in nineteenth-century life, where ideologies of "separate spheres" and the "cult of true womanhood" helped unite women in the domestic or the "female world": "An intimate mother-daughter closeness lay at the heart of this female world. The diaries and letters of both mothers and daughters attest to their closeness and mutual emotional dependency. . . . Expressions of hostility which we would today consider routine on the part of both mothers and daughters seem to have been uncommon indeed. On the contrary, this sample of families indicates that the normal relationship between mother and daughter was one of sympathy and understanding."[6]

Magazine fiction of the 1920s—in distinction to later women's fiction—often portrayed rebellious daughters seeking a new and independent way of life, different from, but not in conflict with, their mothers. These early stories often depicted daughters who were more in conflict with the Victorian and authoritarian *father,* whom they perceived as limiting not only their lives but those of their mothers. Elizabeth Ewen's exemplary work on women on the Lower East Side of New York during the late nineteenth and early twentieth centuries points to the closeness and continuity of immigrant mothers and daughters even in the face of drastic life changes and new social pressures.[7]

The dominant contemporary discourses—stressing struggle and separation as well as the importance of mother/child bonding in infancy—have emerged out of a variety of cultural, political, and psychological discourses. These discourses themselves grew out of substantive shifts and contradictions in the social fabric.[8] The shift to discourses centered on a relationship *constructed in conflict* has its origins both in social shifts as well as in the cultural practices that developed alongside and within those structural changes. To define this relationship *psychologically* and within the terms of a simple dichotomy (bond/separate) is therefore not "natural" but actually quite contrived.

For example, not until the 1940s, which saw both the popularization of Freud and the entry of a significant number of women into the labor force, did the idea of the mother as solely responsible for the psychic health of her children take hold in the popular imagination. Previously, as in the 1937 film *Stella Dallas*, we see mother as responsible for the social growth of her daughter; by 1942, with *Now, Voyager,* and 1945, with *Mildred Pierce*, the mother has clearly become the malevolent agent of her daughter's neuroses. How this shift to a representation of mother as evil force on her daughter's development took place and got frozen into the "common wisdom" is the subject of this book.

## Decoding Mothers and Daughters:
## Methods and Means

This relationship, such a persistent aspect of the popular imaginary and the social narrative, has been interpreted almost solely in psychological terms. Few critics have attempted to chart it as it exists and is constructed in the cultural context of film, television, women's magazines, and popular literature. Typically, in-depth media studies focus on only one specific medium, such as television or, more characteristically, film. In so doing, studies tend to participate in the theoretical segregation of the mass media, avoiding a more inclusive interpretation of media practices. But it is not simply films or television or novels that influence social attitudes and behaviors; the whole range of symbolic practices present in our culture often coheres in certain ways to create what the cultural theorist Raymond Williams called a "way of seeing" or a general "reading" of a relationship or an issue, in this case, the mother/daughter relationship. This book, in including a variety of media forms, presents a more comprehensive picture of the relationship between the media and society and between the different media themselves.

This research takes a cultural studies perspective, arguing for an understanding of representation and the mass media that is both historical and contextual, as well as concerned with the elaboration of central themes that emerge from the intersection of a variety of discursive practices. To study a medium without studying the other popular images within which it interacts is to make of that medium a closed system and thus to limit and constrain the analysis. No medium is an island.

A critical perspective on the media has always been a central aspect of feminist praxis, from the earliest days of Betty Friedan's examination of women's magazines in *The Feminine Mystique* to contemporary feminist film criticism and theory. Indeed, the last fifteen years have witnessed a phenomenal growth in the area of feminism and representation, traversing all types of cultural arti-facts, including film, television, and advertising.[9] Literary criticism in particular has responded to a growing feminist movement.[10] With the introduction of women's studies into the academy, we can now almost point to an alternative feminist literary "canon." The language of feminist film criticism—particularly in its Lacanian versions—has entered into the critical vocabulary of film theorists on both sides of the Atlantic and has found a home within film schools and media courses. In recent years, feminist critics have examined that peculiarly home-based and ubiquitous medium of television and are beginning to explore the complex relations be-tween TV families and "real" families, between soap opera and everyday life. Women's magazines—long ignored and trivialized—have now been recognized as the powerful forces they are in shap-ing and structuring commonsense understandings of femininity. And the ever-present figure of the advertising image that appears as so much "background" information has been deconstructed and criticized both for its portrayal of women and for the consumerist ethos it so vividly and successfully promotes.

Feminist critics have been quick to point out that the represen-tation of women in this media-saturated society is particularly fraught with contradictions and dilemmas, for it is women who more often than not are the "imaged" in our culture. In this society of the spectacle, women's bodies *are* the spectacle upon which rep-resentation occurs. Yet women are in this strange and unique posi-tion of also being spectators, consumers of their very own image, their very own objectification. At the same time that we witness our own representation, we are denied a place in that process of representation; we are denied a voice so that more often than not those images of ourselves that stare at us from the glossy pages of the women's magazines or from the glowing eye of the TV screen are not of our own creation. They are, in more senses than one, truly "man-made."

It is thus no accident that the feminist project has been from the beginning deeply concerned with "the cultural." Even the first, founding texts of this "second wave" of feminism (Betty Friedan on women's magazines, Kate Millet and Simone de Beauvoir on fiction) delved into how the everyday objects of cultural consumption are as much a part of the maintenance of patriarchal social relations as are the inequities of a sexist workplace: "One of the major theoretical contributions of the women's movement has been its insistence on the significance of cultural factors, in particular in the form of socially dominant representations of women and the ideological character of such representations, both in constituting the category 'woman' and in delimiting and defining what has been called the 'sex/gender' system."[11]

This book locates itself in this tradition of feminist cultural criticism yet departs from it in a number of important ways. Feminist cultural criticism has tended to oscillate between two approaches. First is a largely quantitative and empirical sociological approach that focuses on media *content* and that is often tied to reformist cultural strategies, such as demanding more women producers and writers or more representations of women at work. Second, and more recent, is a rather eclectic approach that merges Lacanian psychoanalytic frameworks with semiotic methods in a largely textual "close reading" of a filmic (or televisual) "text," focusing less on content or character than on form and structure. My approach, while drawing on aspects of both perspectives, eschews both the quantitative and the textual in favor of a historical, contextual, and intertextual approach that stresses the ideological thematics of particular representations and their relationship to the social milieu in which they emerge.

There is an abundance of criticism—both feminist and more mainstream—examining the representations chosen for this book. Feminist critics such as E. Ann Kaplan, Annette Kuhn, Teresa de Lauretis, Molly Haskell, Laura Mulvey, Mary Ann Doane, Maria LaPlace, Linda Williams, and Andrea Walsh among others have produced numerous thoughtful and substantive analyses of many of the texts I reexamine here.[12] Although I present a rather different angle on these same texts (and introduce new texts such as "Maude" to the "critical canon"), I have been greatly influenced by the work that has preceded my own and owe a serious debt to the legion of feminist film and culture critics who have opened up these classic Hollywood films to a newly critical gaze.

Indeed, all studies have their limitations, and this one is no exception. One could exhaustively examine all the available material on the subject and then come to a conclusion or set of conclusions. This study, conversely, starts from a felt conviction that we live in a society that, through both the mass media and the more traditional agents of socialization (family, church, education, politics), compresses the mother/daughter relationship into the narrow vision of psychology, framing it within the dichotomous boundaries of "bonding" and "separation" and thus actively constructing a relationship to be inherently conflictual, forcing women apart, and rendering this prophesy self-fulfilling. My examination of hundreds of films, television programs, women's magazines, and popular psychological treatises has convinced me this is the case. This is, then, an impressionistic, highly selective, and critical foray through films, television shows, magazines, and other popular sources that have foregrounded mothers and daughters and contributed to what I understand to be a very specific cultural ideology.

The cultural data were chosen around a number of central criteria. In the first place, the representation (film, TV show, magazine article) had to have something to do explicitly with mothers and daughters. It had to be concerned with adult mother/daughter relationships, or at least young adult daughters and their mothers. Infants and young girls were not substantively considered for this study. For the films and TV shows, the mother/daughter relationship had to be a central aspect of the narrative and figure prominently in the self-representation of the images themselves (e.g., *Terms of Endearment* placing itself culturally as a film about mothers and daughters). The films analyzed are almost all well-known, successful, mainstream Hollywood films that achieved box office success when they were released and have garnered a lasting place in the annals of film history. In the attempt to point not to the impact of particular films or television programs, but rather to the culturally inscribed "ways of seeing" that characterize certain historical periods, my focus was on those large-scale, culturally salient representations that, in their vast audiences, must have helped shape the public consciousness of mothers and daughters.

Magazine articles were chosen through the *Readers Guide to Periodicals* from 1930 to 1990, under the headings "mothers and daughters," "mothers," "family," and anything related to the subject of women and women's lives. A wide review of the magazines resulted in a narrowing of material to that which specifically addressed the mother/daughter relationship. My focus is primarily on women's magazines, but other popular magazine articles are occasionally included to elaborate certain themes and directions. The focus, even when doing close and detailed analysis, is not on texts but rather on discourses of mothers and daughters.

The arguments and analyses set out here are understood as "discourses" precisely because of how feminist work on the mother/daughter relationship has traversed a multiplicity of formations, both theoretical and cultural. To call them "ideologies" or "theories" (although they may be ideological and are often theoretical) belies the interdisciplinary and broad ranging way feminist work on mothers and daughters has emerged. The openness of the concept of "discourse" allows for an investigation of how very different discursive practices (from psychology, from feminist theory, from popular culture) cohere or intersect to produce certain generally agreed upon, or "commonsense," understandings of the mother/daughter relationship.

These representations are placed in a historical context because, without this contextualizing, analyses of mass images become sterile and limited in their range of explanatory vision. The intersection between these representations and the larger social context creates a "way of seeing" that is almost like common sense and that appears to be natural and inevitable. The mother/daughter relationship provides an especially good "location" to work through these questions of feminism and representation because it is a significant subject of both feminist inquiry and popular culture. Through the lens of the mother/daughter relationship, we can address larger issues around the representation of women generally and the impact of a social movement on the structures of representation. In this cultural history, the primary question is necessarily centered around change: To what extent have the representations of mothers and daughters changed during the postwar period? Has the feminist movement of the last fifteen years impacted the dominant media institutions and their picture of this relationship? Have popular films, television, and literature altered their representation of the mother/daughter relationship as a response to feminist demands and ideologies?

If we can posit that the mother/daughter relationship has most consistently been represented as one of conflict and struggle (e.g., *Mildred Pierce*) or, alternately, of maternal martyrdom and daughterly transcendence (e.g., *Stella Dallas, I Remember Mama*), then can we also posit that the feminist critique of sex-role stereotypes and, specifically, of familial arrangements and the institution of motherhood has offered up new fictional renderings of the mother/daughter couplet? Have the institutions of the mass media moved beyond the limiting genres of "mother-blame" or "maternal sacrifice"?

On another level, the question of change relates to the media forms themselves. Is one medium (e.g., television) more likely to present a more varied and "positive" view of the relationship than another medium, and why might that be so? For example, the structure of television sitcoms stresses character over narrative, thus mitigating the possibilities of structural change and substantive transformation. Does this mean that we might see more varied character development of mothers and daughters yet less dramatic change in their relationship generally? Television, particularly daytime television, is often considered a more "familial" medium, addressing a proportionately larger female audience. Does this mean that the thematic concerns of television will allow the mother/daughter relationship to be more fundamental and central to television content?

Each chapter focuses primarily on one medium, although all include a variety of media forms in the analysis. Fundamentally, the choice to proceed this way was dictated by the media themselves. For example, Chapter 2, dealing with the transition from the 1930s to the 1940s, necessarily focuses on film and women's magazines because TV was effectively nonexistent until the postwar era. In addition, film scholars have pointed to these years as representing the heyday of the Hollywood film industry, a time when the studio system dominated, and the genres and styles familiar to later audiences became solidified and established in the consciousness of everyday film goers. The focus in later chapters shifts to television as that medium came into its own and increasingly defined the parameters of public consciousness, somewhat displacing film as the dominant media form. Women's magazines emerge more strongly in the 1970s and 1980s as the relationship of mothers and daughters becomes highlighted by the growing women's movement. Before the "feminist era," one would be hard pressed to find many articles in women's magazines dealing explicitly with relationships between adult (or even young adult) mothers and daughters. This book therefore moves both synchronically—across different media and genres—and diachronically—through different historical and social shifts and transitions.

## From Persephone to *Mommie Dearest*

The Greek myth of Persephone and Demeter dates back to approximately 650 B.C., to the Homeric "Hymn to Demeter." Demeter was the goddess of grain, corn, and the harvests, and the sister of Zeus and Hades. Her daughter Persephone (also known as Kore—the maiden) was abducted and raped by Hades, god of the underworld, who took her with him to his kingdom and forced her to become his queen. She was out picking flowers one day (the beautiful, many-petaled narcissus) that had been planted there by Zeus to lure the girl for his brother Hades.

Demeter heard but didn't see her daughter, and no one would tell her what had happened (no one would speak of the rape, mention the violation, name the trap) until an old goddess, Hecate, told her of Persephone's abduction. She was racked with grief over the loss of her daughter and searched day and night for her until she ended up at the palace of Eleusis, where she disguised herself and became a nursemaid to the infant prince. There she was discovered to be a goddess. She ordered a temple built in her honor, to which she retreated, gave in to her grief, and refused to do her job—refused to let the grain grow and the harvests bloom—until her daughter was returned. Zeus finally relented because the land was barren and all life was in jeopardy. He sent Hermes down to the underworld to tell Hades to return the girl to her mother. Persephone was returned to her mother, but she had to visit Hades once a year because she was tricked by Hades into eating addictive pomegranate seeds. Demeter then allowed the flowers to bloom and the corn to grow, but only for those months when her daughter was with her. It was this return of the daughter to the mother—this reunion—out of which one of the most sacred rites of ancient Greek life was constructed: the Eleusinian mysteries.

Part of the work of understanding the mother/daughter relationship centers on interpreting this myth. It has been interpreted variously as a cyclical story of birth, death, and renewal or a metaphor for the loss of virginity and the entrance into female adulthood. More recently, Adrienne Rich has pointed out that it is primarily a story of abduction, of unwilling and violent separation of mother and daughter, of the power of patriarchy as it asserts itself into the innocent life of a girl child picking flowers.

But there is something more important than interpreting this myth and constructing alternative myths in its place. Whether the story of Demeter and Persephone is the grand metaphor for the mother/daughter relationship is not really the question as I seek here to dispel all grand narratives. Rather, the move is to a radical demystification, a tearing down of those great edifices of narrative and myth that tell us "this story and no other." It is expressly this social construction of the mother/daughter relationship that I seek both to examine and to assert, to render those naturalized narratives suspect and awkward in their claim to universality and truth.

From this venerable Greek myth of Persephone and Demeter to the modern fable of maternal malevolence embodied in contemporary films such as *Mommie Dearest,* the narrative of mothers and daughters has largely been portrayed in terms of conflict and the ambivalent struggle of separation. Just a brief glance at popular images of mothers and daughters would bear this out. We might find Bette Davis as the dominated daughter in *Now, Voyager* struggling to overcome her mother, the incarnation of repression and sexual denial. It is no accident that Bette is "saved" by the dual efforts of a male psychiatrist and a dashing lover. Or there is the classic film noir, *Mildred Pierce* (with Joan Crawford in the title role), in which Mildred's desire to provide for her daughter backfires because she is, well, *too* self-sacrificing. If Mildred's greedy, insufferable daughter Veda is the epitome of the "bad seed," we are told right from the start whose fault it really is . . . by her father. Or there is Lana Turner in *Imitation of Life* as the perennially guilty mother whose adolescent daughter fancies her lover while mom is away making a film, thus indirectly chastising her mother for her neglect. Lana finally sees the light when an angry Sandra Dee tells her that nothing can replace a mother's love and round-the-clock attention—not horses or cars or the finest education. Lana weeps, quits the world of work, goes to her daughter's graduation, and marries the simple but decent man of her dreams.

In our own dubiously "postfeminist" 1980s, we have Shirley MacLaine and Debra Winger in *Terms of Endearment* as a mother and daughter locked in a repetitive cycle of mutual need and denial, resolved only by the daughter's tragic death and relinquishment of her children to her newly maternal mom, already "saved" by the lecherous but loving spaceman, played by Jack Nicholson. In the eerie recent film *The Stepfather*, a single mother and her daughter living without a man become perfect targets for a crazed killer stepfather. In the 1990s tell-all Hollywood saga *Postcards from the Edge*, former movie queen mom virtually causes her cynical daughter's drug overdose by her early maternal neglect and bossy grandstanding. Blame here is not simply psychological, but chemical as well; alcoholic mom is revealed to have given baby daughter sleeping pills during her own tumultuous divorce, thus setting both the psychic and the biochemical stage for daughter's tawdry slide into the world of "B" movies and drugged debauchery.

These are but a few of the mainstream images of mothers and daughters in our culture. The message, contradictory as it sometimes is, comes through loud and clear: Too much mother love can lead to symbiosis, too little, to maternal deprivation. The daughter's mandate to separate from her mother is represented not as a natural process of growth and maturation, but as a wrenching experience that must be endured in order to reach the "other side" of men and marriage. It is no accident that in almost every mother/daughter film where this struggle for autonomy is the central theme, a man (a lover, a future husband, or, more ominously, a psychiatrist) is the one who forces the daughter out of the maternal grasp and leads her into the world of adult femininity. The options presented to these fictional daughters are to sink even further into the domestic and nonsexual world of their mothers or to fly bravely from the maternal nest into the waiting arms of a strong man. The rigid dichotomies constructed by these images are painfully clear and have become—collectively—the reigning ethos of Hollywood: "mother" versus "woman," nurturance versus sexuality, public versus private.

These rigid dichotomies limit and constrain both the representations of mothers and daughters and our lived experience. This book challenges these dichotomies by placing the mother/daughter relationship firmly within culture in its most inclusive sense. This contextualization "denaturalizes" our commonsense assumptions about mothers and daughters by pointing out in detail how this relationship is socially constructed in relation to specific ideological and political trends, such as the "cult of the domestic" in the 1950s and the resurgence of an antifeminist "familialism" in the Reagan and Bush years. By examining the mother/daughter relationship culturally and historically, I shed new light on the mass media, feminism, and the mother/daughter relationship.

## Chapter Two

# From Sacrificial *Stella* to Maladjusted *Mildred*

## De(class)ifying Mothers and Daughters

*"Mrs. Vale, if you had deliberately tried to ruin your daughter's life you couldn't have done a more complete job."*
—Dr. Jacquith, *Now, Voyager,* 1942

Representations of the mother/daughter relationship have survived many permutations to arrive at this classic juncture of blame and guilt. Yet it is possible to locate a specific moment when this new paradigm of inevitable conflict took hold in the popular imagination. Typically, we look to the fifties as the period in which circumscribed conceptions of mothering and "women's place" cohered within the context of a new familialism and domesticity. Indeed, excellent feminist scholarship has detailed how the domestic ideologies of the fifties developed in the wake of enormous changes in women's relationships to work and family that occurred during World War II.[1] Central to this "back to the kitchen" motif was a restructuring of the maternal role and the development of ideologies of mothering that left women little room for self-definition outside of those very narrow strictures.

Feminist scholarship, then, usually focuses on the backlash effect that followed the wartime experience. Yet by looking back to the thirties and forties rather than the forties and fifties, we can discern the cultural changes that took place before the full elaboration of fifties domesticity. This earlier shift paved the way for that

overblown version of the nuclear family that so thoroughly popu-
lated the cultural landscape of what we neatly call "the fifties."

The relationship of mother and daughter affords access to these
popular conceptions and ideologies of woman's identity, particularly her identity as mother. Questions of female sexuality, maternal
activity, and subjectivity are often expressed within the context of
this relationship. Hollywood genre films, always a rich source of
popular knowledge, are central to the construction of domestic ideologies, particularly in the Hollywood heyday of the late thirties
and forties. The intersection of these two sites of discourses on female identity—mass audience Hollywood film and the mother/
daughter relationship—illuminates the extent and seriousness of
the transformation into the postwar world.

I focus primarily on three films, *Stella Dallas*, made in 1937,
*Now, Voyager*, made in 1942, and *Mildred Pierce*, made in 1945, to
examine the shift in discourses of the mother/daughter relationship
from the context of depression era America to a nation absorbed
with the war effort and already deeply concerned about the implications of "Rosie the Riveter." These three films, though not the
only ones I could have chosen for this study, are significant on a
number of levels. First, all three, and particularly *Stella Dallas* and
*Mildred Pierce*, are widely recognized as "classic" Hollywood depictions of mothering and the mother/daughter relationship. Second, all three films enjoyed enormous success and thus stand out
as truly "mass" entertainment. Finally, all three films have been
central texts within feminist film criticism and have been commented on widely. Although this chapter is not intended as a sum-
mary of the various debates and positions articulated around these
films, I refer to the work of Kaplan, Williams, LaPlace, and others
to elaborate my somewhat different reading of these films in the
context of changing representations of the mother/daughter relationship. The focus on these three films is thus meant to be *symptomatic*, to use these celebrated films as emblems of what I understand to be a fundamental and drastic shift in the representations of
mothers and daughters. Counterexamples exist, but I remain convinced of the significance of this transformation.

This shift from a sacrificial model of mothering a daughter to a
model of malevolence and psychopathology speaks to an increasing
anxiety toward the end of the war around women, sexuality, and

the nature and status of "mothering" in a postwar society. Many historians have argued, convincingly, that the backlash that followed women's participation in the labor force had already begun during the war and that ideologies of maternal neglect and the deprivation caused by working mothers began almost as soon as women entered the wartime economy. The change in representation also signals a broader postwar desire to move away from class-based discourses (so prevalent during the thirties) and toward a sanitized version of the pluralistic American dream, replete with suburban idylls, postwar consumerism, and a rejuvenated familialism.

## My Heart Belongs to Mama: *Stella Dallas* and the Politics of Class

In many ways, *Stella Dallas* signifies an end not only to a certain kind of representation of mothering and the mother/daughter relationship and an end to a kind of genre, which became increasingly unpopular as the years progressed, but also an end to a *social* representation of family relationships. Instead, what we increasingly see as the years progressed is the personalization and psychologization of the mother/daughter relationship, removing that interaction from the larger field of social and class relations, which continued to shape cultural production as late as the 1937 "weepie" *Stella Dallas*.[2]

In this film, Stella (played by Barbara Stanwyck), a fast-talking, upwardly mobile (she's taking night business courses to "improve" herself), working-class girl from a small New England mill town, hooks the upper-class and correct Steven Dallas. From the beginning, Stella is depicted as different from her family, particularly from her mother, a hunched over, beaten down wife and mother whose visual resemblance to a depression era Dorothea Lange photo is striking.

The birth of their baby girl, Laurel, signifies the real beginning of this narrative. Stella's husband quickly moves to New York in exasperation over her refusal to become appropriately upper class, and the girl is brought up by her mother, although the father remains very much in the picture. Steven Dallas's initial move away from his wife—his frustration with her working-class ways—is in direct contradiction to his earlier claims of wanting her to remain

Fig. 1. Barbara Stanwyck and Ann Shirley as the loving mother and
daughter in the heartrending tale of a sacrificial working-class mother who
gives up her daughter in the melodrama *Stella Dallas*. (Samuel Goldwyn,
1937: photo courtesy of Museum of Modern Art Film Stills Archive)

"just as you are." Stella's desire to ascend is never masked: she is
clear with Steven about her wish to learn from him the ways of the
bourgeoisie, tellingly described as being "like the people in the
movie." Yet he changes his tune as soon as her incorrigible working-
class ways begin to impinge on his life-style.

Through a series of humiliating and poignant events, Stella rec-

Fig. 2. Stella bids farewell—for the last time—to her devoted daughter as she gives her up to high-class society and nuclear family bliss. (Samuel Goldwyn, 1937; photo courtesy of Museum of Modern Art Film Stills Archive)

ognizes that she is inadequate to bring up a "proper" girl and concocts an elaborate scheme to place Laurel in the bourgeois family of Steven and his new wife. In the final scene, which many spectators remember as both compelling and disconcerting, Stella stands in the rain outside the house where her daughter is being married, looking in on the scene of wedded bliss.

The mother/daughter theme in *Stella Dallas* is worked through or intersects with a pronounced class theme, something that should not be surprising given the depression era in which it was filmed, when questions of equality, class mobility, and governmental responsibility came to the fore. Indeed, a whole genre of class-conscious films was produced in the thirties, many of which focused on women and their families.[3] Questions of maternity and social class are intimately linked in many of the early maternal melodramas. In a time of deprivation and hardship—of sacrifice—a powerful narrative of social ascendancy asserts itself strongly and often depends on some sort of parental sacrifice, typically of the mother.

This linking of class and motherhood has disappeared in more recent films as the mother/daughter relationship has increasingly
come under the master discourse of popular psychology.

Stella is first and foremost a *working-class* woman motivated by
her desire to move up in the world. In depression era America, the
message is that the mother's (Stella's) generation cannot transcend
their class origins, but they can enable their children to ascend. It
is through her father that Laurel accesses bourgeois values and
moves away from her (depression) mother. E. Ann Kaplan thus
rightly argues that Stella is doubly punished—as a mother and as a
working-class person: "The film punishes her first by turning Stella
into a 'spectacle' produced by the upper-class, disapproving gaze (a
gaze that the audience is made to share through camera work and
editing), but secondly, and most devastatingly, by bringing Stella to
the recognition that she is an unfit Mother for her daughter."[4]

In this reading, *Stella Dallas* is understood as a virtually seamless representation of the mother/woman dichotomy that is such a
mainstay of patriarchal thought and culture. Other feminist film
critics, like Linda Williams, argue for a more contradictory reading
of Stella that centers on the positive aspects of the mother/daughter
love depicted in the film and the strangely triumphant look Stella
walks away with at the end of the film: "We see instead the contradictions between what the patriarchal resolution of the film asks us
to see—the mother 'in her place' as spectator, abdicating her former position *in* the scene—and what we feel as empathic identifying female spectators can't help but feel—the loss of mother to
daughter and daughter to mother."[5]

Both analyses center on the mother/woman dichotomy as the
central problem in the film, making this film one more example of
a representation supporting and constructing the belief that to be a
mother is to be asexual. Many critics, such as Kaplan, have therefore understood Stella as "resisting"—albeit unsuccessfully—both
her role as mother and the narrative's repression of her sexuality:
"Stella's resistance takes the form, first, of literally objecting to
Mothering because of the personal sacrifices involved (mainly sen-
sual pleasures); second, of expressing herself freely in her eccentric
style of dress and being unabashedly sexual; finally, in growing too
attached and needful of her daughter."[6] Although this mother/
woman dichotomy is a significant issue for all "maternal sacrifice"

films—indeed, for almost all popular representations of women—the relationship between class and ideologies of motherhood is perhaps more significant here.

Stella *doesn't* object to mothering. After showing her initial desire to get out and have some fun following the birth of her daughter, the film details her devotion to mothering and her daughter at the expense of any other kind of life. Second, her ways of dress and self-expression are signifiers here of *class*, not of sexuality. For example, when we see her "decked out" and making a spectacle of herself—being made a spectacle of—it is in the context of a rich resort to which she has taken Laurel for a vacation. It is not in the context of trying to express her own sexuality in a coherent way. Her dress reveals her to the rich patrons as "other," as lower class. The audience here seems to be put in a strange position. On the one hand, we are invited to participate in the process of making a spectacle of Stella: she *is* laughable. Yet we also see those who are ridiculing her as mean and vicious: these children of privilege do not compare to the simple and honest Laurel. Laurel's boyfriend is kept out of the ridiculing, signifying that he is one of the decent upper class, unlike the snobs in his midst.

Most significantly, we witness the *daughter's* concern for her mother and her desire to shield her from the slings and arrows of upper-class elitism. As Mary Ann Doane points out in her trenchant analysis of *Stella Dallas,* Laurel witnesses her mother's "otherness," her unsuitability, through the mediation of both an upper-class gaze (the rich kids in the soda fountain) and through the image of her mother reflected in the fountain mirror: "Her gaze mediated via the gazes of others and the mirror, Laurel finally recognizes an accurate or 'proper' reflection of her mother's disproportion. It is as though the closeness of the mother/daughter relation necessitated the deflection of the gaze, its indirection, as a precondition for the establishment of difference."[7]

The central conflict is thus not so much between Stella's wanting to be a "woman" (defined as sexual, active, free, etc.) and her duties as a mother as between two different sensibilities about mothering itself. In fact, Stella sees her identity solely in terms of mothering, as she tells her pal Ed Munn when he once again implores her to be with him: "I don't think there's a man living that could get me going anymore. I don't know, I guess Lolly just uses up all the feelings I got and I don't seem to have any left for anybody else." Stella throughout is explicitly *nonsexual*. She even treats her potential lover, Munn, as yet another object of her maternal affection: he is alternately a "bad boy," in need of maternal admonishment, and a "sad boy," in need of care and nurture. In that sense, she remains a "good" mother.

Yet she explicitly resists the kind of "appropriate mothering" that her husband and the medical establishment try to force her into, as she expresses in an early scene when she returns from the hospital. There, she refuses to allow her maternity to be pathologized, and it is in taking control of her own maternity that Stella's real transgression can be seen: "Why is it that doctors and nurses and husbands always seem to think they know more about this maternity business? Don't you think a mother learns anything in that little room they wheel her into? Or is that just a kindergarten class? Let me tell ya something, I picked up quite a little experience in that room, and it wasn't out of books either. Experience." Here Stella, as her daughter does later in the film, valorizes her own *experience* of birth and mothering over the upper-class learning and establishment ways. So the first conflict we have in the film is between Stella's version of "correct" mothering ("experience," she tells us) and the version promoted by the nurse and her husband (an interesting alliance of male interests and the pathologizing medical establishment). But this scene, which includes a full close-up of Stella and is clearly from her point of view (we don't get a full shot, but only a glance, of the nurse who attempts to boss her, and the nurse's voice is almost disembodied), is immediately followed by another in which Stella's way of mothering is called into question.

Stella is obviously weary of being cooped up and domestic and insists on going out to a dance right after the baby is brought home from the hospital. As she complains to Steven about her boredom, he protests, and she expresses fervently the desire to be "other than a mother" ("Gee, I just want to get a wave and a manicure and get all dressed up again and go hear some music and forget all about doctors and hospitals and nurses"). He asks pointedly, "And babies?" looking over at their newborn infant in the crib. Stella's ambivalence, which disappears after this point, is expressed as she looks over at the baby with Steven, says, "No," and then follows this with a plaintive plea, "Oh Steven, please . . . ." The next shot opens at the club: Stella has gotten her way, but it will be the last time. If Stella ever thought she would get out of mothering, she now realizes her destiny is sealed. And, importantly, the destiny to be "only a mother" is tied up with the destiny *not* to ascend the class ladder, to be "only working class."

Laurel mirrors Stella's emphasis on everyday (coded here as both maternal and working-class) experience when she rushes home to her mother after she hears of her sacrificial plan to "give her up" to Mrs. Morrison, the soon-to-be new wife of Steven: "But good times oh they aren't what make you belong, it's other kinds of times, it's when you've cried together and lived through things together, that's when you seem to love the most . . . it's different." Laurel here validates the routine, commonplace events in domestic life she shares with her mother. Yet "everyday life," familiarity, and continuity lose out to social ascendancy and the newness of Mrs. Morrison and all that her world has to offer. By discrediting that everydayness, which is, after all, the stuff of most women's lives, and was particularly so in the trying times of the thirties, the film thus further invalidates women's social reality. Experience loses out to progress, familiarity to newness, the prosaic to the novel.

Nevertheless, we are invited to empathize with Stella's anguish and pain when she realizes that it was her "lower-class" qualities (Stella as an embarrassment) that led Laurel to insist on leaving the resort. In fact, one of the most poignant moments between mother and daughter occurs during the train ride home, one of the few moments of mutuality, of a glimpse at the shared love between mother and daughter, but a love that is nevertheless doomed as Stella begins to see herself through her daughter's eyes and sees the social situation more clearly: "It is *this* vision, through the daughter's sympathetic, mothering eyes—eyes that perceive, understand, and forgive the social graces Stella lacks—that determines her to perform the masquerade that will alienate Laurel forever by proving to her what the patriarchy has claimed to know all along: that it is not possible to combine womanly desire with motherly duty."[8] More to the point is that it is not possible to combine a strong class identity with (appropriate, bourgeois) motherly duty.

The daughter feels the mother's hurt; the mother translates her own hurt into the implications for her daughter: the sacrifice theme is initiated. At this moment of their greatest shared pain (for themselves, for each other), they also seem most intimate, most deeply connected. The kind of image seen here—the soft music, the daughter lovingly stroking her mother's head, the daughter's head on the mother's shoulder as they sleep together on the train bunk—creates a mise-en-scène usually reserved for lovers. One wonders if the audience would sense this, feel slightly uncomfortable (both at the prospect of such intense female intimacy and at the incestuous implications), and then begin to construct in their consciousness the paramount need for separation: something is wrong with this picture; they must be torn asunder.

Not coincidentally, the mother launches her attempt to propel the daughter into the father's world following this intimate love scene between them. Stella must try several times; her daughter will not leave willingly. To do so would render the daughter less likable and the relationship itself more conflictual, thus de-emphasizing the sacrifice theme and replacing it with a more tortured, psychodrama motif (as in *Mildred Pierce*). When Stella goes to visit Mrs. Morrison to arrange her "gift" of her daughter, we have a repetition of the previous love scene between Stella and Laurel.[9] Mrs. Morrison is caring, concerned, overwhelmed, and very moved by Stella's sacrifice. As the scene progresses, she moves closer and closer to Stella on the couch. By the end, she is almost in Stella's lap, stroking her hand, and gazing lovingly at Stella, as Stella's daughter did to her on the train. In this world, the work of relationships is clearly women's work: they are both mothers, they understand each other, they empathize with each other, and they know what is best. Indeed, Mrs. Morrison has to explain to Steven Dallas why Stella is behaving the way she is (pretending to be having an affair to drive the daughter off). This sisterhood, this "mother knows best," is in marked contrast to what we will see in depictions of the relationship in the late forties and fifties, when maternal decision making is likened more to the opening of Pandora's box than the knowing looks of two mothers.

The mother in *Stella Dallas* can't win: she is bad because she wanted more (be it some form of sexuality, as Williams and Kaplan argue, to retain her class identity, or merely to have an intimate and passionate life with her daughter), but good because she didn't get it. "She proves her very worthiness to be a mother (the desire for her daughter's material and social welfare) by acting out a pat-

Fig. 3. Bette Davis plays the buttoned-up and bitter unwed mother in
*The Old Maid*, pitted against the maternal ambitions of her rich and glamorous cousin, played by Miriam Hopkins. (Warners, 1939; photo courtesy
of Photofest)

ently false scenario of narcissistic self-absorption." [10] The triumph in
her eyes in the last scene is the triumph of sacrifice, a dubious
triumph indeed. [11]

Another film of the 1930s, *The Old Maid*, also portrays a sacrificing mother whose sacrifice, like Stella's, benefits her ascending (il-
legitimate) daughter. [12] Here again issues of maternal sacrifice are
linked with those of class ascendancy. This film too is set in the past,
during the Civil War. Just as Stella must concoct an elaborate ruse
to push her daughter from the maternal home and into upper-class
society, Charlotte (Bette Davis) must construct herself as an "old
maid" (replete with rigid posture, severely pulled back hair, and
high-buttoned dowdy clothes) to conceal her daughter's true identity and allow her to be adopted (both literally and figuratively) by
her well-connected cousin Delia (Miriam Hopkins). The final scene
mirrors the classic closing image of *Stella*. As the daughter marries
into the wealthy aristocracy, Delia (cousin to mother Charlotte and

beloved adoptive mother to Tina) has asked her to give the last kiss to "Aunt Charlotte" as her carriage pulls away. Charlotte's look of amazed gratitude, hand on cheek, eyes misty, is almost as (melodramatically) heartbreaking as Stella's handkerchief-in-mouth, teary, sacrificial bliss.

Three years before *Stella Dallas*, another famous mother/daughter film hit the theaters. The 1934 melodrama *Imitation of Life* starred Claudette Colbert and Louise Beavers in a dual narrative of two mother/daughter couples, one black and one white, who make good on Beavers's pancake recipe and move into high society. I will discuss this film in greater detail in the next chapter, where I examine the 1959 remake. But suffice it here to say that, like *Stella Dallas* (and unlike the 1959 remake with Lana Turner and Juanita Moore), *Imitation of Life* refuses to indict mothering and instead foregrounds the narratives of class and race through which the mother/daughter narratives emerge.

## Modern Daughters: Women's Magazines and the Postflapper Confusion

The relationship of mothers and daughters was not typically the stuff of women's magazines in the 1930s; indeed, it is not really until the mid-1970s and 1980s that the relationship comes to the fore of magazine nonfiction. What is available is of a less coherent mode than later, more ideologically unified magazine articles. Nonetheless, modern daughters and their bewildered mothers are often the subject of articles in the 1930s, a period of postflapper independence and depression era dislocations.[13]

In a 1932 piece in *Forum* magazine, Alice Austin White raises the vexsome subject of "modern daughters" and the anxiety they provoke in their older and more staid mothers. White soothes their ruffled feathers by pointing out that every generation has "represented a sharp divergence from their parents." White chastises her own generation, unduly influenced by the " 'new feminism' of 1890," who brashly refused to "bend our course to please men" only later to discover the error of their ways. In other words, we have all been "youth in revolt." Today's modern daughters will learn the "essence of life" and fall in love and marry. For most mothers and

Fig. 4. Claudette Colbert plays Bea Pullman, doting mother to daughter Susie (Rochelle Hudson) and rising "pancake queen" who puts aside romance to keep little Susie happy in one of the greatest tearjerkers of all times, *Imitation of Life*. (Universal Pictures, 1934; photo courtesy of Museum of Modern Art Film Stills Archive)

daughters, love conquers all because "no marriage could equal the grey exclusion of not being married."[14] A mother of six daughters wants to "speak out boldly for what is called the flapper" whose "untainted heart of youth" is no cause of concern. Rather, the author "marvel[s] that older women, who surely at one time must have been girls themselves, can condemn as they do."[15]

Many magazine articles emphasized the mother's ability (or disability) to help her daughter be popular with boys and eventually become a wife and mother, which will, inevitably, reveal her true calling. Most women's magazine articles were not violent on the subject in the way we see in later years, but they were adamant about it in a "helpful" rather than explicitly judgmental way. In "If I Were That Girl's Mother!" Mary Whitton goes out of her way to place the responsibility for a daughter's popularity firmly on the shoulders of the ever-helpful, uncomplaining mother. In the true spirit of modernity, the mother should not cling to outmoded models of obedience but rather should attempt to "steer her course through the stormy teens that out of it there may emerge a real spirit of friendliness between parent and grown child." Daughter's appearance is all-important, as is that of her family. Mothers should be careful not to embarrass their daughters: "But slippered ease is a dangerous thing for the mother of a girl in the clothes-conscious stage, if that mother wishes to remain her daughter's guardian, guide and friend. So if daughter begins to criticize our clothes, hold back the words of wrath, even at risk of choking on them. It is just possible that maybe mother has been getting slack in her appearance, and that daughter's criticism, unpleasing as it is, may serve as a useful tonic."[16]

This emphasis on the marriageability of young women makes sense, given the tenor of the times. With the advent of the depression and the tight economic straits into which it forced so many families, there was a fear of a disintegration of the family. Specifically, many feared that young people would delay marriage because of a lack of resources. Many writers and popular psychologists urged parents to support young couples to counteract what they saw as an alarming trend. In addition, the fears of women's independence, fostered first by the postsuffrage flapper years and later by the expansion of job and educational opportunities, helped construct a media emphasis on reasserting traditional female duties and responsibilities. In a 1931 article, Marian Castle attempts to domesticate the flapper and thereby contain any real changes she implied by suggesting that youth is always, well, youthful and that although the flappers of yesteryear may not have become exactly like their own mothers, they have harnessed their laissez-faire individualism to the good uses of a lively and rich domesticity: "After this modern mother has done what she can with her comradeship and her bravery and her candor, I think she'll say to herself: Hands Off! I think she'll admit that her daughter is a complete and separate entity. I believe she'll pretend to be very busy with her own life while she lets nineteen plunge into hers."[17]

Estelle Reilly also attempts to domesticate substantive changes and the challenges imbedded in those changes by painting a picture of the "modern daughter" as one characterized by "independence, endurance and aggressiveness." The brazen and forthright young daughter must, in Reilly's estimation, be treated with similar honesty by her mother. Yet Reilly is quick to assert that mother should be seen and not heard: "Restraint is our clearly indicated path."[18] A 1938 *Parents' Magazine* article speaks to mothers who feel their teenage daughters are not confiding in them, arguing that mothers must prove themselves worthy of trust by treating their daughters as they would treat a good friend. The author even chastises mothers who allow their minds to be occupied with other things, thus neglecting the information their daughters *do* choose to impart: "We all do it. Push aside their confidences and enthusiasms and troubles for something that interests us more at the moment and then wonder why they don't tell us more."[19]

Mothers are not always to be restrained with their daughters, particularly when it comes to questions of "success" with boys, given that "All girls want masculine attention. Most girls want to think that they are going to be married one day." Although "no mother of a girl in her teens should expect to be happy," the resourceful mother can help her daughter wedge her way into the bliss of male attention by providing her with ample private space (even if it means giving up her own privacy), dancing lessons, and the best clothes and hairstyles to enable the daughter to be "the center of a pleasant entertainment," making sure that mother stays "as far as possible in the background."[20]

The specter of the overinvolved mother rears its ugly head even in these financially trying times, as demonstrated in a rather typical piece by Eleanor Boykin that asks the pressing question: "Should Mothers Be Matchmakers?" Boykin begins by stating the common wisdom that "Every mother of a girl knows that her daughter's best chances of happiness lie in a satisfactory marriage." Mothers need to do all they can to help their daughters find the perfect mate, even if it means moving into a new neighborhood where the young men are up to par. Overambitious and selfish mothers are the bane of the budding wife's existence, either demanding too much from the daughters (as Ruth Hawthorne feels) or "taking the center of the stage themselves." Although mother-blame is on the rise here, it is generally much less virulent than the "momism" that emerged in the 1940s. Boykin ends her piece by attempting a balance—"Let us be fair and admit that mothers do not deserve the credit for all the happy marriages or the blame for all the unhappy ones"—while maintaining the position of mother as primary socializer of adolescent daughter.[21]

This notion of "balance" and maternal mental health crops up in a 1930 Parents' Magazine piece, "This Business of Being a Mother," where Lovisa Wagoner is concerned to present a more comprehensive picture of motherhood that alerts readers to the limits of maternal endurance and the need for mothers to "escape from the daily grind." Although emphasizing the need for mothers to find outside relaxation ("It is quite legitimate for a mother to feel that she needs to get away from her children occasionally"), this article tries to work out problems of maternal depression within the confines of a rigidly domestic life: "One reason that mothers frequently fall into a rut or suffer from depression is that they are too closely confined by the care of their children. A mother finds her greatest satisfaction, of course, in being with them." To remedy this sorry state, the healthy mother should not only go to the PTA, visit friends, and find religion, but should "take a vacation from herself" so that she can "detach [herself] from the strain of everyday life" and regain her much needed poise.[22]

Barbara Beattie encourages mothers to prepare their daughters for adolescence rather than simply allow them to go on as little girls. Girls need to be tested for "normalcy" so they "approach adolescence fortified by normal reactions." But girls can be handicapped in their attempts at normalcy by an "inability . . . to think and act with any degree of independence." Culpability is obvious: "Too often mothers are to blame for this undesirable characteristic in their daughters, for they consciously or unconsciously want to keep their children young and dependent upon them for decisions and opinions concerning even the smallest details."[23]

Mostly the mother-blame was rather mild, as indicated by the previous quote. I did, however, come across an unusually virulent piece in a 1931 issue of the Delineator. Simply titled "Mothers and Daughters," this article seems markedly out of step with the more benign vision of the relationship evidenced in popular culture of the period. Indeed, it is more reminiscent of the 1940s psychoanalytic themes and perhaps foreshadows the demonization of mothers looming on the cultural horizon. Ruth Hawthorne opens the article with a lengthy retelling of the narrative of Sidney Howard's play

*The Silver Cord,* a typically "momist" diatribe against overbearing, controlling mothers and their cowed sons. But the author of this article rethinks this narrative in terms of mothers and daughters, claiming, "It takes two women to fight this particular issue through or at least bring it out as an issue."[24]

References both to the depression and to the "new woman" of the 1920s permeate this article as the author assures us that "modern young women" still find themselves in the "maternal spider web" in their endless sacrificing for the always demanding mothers. Mother's endless games of power and control are understood by reference to her own failed life, her own disappointments, as she constructs a "will to power, as it is so aptly called by psychologists." By referencing developing ideologies of independence and individual freedom, the author validates the centrality of the mother/daughter struggle over what has typically been thought of as the more crucial battle between mother and son: "A man and a woman, struggling over the pawn of the man's life and freedom, are far more cosmic in their implications than two women bickering over whether one of them shall go to a dance with George or stay at home and read aloud to mother." But Hawthorne is convinced that the situation between mothers and daughters is "more tragic" because the son can, after all, escape from mother into the world of business, while the daughter cannot. The author sees hope both in daughters who are openly flaunting their mother's rampant authority and in mothers who are valuing independence and responsibility. Nevertheless, "all old orders change slowly, and we have had the sacrificial mother—waiting around for her daughter to grow up enough to be sacrificial in her turn—written in our book of rules too long for it to be an easy change."[25]

## Malevolent Moms and Desperate Daughters: The Viper Years

By the forties, the mildness of women's magazine articles and the gentleness of the maternal melodrama begin to recede. Forties films were filled either with wartime propaganda or, as the war came to a close, with the urgent need to recuperate women into acceptable postwar family life. This shift, from a more benign view of the mother/daughter relationship to one steeped in psychological condemnations, seems fundamental here. It entailed a shift away from a focus on class and toward a focus on sexuality, as Michael Renov has pointed out: "In the context of American social life during the World War II years, it was sexual difference rather than class conflict that constituted the crucial problematic to which countless cultural artifacts and public utterances were addressed."[26]

By 1942, a year that witnessed the publication of Philip Wylie's *Generation of Vipers*, one of the most virulent attacks on women in the last fifty years, we get a very different sort of representation of mothers and daughters than in the prewar years. Wylie's book remains one of the most astoundingly misogynist tomes in recent memory. His basic thesis—that America was being weakened from within by a horde of omnipotent "moms" who turned men into sniveling company dolts and women into awful moms-in-training— found a home in the mid to late forties.

Generally, the architects of "momism" focused on the deleterious effects of overprotective/domineering/smothering moms on the men of the nation. The concern was primarily with mothers and sons. Although "moms" created cowardly men unable to fight bravely for their nation, the effect on girls is understood more as a reproduction of mom herself: "And it is not always the son who suffers. I have known many a young woman who has realized that she was being dominated by her mom, and upon the mom's death experienced a feeling of freedom and relief, but ultimately has lived strictly according to her mom's selfish code."[27]

For Wylie, Edward Strecker, and their ilk, the psychic health of girls was of little concern when such weighty problems as the moral fiber of the nation were at issue. Daughters were thought to be victims of moms too, but the model here was one of endless generational reproduction rather than specific and deadly aberration: "In most cases, a mom is a mom because she is the immature result of a mom."[28] Yet the implications of the ideology of momism on the mother/daughter relationship are profound and far-reaching.

*Now, Voyager* (1942) pulls no punches in its portrayal of maternal evil and its deleterious effects on unwitting daughters. Most critics have not focused on the mother/daughter aspects of this film, tending instead to see it in terms of the explicit psychiatric narrative or the hopeless love story of Charlotte (Bette Davis) and Jerry (Paul Henreid). But insofar as the story is a classic Cinderella one, with Bette Davis as the ugly duckling virtually imprisoned by her tyrannical mother, we must understand her quest, and thus these secondary narratives, as motivated by the desire to grow up and away from the maternal nest.

*Now, Voyager* contains an impressive cast including Bette Davis, Paul Henreid, and Claude Rains. It tells the story of Charlotte Vale, a spinster living in fear of her domineering and tyrannical mother, who, since the death of her husband, has kept Charlotte a virtual prisoner in their Boston Brahmin mansion. Charlotte is the archetypical spinster: shy, unattractive, overweight, with strange and quirky hobbies that signify her "otherness" (woman without man).[29] Enter the hero, this time in the split form of a psychiatrist who promptly diagnoses the mother's guilt and viciousness ("Mrs. Vale, if you had deliberately tried to ruin your daughter's life you couldn't have done a more complete job") and an inaccessible lover who proves to the ugly duckling that she is indeed a swan.

The discourse of psychiatry is pronounced and explicit here: Dr. Jacquith is presented right off as the expert who can cure Charlotte of the neuroses her mother has produced in her. But, significantly, the figure of the mother is the block to emotional cure: she distrusts the medical profession, as she informs Dr. Jacquith, and shames Charlotte in her meeting with a psychiatrist. In this scene, when the doctor is brought to the house by Charlotte's sister-in-law to examine Charlotte, Mrs. Vale expresses her contempt for the profession and, in doing so, reveals a decidedly outmoded understanding of psychiatry:

*Mother:*  "Probably one of those places with a high-wire fence and yowling inmates."

*Dr.:*  "Well now, I wouldn't want anyone to have that mistaken notion. Cascade is just a place in the country. People go to it when they are tired. . . ."

*Mother:*  "The very word psychiatry, Dr. Jacquith. Doesn't it fill you with shame? My daughter, a member of our family."

*Dr.:*  "There's nothing shameful about my work or frightening or anything else. It's very simple really what I try to do. People walk along the road, they come to a fork in the road, they're confused, they don't know which way to take. I just put up a signpost. Not that way, this way."

During this speech, the doctor is first standing, and the mother is looking up at him. This pattern is repeated throughout the film.

Toward the end, though, he is positioned between Charlotte's chair and the mother's chair, as if to signify his role as mediator between the two warring women, and the close-up at the end of his little discourse on psychiatry further establishes his position of mastery. More important, this speech affirms the mother's backward idea of psychiatry and produces a very benign and innocuous perception of the psychiatric enterprise: the sanitarium is just a place in the country, and the doctor is simply a traffic warden of the soul.

This attempt to normalize psychiatry is consonant with the more general explosion of popular psychology onto the cultural scene.[30] In a period when "the advice of experts" was increasingly becoming the commonsense culture of American everyday life, the mother's resistance to the doctor can be seen not only as a holding on to her daughter (which is wrong, of course), but as an impediment to progress (which is also wrong, of course, especially in a soon to be postwar economy).[31] If Stella is the impediment to social mobility and class ascendancy for her daughter, the aristocratic Mrs. Vale is the impediment to social health/social control; in holding back her daughter, she may just hold back the nation. The "old-fashioned," commonsense parenting approach of the mother is shown to be overpowering, exclusive, smothering, and unhealthy. It is associated with the rigidity the mother expresses in the first few minutes of the film as she berates the erring servants. Stella's mothering was merely "not enough" for her daughter's social growth, but the mothering of the evil Mrs. Vale is clearly malevolent. Charlotte needs treatment, expert help, so she may "grow free and blossom," as the doctor puts it.

Indeed, the mother here is very visibly the figure of Victorian repression: She is consistently dressed in a clearly Victorian costume with tightly buttoned collar and lace around her wrists and neck. She "matches" the Victorian furniture in her relic of a mansion. She is altogether anachronistic, an obsolete old woman who is the physical embodiment of an era long surpassed.

Charlotte does get "saved" by the good doctor, but medicine alone cannot right the wrongs of a woman-dominated woman: enter the other hero, this time in the dashing figure of Jerry (Paul Henreid), a sorrowful and lonely man whose "sick" wife sounds suspiciously like Charlotte's neglectful mother. The curative powers are now placed onto Charlotte: they fall in love, and Jerry is reborn, but he will never leave his wife (duty before desire).

The shipboard affair between Charlotte and the long-suffering but noble Jerry is the first of many scenes that are repetitions: Charlotte here is repeating a disastrous sea journey she had as a young woman on which her repressive mother cut off her affair with a sailor. In this flashback scene, the connection between Mrs. Vale's repressiveness and class becomes apparent. Charlotte's suitor is unsuitable, a common man whom Charlotte must avoid just as she must avoid the other tourists on board. Apparently, this aristocratic elitism was dissonant with the forties wartime emphasis on a sort of pluralistic patriotism.

Now cured, Charlotte repeats the journey. This time her sexuality fully "blooms" sans the restrictive presence of her mother. But most important, Charlotte gets to "redo" her mothering when she takes Jerry's lonely daughter under her wing (they meet at the sanitarium, where Charlotte has gone for a tune-up after her mother has conveniently died in a moment of rebellious confrontation) and makes her well through the love and attention that neither "girl" received. In this film, the only good mother is a pseudo one: Charlotte gets the chance to "do mothering right" where two mothers have so profoundly failed: "While biological mothers in the film are distinctly lacking in mothering skills . . . Charlotte turns motherhood into a profession—part psychotherapist, part nurse, part charming companion."[32] In doing so, she must renounce her sexuality: Paul will never leave his wife.

The film ends with the classic cigarette lighting scene in which Charlotte tells Jerry, "Oh, Jerry, we have the stars, let's not ask for the moon." The stars presumably are the shining light of motherhood, and the moon is the murky and changing passions of adult sexuality. Charlotte thus becomes an advertisement for the "constructed mother." In this film, as in much of the culture at large, maternal instincts are depicted as often aggressive and destructive; one must *learn* how to be a good mother.[33] Charlotte has learned, as the happy child proves. And that, of course, is the happiness Charlotte seeks.

The merger in this film of the psychiatric discourse and that of mothering is striking. They depend on each other for their legitimation. The former depends on the figure of the "unhappy couple" of the evil mother and the neurotic daughter to justify the therapeutic intervention. Indeed, the strong, male voice of the doctor serves as an omnipresent reminder to Charlotte of how to conduct herself. As Charlotte returns home from her second sea voyage—the one on which she is reborn—she goes upstairs to see her mother. Right before she enters the room, the doctor's disembodied voice-over gives her strength: "Just remember that honoring one's parents is still a pretty good idea. You're going to be a shock to her. I advise you to soften the blow. Give her a little time to get used to you. Remember that whatever she may have done, she's your mother."

Charlotte enters the room and finds it difficult to resist the overpowering mother, and we sense a failure in her future. In the nick of time, she receives flowers from Jerry and thus finds the power to resist, to be her own woman. Thus two men give a woman the strength to fight off another woman. Charlotte is now able to give her triumphant "I'm my own person" speech to her furious mother: "Mother, I don't want to be disagreeable or unkind. I've come home to live with you in the same house. But it can't be in the same way. I've been living my own life, making my own decisions for a long while now. It isn't possible to go back to being treated like a child again. I don't think I'll do anything of importance that will displease you. But mother, from now on you must give me complete freedom."

Mother does grant her complete freedom, forties style: she throws herself down the stairs in defiance of her daughter's defiance. In this scene, Charlotte is off camera during her grand speech, and all we see is the back of the mother, tapping her laced hand on the daughter's bedpost, while Charlotte's voice emerges from an adjoining dressing room. Charlotte's inability to face her mother signifies the incompleteness of her cure. The full resistance can occur only after Charlotte herself is "full" with a man and child (Jerry and his daughter) and the mother has completely disappeared from the family picture.

What is striking is the explicitness of both discourses. Charlotte even mocks the psychiatrist when she first meets him ("She locks the door, doctor. Make a note of it. Its significance."). But it doesn't take much for the good doctor to break through Charlotte's "defenses" and whisk her away for a cure at Cascade, mildly described as a "place in the country." Throughout the film, Charlotte refers to her "repression," her "inhibitions." She becomes the advertisement for the new psychology, even suggesting that Jerry send his daughter to Cascade.

Perhaps it is the aristocratic setting of the film—replete with Victorian mansion, servants, and ocean cruises—that allows for a more explicit discourse of psychology and maternal evil. Released from any financial concerns (except Charlotte's mild anxiety over her inheritance), Charlotte and her mother can now immerse themselves fully in psychological concerns. Although psychology has most assuredly replaced class here as a central narrative theme, the aristocratic upper classness of Mrs. Vale is depicted as part of her anachronism. Her snobbery is part of what oppresses the daughter, although she seems to live off her mother's beneficence without excessive guilt.

In a crucial scene, when Charlotte refuses to be scared by her mother, refuses to give in, she uses this as ammunition: "Dr. Jacquith says that tyranny is sometimes the expression of the maternal instinct." At this point, when Charlotte confronts the agent of her oppression, the mother has a heart attack, slumps in her chair, and dies. Although Charlotte now believes she killed her mother ("I did it, I did it"), symbolically the mother has been killed by the burden of the new psychiatric "truth."

As Karen Anderson points out in her book on wartime women, a good deal of the anxiety expressed about the working mother both during the war and with much more vigor afterward was related to the fear that the much vaunted "maternal instinct," which had always been a bedrock of biological arguments about "women's place," was perhaps not so firmly ingrained as had been previously thought: "The fear expressed about women rejecting their children, especially by psychologists and social welfare officials, reflected a surprising anxiety about the presence or strength of the 'maternal instinct.' Similarly, the apprehension regarding the abandonment of feminine roles belied the conventional wisdom regarding an ostensibly immutable feminine personality."[34]

Even many of the women's magazines, in the rush to adapt psychology to a popular, female audience, stressed that mothers ought not to rely so firmly on their "maternal instinct," but instead should depend on more reliable sources, as this article from a January 1945 *Good Housekeeping* implies: "The average woman tends to accept her offspring at face value and to depend on her Mother's Intuition to keep her informed of what's going on—and not, as she should, on observation, psychology, and the ability to face facts."[35] This mutation from Stella Dallas's intuitive knowledge of what to do for her

Fig. 5. Bette Davis appears again, this time as the mother-oppressed Charlotte Vale in the classic melodrama *Now, Voyager,* here confronting the demon as she announces her newfound independence. (Warner Brothers, 1942; photo courtesy of Photofest)

daughter (even how to sacrifice) to a new construction of inherently evil motherhood (maternal instinct as flawed and thus in need of medical intervention to set it straight) can be seen as an attempt to avoid the implications of changing social/sexual relations by deflecting the real transformations in the body politic (particularly women's increased involvement in the paid labor force) onto the question of maternal instinct.

Bad maternal instinct must be eradicated and replaced with the sentiments of the constructed/scientific mom (Charlotte), whose "good mothering" to her pseudodaughter (Jerry's daughter) is very clearly the result of "observation, psychology, and the ability to face facts." They do, after all, meet in the mental institution under the watchful eyes of the expert/psychiatrist (Charlotte even refers to him as "God"). In the war to liberate daughters from their fearsome mothers, psychiatry is clearly the best weapon.[36]

In a 1944 film, *Mr. Skeffington,* Davis is again paired with

Fig. 6. Pseudomom Charlotte finds her own mother-neglected little girl
to save in lover Jerry's (Paul Henreid) "ugly duckling" of a daughter.
(Warner Brothers, 1942; photo courtesy of the Museum of Modern Art
Film Stills Archive)

Claude Rains; but this time she is the vain, rejecting mother, and
Rains is the long-suffering Jewish husband, Job Skeffington, who
raises their daughter in Germany while party girl Fanny (Davis)
devours younger and younger men. Youth conscious mom is star-
tled by the sudden arrival of her now grown daughter, and when
the ravages of diphtheria take their toll, she is eventually taught the
error of her decidedly nonmaternal ways. Although it is clearly too
late for repentant mom to make it up to the daughter she aban-
doned, her maternal instinct is now reawakened, and she is re-
deemed through the return of Job, now blinded and weakened after
years in a concentration camp.

## Rosie the Riveter Revisited: Too Much
## Mother/Too Little Mother

In 1945, another important mother/daughter film with another
powerful female star at its helm emerged to complete the shift from

benign to aggressive, from sacrificial to overpowering, from class conflict to psychopathology.

*Mildred Pierce* is the story of a woman who moves up from slaving housewife to owner of a chain of restaurants. This method of class ascendancy (entrepreneurial, suburban, referencing the mass consumption of the future with its chain store motif) contrasts with Stella's more traditional rise via marriage. But Mildred's rise to the top is only one part of the narrative. Mildred's relationship with her greedy and malicious daughter Veda moves the narrative and is the catalyst for the climactic finale. Almost every motivation for Mildred's actions—from leaving her husband to marrying the aristocratic moocher, Monty—originates with her devotion to this daughter above all else in her life. Yet this is no straightforward maternal sacrifice film in which the mother's sacrifice is at least rewarded (à la *Stella Dallas*) by seeing the daughter go happily off into the sunset because Mildred's daughter ends up being arrested for the murder of Mildred's second husband, Monty. Ironically, it is the mother who goes off into the sunset in this film, reunited now with her original husband, Burt.

*Mildred Pierce* is a particularly interesting film not only because it is a strange combination of film noir (a traditionally "male" genre) and melodrama (a traditionally "female" genre), but because it offers a reading of the mother/daughter relationship that inhabits two worlds, two paradigms.[37] *Mildred Pierce* is certainly a film operating very much within the "back to the kitchen" mode of the late war and immediate postwar years (many of the scenes are literally set in kitchens, both public and private). It is a harsh condemnation of working women; more precisely, of working *mothers,* for this new labor pool (white, middle-class mothers) provoked the greatest outcry during and after the war. Even the war propaganda in the women's magazines, while urging women to work as a patriotic duty, constructed a strict hierarchy of admissible female labor, with single women at the top of the list and mothers with young children at the bottom, as a sort of last resort. While debates about working women raged, one position seems to have been shared by all, even the supporters of full participation in the labor force: women with young children should not, unless absolutely necessary, work outside the home. The age usually stated was three years, not coincidentally a crucial age for Freudian theory, which was becoming increasingly popularized.

This disapproval of working mothers was widespread in the late war and postwar years. The ferocious attack on working mothers seemed to begin as soon as women began working in the defense industries: "Scare stories about 'latchkey children' and 'eight-hour orphans' filled the newspapers and magazines, even though most surveys showed that the vast majority of working mothers made arrangements for the care of their children before they took jobs."[38] Released in 1945, when men were returning home from war, this film demonstrates the commitment to placing women back in their "proper" place. As Linda Williams has noted, the film's avoidance of specific references to the war allows for both a reflection and a repression of women's wartime experience: "Some of the most important issues raised by the war are not reflected in the films about the war. It is as if only those films that could both reflect *and* repress could also *manage* these issues so important to women's new wartime experience."[39]

*Mildred Pierce* is also a film about maternal sacrifice; as Mildred tells us in no uncertain terms, "I've done without a lot of things— including happiness sometimes—because I wanted her to have everything." Mildred is endlessly doing for her daughter, giving more and more. Yet, while Stella's sacrifice pays off (Laurel marries the man of her dreams and enters into the upper-class world), Mildred's sacrifice not only backfires, but is seen as slightly unhealthy. What was a sign of love and devotion in *Stella Dallas* is now a sign of smothering, overinvolvement, and, ultimately, pathology. This film invokes the resurgent spirit of popular psychology in that it clearly places blame on the mother for the wretched way her beloved daughter has turned out, a popular sport in the 1940s.

The way these two discourses—on maternal sacrifice and maternal deprivation—work hand in hand produces the ideological moment of the film. This moment speaks directly to the aggressive ideological work of the late war and early postwar years, a work predicated on the disjuncture between the rise in working women and developing images of domesticity. In other words, the media were actively *working* to construct an ideological edifice that would

safely enthrone Rosie the Riveter as a patriotic heroine while cur-
tailing the radical potentials embodied in both the image and reality of "Rosie." This gap between the lived experience of women and
the images of their lives in the mass media was a persistent thorn in
the side of the culture industry that films like *Mildred Pierce* tried
their best to reconcile.

Mildred's sacrifice seems to backfire, spoiling and warping the
very child she purports to adore. Even Mildred's vapid husband
Burt wonders if it isn't perhaps a bit "abnormal" that Mildred is so
devoted to and sacrificing for Veda. In the first flashback scene,
Burt tells Mildred that she's "trying to buy love from those kids and
it won't work" and concludes, "There's something wrong Mildred,
I don't know what, I'm not smart that way but I know it isn't right."
Throughout the scene, the camera follows Mildred's movements as
if she were the changeable, unstable force, and Burt appears as the
constant and steady presence, commenting knowingly on the errors of his wife's daughter-obsessed ways.

There is a sort of double assault going on here, as mothers are
blamed for both their psychological and social mishandling of their
children. This film is responding to the growing trend in popular
psychology to place the full responsibility for the child's psychological health firmly on the mother's shoulders. As E. Ann Kaplan
notes:

In the post-war period both the maternal melodrama and the woman's
film undergo marked changes. Indeed, the maternal sacrifice theme may
be said to have all but exhausted itself, its essentially nineteenth-century
ideology being finally archaic. In its place, we have a different kind of
male Oedipal drama that focuses either, as in film noir, on the threat of
female sexuality (now seen as extremely dangerous), or on the Mother's
inadequacies, especially her inability to foster psychic health. *Mildred
Pierce* and *Now, Voyager* may be seen as setting the pattern for 50s and
later films in their portrayals of the alternately masochistic and sadistic
Mother. Close Mother-daughter bonding is now seen not merely as "unhealthy" but as leading either to evil, or to neurosis.[40]

Motherhood here is dangerous, suspect, almost unnatural. The
men in the film repeatedly tell Mildred that "something is not quite
right" with her doting closeness with Veda.

Not only are mothers presented as fully responsible for the psychological health of their offspring, but, with the growing concern

Fig. 7. (Too) hardworking restaurateur Mildred (Joan Crawford) finds out in *Mildred Pierce* the violent way that too much mother love can produce killer daughters. (Warner Brothers, 1945; photo courtesy of Museum of Modern Art Film Archives)

over rising rates of juvenile delinquency during the war years and after, mothers were targeted as responsible for the social behavior of their daughters as well:

Many expressed concern that the problems of child neglect and juvenile delinquency might have been intensified by the loosening of family ties, the separation of families, the rising divorce rate, the employment of teenagers at high salaries, and, most particularly, the expanded employment of mothers. . . . Most law enforcement and other officials cited parental neglect as the most important contributor to increased juvenile delinquency and contended that working mothers were a primary cause of such negligence.[41]

Even the head of the FBI, J. Edgar Hoover, contributed to the growing sense that there was a relationship between the spread of juvenile crime and the increasing numbers of women in the work force. Hoover gravely informs us that mothers are "our only hope" in the battle against the decline of wholesome youth, a problem

exacerbated by the absence of fathers during the war: "At this point
the war enters the picture by placing a double burden on mothers.
Fathers who might be roused by a campaign of education to become not only examples but preceptors for their children are in
many instances away at war or at war work. . . . If the drift of normal youth towards immorality and crime is to be stopped, mothers
must do the stopping." He goes on to inform us that the "happy
home" without juvenile delinquency "is the home where the child
rushes in and calls, 'Mother!' and gets a welcoming answer." [42]

One question haunts the film: Why is Veda the way she is? Is she
just a "bad seed" who somehow emerges from nowhere to haunt
her innocent mother? Or does the film lead us to believe that, in
some very profound sense, Veda's greed and evil are directly attributable to her mother, a woman seemingly obsessed with giving the
child "all that she never had"? Mildred's working is never directly
denigrated; indeed, the denigration she receives from Monty and
Veda is shown as mean, ungrateful, and snobbish. But the narrative
works in such a way as to be critical of Mildred's status as business-
woman without directly confronting the issue, a strategy perhaps
more disturbing in its subtlety. Why does Mildred go out to work?
She must support her family. Why must she support her family?
She has kicked her husband out of the house. Curiously, we see
that Mildred had always worked—baking pies for neighbors. But
this work is "acceptable" because it is done within the confines of
the family kitchen and to supplement the husband's meager income. Mildred becomes both more dangerous and more powerful
once that same labor is released from its domestic environment
and made "public." This tendency is consistent with government
propaganda and the policies of the wartime Women's Bureau:
women working was an unfortunate necessity, and when it was necessary, at least it should be in work appropriate to their sex, such as
cooking.

The narrative not only indicts Mildred's status as working
woman; it also links that labor with her failures both in love and in
mothering. Why has she kicked her husband out of the house?
Here again we return to Veda, for it is over a fight concerning her—
how Mildred is spoiling her—that Burt Pierce leaves. Indeed,
even his involvement with another woman, which is also central to
their breakup, can be seen as attributable to Mildred's overinvolve-

ment with her daughter and subsequent neglect of her wifely duties. Mother/daughter intimacy is almost always at the expense of husband/wife intimacy: here again the mother/woman split dominates the narratives of popular culture.

Veda has turned on her mother, but is there any way for a 1940s audience, familiar with Philip Wylie's *Generation of Vipers* and his battalion of imitators, to understand this other than as the (perhaps well-intentioned) bad mothering of Mildred? After all, we know Mildred is bad because she has, through her involvement with her work and a man romantically, allowed her younger daughter to die. Kay, the "good" daughter, mysteriously contracts pneumonia and dies in a single day—the single day that Mildred happens to be out with another man and her estranged husband Burt has the kids. Indeed, as soon as her husband walks out, Mildred becomes fair game to every man who enters her life: the tawdriness of the scene with her husband's old partner, coming as it does on the heels of Burt's departure, only reinforces the idea that now Mildred is somehow "unclean." She is clearly held responsible for her uncleanliness (and for Kay's death), yet curiously seems to show little long-term remorse or grief.

Not only is Mildred punished by the loss of her other daughter, Veda, at the end of the film, but she is further punished as the daughter steals away the mother's lover. The theme of mother/daughter sexual rivalry has been a staple of popular culture, but *Mildred Pierce* adds a strange twist: it is a completely one-sided rivalry. In the context of 1940s ideologies of irresponsible mothering, Veda's involvement with Monty can be seen as an indication of maternal deprivation in two senses. First, if Mildred weren't so busy making money, she would be more aware of what is happening right under her nose (indeed, it was she who pushed the two together). Second, if Mildred were more of a mother, more attentive to her daughter's emotional life, the daughter wouldn't have to turn to Monty to get her mother's attention, and perhaps the murder wouldn't have even taken place.

Mildred's last attempt at sacrifice (to take the rap for that murder) is doomed from its noir start; the true killer must be found out by the masterly—yet almost anonymous—male detective ("Not this time, Mrs. Berrigan. This time your daughter pays for her own mistakes.") As many film critics have argued, the noir part of this film seems in many ways to outweigh its melodrama counterpart and sets the tone (the film begins in noir fashion—a gunshot, a man dies, a suicidal woman on a pier on a dark and rainy night) for the guilty-woman resolution (not of murder, but of bad mothering, which led to the murder) that is so much a part of film noir.

Clearly, the change here is from a more complexly layered representation of the mother/daughter relationship where attachment itself wasn't necessarily suspect (*Stella Dallas*) to an image of this relationship that presents intimacy and attachment as inherently debilitating and essentially unhealthy. The attachment was clearly mutual between Stella and Laurel, and the poignancy of the film derives at least in part from the audience's knowledge of the very palpable and mutual love that existed between the mother and daughter.

Mildred's attachment, conversely, is coded as "overinvolved" and rejected by the daughter, who moves out of the house to live on her own and become a nightclub singer (a plot device used to great effect in another classic mother/daughter film, *Imitation of Life*). The difference in the two films is graphically visualized in a brief comparison of two similar scenes. In *Stella Dallas*, the scene is the already mentioned one on the train, an unusual depiction of mutuality and love. The counterpart in *Mildred Pierce* takes place right after Mildred's husband has left and Mildred is upstairs in the girls' bedroom, saying goodnight to Veda. Similarly lit, the mise-en-scène, like that of the earlier film, evokes a romantic environment. Yet this scene exposes the daughter's greed (not her love and concern for her mother) and depicts the mother's sacrificial intent as a desperate attempt to hold on to her unloving daughter. Their words of love ("I love you, Veda." "I love you too, Mother.") are brutally parodied as Mildred reaches over to kiss her daughter, and the daughter utters the unforgettable line, "But don't let's get sticky about it." What a contrast to the bittersweet tenderness of the train scene in *Stella Dallas*.

*Claudia* (1943), starring Dorothy McGuire, Robert Young, and Ina Claire, spells out very straightforwardly the new concern with "too much" mother/daughter attachment. It does so in the form not of film noir, as in *Mildred Pierce*, or classic melodrama, as in *Now, Voyager*, but rather in the jokey, light form of a sort of comedic, sitcom melodrama. *Claudia* was the first of several films to be made

Fig. 8. Poor Claudia just can't seem to get over her "mother thing."
Dorothy McGuire plays the naive girl/woman who must "let mom go" so
she can team up more vigorously with paternalistic hubby Robert Young
in *Claudia*. (20th Century-Fox, 1943; photo courtesy of Photofest)

by the McGuire/Young team. In this early one, McGuire plays a
recently married young woman who has moved with her husband
to a farm in Connecticut, outside of New York, where he works as
an architect. The character of Claudia is a staple of Hollywood films:
the not quite grown woman-child, almost tomboyish, innocent
babe in the woods. Visually, the contrast between Claudia, with her
flopping hair, simple gingham shifts, and boyish figure, and her
husband David, with his pipe, suit, and paternal manner, could not
be more striking.

The catch with this film is that Claudia's "immaturity," her inability to grow up and be a mature wife (and mother), is directly referenced by her ties with her mother. Claudia's mother has been visiting for the weekend but has left unexpectedly to return to New
York. Claudia is curious, and sends her husband to find out what
the story is. In this interchange, the subject of Claudia's overattachment to her mother is made explicit, as is the position of the mother
vis-à-vis this "problem."

| | |
|---|---|
| *Mother:* | "Oh, David, Claudia's worse than a detective. I never have been able to fool her." |
| *David:* | "Well, she certainly has herself an overdose of mother image." |
| *Mother:* | "Yes, I wish she hadn't." |
| *David:* | "I wish she hadn't too." |
| *Mother:* | "That's why I was so glad about you buying this house." |
| *David:* | "The only thing she doesn't like about it is leaving you in New York." |
| *Mother:* | "That's the best thing that could have happened to all three of us." |

Here the stereotypical attachment issue manifests itself alongside the rather strange image of the mother and son-in-law bonding around the overattachment of the daughter to the mother. This is interesting because most films depict daughters struggling to break free of their "overinvolved" mothers. In this film the mother is enlisted as an aid in the separation, rather than an impediment, and in alliance with the male "rescuer" rather than in opposition to him. Nevertheless, the necessity for the separation remains the same.

As in *Now, Voyager,* the daughter's independence from the mother is directly related to the daughter's ability to be successfully heterosexual: that is, to be a good wife and mother. Growing up is explicitly related to separation, as David makes clear in the film: "Now listen darling, when are you going to grow up and stop being a Mama's Girl?" And Claudia certainly doesn't refute his analysis of her problem; she too sees her attachment as "unhealthy": "Yes, I know it's not good. Someday when I'm an old woman I'll develop a twitch in one eye and you'll hype me to the doctors and he'll say it's because I have an attachment to my mother."

The mother's "secret" is that she has an "illness" and is going to die. This is perhaps the only melodramatic element to the narrative. Not coincidentally, this revelation occurs at the same time Claudia finds out that she's pregnant, making it more difficult for her to tell Claudia she's dying:

| | |
|---|---|
| *Mother:* | "Oh, it'll be so hard to tell her now. I'm a coward, David." |
| *David:* | "When it comes to Claudia I think you are at that. You haven't got the insides to let her do her own suffering." |

| | |
|---|---|
| *Mother:* | "She's not disciplined to pain. Life's been gentle to her up to now." |
| *David:* | "And you want to go on taking the hard knocks and leaving her the easy ones." |

Although said with much less venom, this is not that far from Mrs. Vale's claim in *Now, Voyager* that "I've always made decisions for my little girl. Always the right ones." Although in this case the roles are rather reversed (mother here is not the evil force of repression, but wants to see her daughter "free" herself from her), the message is still the same: to be an adult is to be separate from mother and attached to men. Dr. Jacquith's assertion that the daughter must be allowed to "grow free and blossom in her own right" is consistent with the discourse here about self-determination.

The daughter does know about the mother's illness, and this knowledge is what propels her to "grow up":

| | |
|---|---|
| *Mother:* | "She knows, David." |
| *David:* | "Yes Mother. She knows." |
| *Mother:* | "And she's let me go?" |
| *David:* | "I think so." |
| *Mother:* | "Ohh, it makes all the difference David." |
| *David:* | "Does it Mother?" |
| *Mother:* | "Yes. It's like a miracle. It's as though she were the mother and I were the child." |
| *David:* | "Well, maybe that's the way it should be. If it's . . . right." |
| *Mother:* | "It's right David. Suddenly I'm quite sure of that." |

So "letting go" is here the sign of maturity: the "way it should be." The ending reiterates this once more. As the mother walks upstairs, a sort of farewell occurs between her and her daughter. Standing looking up at her mother ascending the stairs (to her death), Claudia says, "So long, Mrs. Brown." And the mother replies, "So long, Mrs. Naughton," as if by calling each other by their married (male) names, they acknowledge each other's grown-upness. The mother continues up the stairs; Claudia stands on the landing while her husband enters the frame, and the couple is framed in a shot. The camera then pulls back as Claudia walks down the stairs, and her husband follows. The two then face each other, and David says, "Hello darling," to which Claudia replies, "Hello David," followed by a fade-out. Moving from the close-up of mother and daughter (separately) saying goodbye to the coupled, two-shot of the husband and wife saying hello could not be clearer: the mother has died so that the daughter can be free to be an adult wife to her adult husband—good-bye mama (immaturity, presexuality, boyishness, innocence, enmeshment), hello hubby (adult sexuality, maturity, coupleness, sophistication, emotional distance).

## War Workers and Mothers in Training: Togetherness on the Home Front

The women's magazines of the war years paint a more benign picture of the mother/daughter relationship. Although the introduction of psychology and the rise of the experts found their way into the magazines, the conflict rendered so explicitly in both *Now, Voyager* and *Mildred Pierce* seems almost absent. Instead, we find an approach that has to do with the "new" responsibilities daughter must take on as mother enters the labor market. Primarily, these are organized around domestic tasks as daughter is urged to stand in for mom, acting as mother and housewife for dad and the boys: "With mothers doing war work . . . and with household help fast vanishing, lucky is the family that boasts a daughter! And lucky is the daughter who can learn at home the art of planning, buying and preparing meals for a family."[43]

Magazines such as *Good Housekeeping* promoted the idea of daughter as mother/housewife in training with regular sections such as "Cook's Kindergarten" and "Homemaker's Kindergarten" that paraded headlines like "Susan makes hot cross buns" and "Susan does the dishes in record time." Ads for household products often included mother and daughter using them together, marveling at how quickly the housework will now be done, or sharing war work, as in the ad series for "Tangee Natural Lipstick" ("mother does the seeding—daughter, the weeding"). Clearly, the aim was to present the woman war worker as fulfilling her patriotic duty and, most important, remaining devoted to the family and not producing significant disruptions: "Advertisers conveyed the message that employed women would not disrupt the family. . . . War workers were often shown in housewife/mother roles—working with or taking care of children or doing housework in factory coveralls. Children pictured in these scenes cheerfully helped their mothers with household tasks, especially young daughters who were frequently dressed in coveralls and kerchiefs themselves."[44]

However located in the domestic this vision might be, what emerges from the women's magazines is both a sense of mother/daughter togetherness (be it in war work or in housework) and, to a lesser extent, mother serving as role model (albeit a "superwoman" one) for daughter. Except for the explicitly war-focused films, we see no consistent cinematic counterpart to the "togetherness" motif found in magazines.

The reasons for this discrepancy in media representations are in many ways quite simple. The women's magazines, very much like Hollywood films of the period, were explicitly enjoined in the war effort by the direct "guidance" of the propaganda efforts of the Magazine Bureau, which published the bimonthly *Magazine War Guide* from 1942 to 1945. Writers, editors, and publishers sat in on meetings of the bureau, received instructions for "helpful" and "patriotic" plot lines and characterizations, and were generally caught up in the combined war efforts. Indeed, this tie-in helped smooth the way for the astoundingly "back to the home" tenor of postwar magazine fiction and nonfiction:

The close connection between propaganda groups and the magazine industry throughout the war made unnecessary specific instructions to encourage the movement of women back to the home and to female fields in the labor force during demobilization . . . fiction and advertisements during this period portrayed war workers leaving their jobs for domesticity, office work, and unskilled jobs in manufacturing. This largely resulted from information writers had received from the government for two and a half years—information based on the assumption that new women workers would not remain in the "male" occupations once veterans returned and the dominant perspective of which highlighted the needs of the country.[45]

Like other media, magazines began to shift in midwar toward a more overt concern with the perils that the working mother offered to the smooth functioning of the family: "[T]he initial idea that working mothers could raise happy children was replaced by tragic portraits of families breaking under the strain of mother being away. By the spring of 1944, ads began dramatizing the unhappiness of children with war-working mothers."[46] Yet editorials and nonfiction articles in the women's magazines continued to print pieces that provided very supportive views of working mothers. In an article entitled "Girls in Overalls" in the March 1943 edition of *Parents' Magazine*, Josephine Von Miklos writes very positively about women's work and cites reasons other than the patriotic for their continued involvement after the war. Stella Applebaum in February's issue of *Parents' Magazine* also argues strongly for the value of mothers at work, again stressing not only the patriotic but the personal and psychological benefits.[47] Nevertheless, by the late forties, the magazines too began to blow the horn of maternal neglect, deprivation, and the ever present "momism."

This is not to say that the shift from the sacrificial model to the malevolent model was straightforward and without deviations. Indeed, while the shift remains a dramatic one, there are a number of important exceptions, particularly in the war films of the mid-1940s. In both *Since You Went Away* and *The Best Years of Our Lives*, daughters are not the victims of maternal love gone awry, but rather the helpful and nurturant mothers in training, keeping the home fires burning while dad is off making the world safe for democracy. Like much of the wartime advertising that depicted daughters side by side with valiant victory gardening moms, these wartime films served to locate teenage and young adult daughters as mature and responsible apprentices to the arts of American domesticity. Mothers and daughters are often shown sharing domestic tasks such as preparing breakfast for a returning, drunken soldier in *The Best Years of Our Lives* or wearing matching aprons as they cook together in the kitchen of *Since You Went Away*. Indeed, mothers and daughters are here shown to be united in their war efforts and their desire to maintain a haven for the returning vets. In *The Best Years of Our Lives*, the good daughter is explicitly contrasted with the slatternly wife of the returning vet with whom she has fallen in love. Domestic charms win out, of course. Jane, the patriotic daughter of *Since You Went Away*, provides her mother with an example of bravery by working in the vets' hospital, thus gently pressing mom to do her part for the war effort by welding at the local munitions factory. In this wartime ethos, danger and discord are signified outside the world of putative domestic bliss or in

Fig. 9. Mother and daughter sharing the joys of domesticity and keeping the home fires burning in *Since You Went Away*. (United Artists, 1944; photo courtesy of Museum of Modern Art Film Stills Archive)

the figure of (unpatriotic) independent women who have (selfishly) neglected to keep the haven heavenly.

There are, of course, more significant exceptions. But the exception is, in itself, telling. The film *A Tree Grows in Brooklyn* stands out as a somewhat different representation of mothers and daughters located outside of the two paradigms discussed thus far. Starring Dorothy McGuire as Katie, the mother, and Peggy Ann Garner as her daughter Francie, about twelve years old, *A Tree Grows in Brooklyn* is set in the tenement slums of 1920s Brooklyn.[48] The earlier date is significant because more "positive" mother/daughter relationships are often presented in films that locate them in an earlier era.[49]

The plot is relatively simple: a young family struggles to make ends meet in the slums of Brooklyn. Although *A Tree Grows in Brooklyn* is most often thought of as a touching coming-of-age story, this narrative of the young girl's development is intimately tied in with the narrative of both mother and daughter and daughter and father. A neat split is set up early on between the hardworking, down-to-earth, pragmatic mother who essentially supports the family and the often unemployed, often drunk, funny, dreamy, lively man who is her husband. The children fall on either side, the boy—a street smart young tough—identifying with the mother, and the daughter—dreaming of being a writer—identifying with the adored father. This "pairing" is accomplished through both the dialogue and the visual aspects. In one scene, where mother and father are arguing over the future of Francie's schooling (Francie wants to transfer to a fancier school, and dad wants to lie to get her in there), the camera literally shows the mother and son and then cuts to the father and daughter, reinforcing the explicit message of opposition and alliances. Not until the end of this scene, when mother gives in, are all four shown within the same frame. The coming-of-age narrative is thus connected with the realignment of this familial mise-en-scène so that the daughter becomes reattached to mother.

One crucial difference emerges between this and the other films discussed thus far: the reversal of the motif of separation from mother as the hallmark of adulthood. Here Francie's move into womanhood is accessed not through the world of men, but through a new and deeper connection with her mother, a connection effected by a more realistic appraisal of the mother's life and her choices and, very crucially, by a sense that the daughter matters to the mother, that she can be a nurturer and caretaker.

The narrative can be seen as a move from daddy's girl to young woman rather than a move into a similar adoration of mother. Francie's adoration of her father is an Electra complex gone overboard: she enacts scenes with him that are completely inappropriate to their relationship as father and daughter. In one scene that sets the tone for their relationship, Francie rushes to the door as her father comes home, and they proceed to create a mise-en-scène of husband and wife (he even comes up behind her and kisses her) as she caters to his domestic needs ("I love to iron for you, Papa"). He gives her his fervent "things are going to be different one day—you won't have to iron for me" speech, which he should be giving to his wife. As Francie stands ironing, he reinforces his treatment of this child as woman/wife: "You know something, prima donna, you're going to make somebody a mighty fine wife some day."

The contrast to this ideal husband/wife couple can be found in the scene immediately following, in which father goes up to tell mother, who is cleaning the steps, about his job and is disappointed at her less than enthusiastic response. As she "diminishes" the father, the camera cuts away to the daughter, gazing up lovingly at him, and he descends the stairs to waltz out with the daughter (singing "Here Comes the Bride!") while the mother looks on.

If the film stopped with this, if it produced the idea of pop as a great and fun guy and mom as a hard and uncompromising wet blanket, it would be no different from the majority of films on mothers and daughters. But as the film progresses, it also becomes infinitely more complex in its portrayal of a mother placed in an impossible position and a daughter infatuated with father but slowly learning the reality of mother's life. Mom is chastised for, as her mother puts it, forgetting "to think with your heart," and we agree with Aunt Sissy's concern over mother's statement that "My kids is going to be somebody if I got to turn into granite rock to make them." But this is never presented as the mother's inherent failing. To the contrary, not only is she shown to struggle personally with this question of her "hardness," but the hardness itself is seen as a consequence of a difficult situation: the prospect of a new baby, an out-of-work, dreamy husband, and the overwhelming reality of poverty.

After the father's death, the mother/daughter narrative surfaces more explicitly. The daughter resents the mother for his death, and the mother works to regain her daughter. The birth of the new baby not only is the catalyst that brings Francie back to her mother, but it is the moment that signifies her move into adulthood. Francie is now needed, as her mother tells her in the crucial scene that marks the beginning of the reconciliation. They are in the hospital where Aunt Sissy is having a baby, and Katie speaks to her elusive daughter about her need for her help when she has *her* baby at home:

Katie: "It isn't going to be long now. For me, I mean, with my baby. We can't come to a hospital. There isn't even going to be enough money for a woman to come and help. I'm going to need you Francie. Don't ever be far away. Neely—well, a

> boy ain't much good at a time like this. I'm counting on you
> Francie. You won't forget that will ya?"
>
> *Francie:*     "All right Mama, I'll remember."

In this scene, as in the next one, where Katie is giving birth, Francie is standing, and her mother is either sitting or lying in bed, as if to symbolize the new power of the daughter. But unlike that depicted in many other films, it is not a power gained at the mother's expense, as in *Now, Voyager* when the psychiatrist looks down on the mother upon announcing her culpability. Conversely, we have here a power gained through an understanding of the mother's life.

The labor scene is one of the most moving film moments between mother and daughter. As the daughter begins to help her mother through her pain, both share a bit of each other's life: Francie reads her mother her essays, and the mother talks of her choices, the limitations of her life, how she misses the father. The knowledge that her mother needs her empowers both the daughter ("She only wants me now," she says to her brother) and the mother.

In an extraordinary speech by Katie, she speaks of the double binds mothers are put in, having to hold the family together in the midst of adversity and then being forced to make decisions that seem punitive and oppressive:

> *Katie:*     "It's so nice to have a visit from my daughter. I didn't want
> for you to have to grow up so soon. I didn't want for you to
> have to quit school. I tried to tell him that. He didn't mind
> about the baby but he never forgive me for wanting you to
> quit school. I told him, and he just went out. You never forgive me either."
>
> *Francie:*     "Please don't Mama."
>
> *Katie:*     "He would've bought you dolls instead of milk. I don't know,
> maybe you would've been happier, I don't know. I never
> would've thought of givin' ya that school like he did. And all
> them fine compositions of yours. I never read one of them.
> I should've had time. Johnny did. But I couldn't do no different. I don't know how I could do any different."

Later she continues to express this double bind as she is in the throes of labor and speaks at random about her life: "Who'll cry for me like that if I died. . . . I never did a wrong thing in my life but it ain't enough. . . . Oh, Sissy, I didn't mean to be hard like you said. . . . If Johnny was here he could go to your graduation and I'd go to Neely's but I . . . I can't tear myself into two pieces . . . how'm I going to do both?"

The reunion of mother and daughter is not a simple matter of hugging, kissing, and bittersweet tears. The reunion, if one could really call it that, is about mutual recognition, a sharing of experience, and a deeper understanding of the choices mother was forced to make. There are no great epiphanies in this scene of coming together; yet the coming together is apparent in the daughter's caretaking, in the mother's expression of the double binds, and in the way this scene is tied to the daughter's coming of age.

This exception can be explained on a number of levels. First, *A Tree Grows in Brooklyn* was adapted from a best-selling "serious" novel (it was a Book of the Month Club selection), and it retains a certain literariness and staginess, as do films like *I Remember Mama* and *Little Women*. Second, it was not a classic genre film and thus was not subject to the strictures of most genre productions, such as the centrality of a narrative resolution centering on a male agent. More important, this exception provides an interesting contrast to the genre films discussed previously in that its historical, ethnic, and working-class setting allows this film to present a relationship that is both moving and complex and that renders neither mother nor daughter absent. The working classness and ethnicity allow for more space for mother/daughter mutuality in the context of a society still struggling with the incompleteness of the much vaunted "melting pot." The generic formulation here, a sort of ethnic historical one, subverts and rearranges the dominant cinematic codes in a way that "in the present" genres are unable to, given their rootedness in the dominant ideologies of the time. Perhaps all this suggests that the psychologizing is a primarily middle-class phenomenon.

What emerges from this overall transformation, then, is twofold. On the one hand, the move from *Stella* to *Mildred* signifies a shift from a vision of all-giving motherhood that locates women as sacrificial caretakers who derive deep pleasure from that sacrifice to an image of motherhood slightly off, possibly unhealthy, and almost certainly responsible for the psychic health (or, more often, ill health) of their offspring. On the other hand, the change is not just in images of motherhood (from sacrificial and benign to overpower-

Fig. 10. Mother and daughter find a tenuous and gritty resolution amid adversity and the empowerment of daughterly care in *A Tree Grows in Brooklyn*. (20th Century-Fox, 1945; photo courtesy of Museum of Modern Art Film Stills Archives)

ing and controlling) but in the way the discourses of motherhood refract and interact with other significant social discourses.

The story of Stella's mothering is also a story of class, an uneasy story that applauds class ascendancy (and sees it as accessed through the father) but still maintains a sharp criticism of bourgeois "expert" values and modes. The story of Mildred's mothering (like Mrs. Vale's and Mrs. Brown's), on the other hand, is a purely psychological story. Even Mildred's class ascendancy is directly tied to her unhealthy desire to "give her daughter all she never had." Stella's original move up the class ladder was propelled by her own desires. Mildred is punished both for wanting too much for her daughter and for daring to think that a working mother/single parent can join the ranks of the entrepreneurial upwardly mobile. Linda Williams points out how the background of the war served to change the original intent of the novel written by James Cain and turn Mildred's mobility into an altogether more problematic affair:

"The indirect evocation of wartime ideology operates to judge Veda's—and by extension Mildred's—materialism harshly. In the original novel, Mildred's materialism encounters no such censure, because it arises directly out of her experience of want and social humiliation during the Depression. Similarly in the novel, Mildred's excessive mother love and spoiling of Veda appears misguided, but it leads to no crime."[50] The class motive for Mildred's working is now replaced with a basely materialist and neurotic one. Class as providing the context for the mother/daughter interaction thus disappears as that relationship is increasingly portrayed as having no context other than itself.

Although this metamorphosis in the representations of the mother/daughter relationship is significant and speaks to the strength and persistence of the postwar backlash and domestic surge, it is also important to stress the continuities. For all the daughters in these three films, the sign of their difference from their mothers is their popularity. Laurel's popularity in the "in" group crowds her less fashionable mother out. Charlotte's ability to be popular with the "common" cruise goers distances her from her more standoffish mother. Veda's worldliness and swirl of parties and polo matches stands in severe contrast to the life of her hardworking mother. This issue of popularity, and the mother's ability to access it for the daughter or deprive her of it, not only persists in the film images of the period but crops up continually in the women's magazines of the late thirties and forties. The connection between the new concern with popularity and the popularity of psychology is striking, as this passage indicates: "Somebody with a desire to help harassed young girls ought to endow, for mothers, a number of classes in advertising and public relations. The purpose would be to teach women how to speak of their daughters so that they seem well adjusted and worth knowing, rather than walking problems with a low popularity rating and enough complexes to supply a psychology textbook."[51]

But the most critical continuity, and the most lamentable one, is the legacy of loss in these films. In all the films discussed here except *A Tree Grows in Brooklyn,* indeed, in most representations of the mother/daughter relationship, mother and daughter are torn asunder, forever to be deprived of each other's company. Stella's daughter is forever lost to her, Mrs. Vale and Mrs. Brown die, and

Veda is booked for murder. In all these films, narrative resolution is firmly anchored to a permanent separation of mother and daughter, a separation that is both psychic and physical.

At least with *Stella,* we experience the loss of mother to daughter (and daughter to mother) as sad, wrenching, unhappily necessary. As Andrea Walsh points out, we do get some sense of Stella's activity, her decision making, her subjectivity: "These *sacrifice* films, though rarely feminist in ideology, are based on a feminist assumption that women can make choices. . . . They are, to an extent, authors of their own destiny. The fact that they are depicted as choosing subjects may be as important as the *content* of the life styles they choose."[52]

Conversely, in the other films, the loss is never depicted as loss, much less as choice, but as the *inevitable* separation of daughter from mother. Neither option constructs a discourse of constancy and mutuality. In the move from sacrificing *Stella* to maladjusted *Mildred,* we may have relinquished class and acquired psychoanalysis, but one thing remains constant: we have lost each other.

## Chapter Three

# Father Knows Best about the Woman Question

## Familial Harmony and Feminine Containment

Lora: ". . . Yes I'm ambitious, perhaps too ambitious, but it's
  been for your sake as well as mine. Isn't this house just a
  little bit nicer than a cold-water flat? And your new
  horse, aren't you just crazy about it?—"
Susie: "Yes, but—"
Lora: "And that closet of yours—"
Susie: "Has all the dresses fit for the daughter of a famous star."
Lora: "Now just a moment young lady. It's only because of
  my ambition that you've had the best of everything.
  And that's a solid achievement that any mother can be
  proud of."
Susie: "And how about a mother's love?"
Lora: "Love! But you've always had that!"
Susie: "Yes, by telephone, by postcard, by magazine interviews,
  you've given me everything . . . but yourself."

  —Imitation of Life, 1959

As we've moved from the thirties through the wartime years, we
have seen that the representations of mothers and daughters under-
went profound shifts. Fundamentally, the move was from an
idealized dream of the mother as sacrificial lamb to her daughter's
social ascendancy to a much harsher nightmare of the mother as
malevolent force on her daughter's struggling psyche, particularly
as the war came to a close, and the specter of a more permanent
working mother provoked anxiety. Moving now to the years after
the war, to the late forties and fifties, we face the question of how
the culture industry "handled" the personal and social turmoil that
now characterized almost any discussion containing the terms
"woman" or "mother."

 The years after World War II are crucial to any examination of the mother/daughter relationship, for it is roughly between 1945 and the early 1960s that we witness the hardening and solidifying of what Betty Friedan was to call "the problem that has no name." Indeed, Friedan's ground-breaking book, *The Feminine Mystique*, detailed for the first time the tremendous backlash experienced by women during the postwar years. Her chronicle of middle-class, white women gone slightly mad under the pressures of suburban isolation and severely circumscribed lives opened the door for both a resurgence of women's activism in the seventies and a reexamination of what was hidden under the pleasant facade of fifties consensus.

It is a particularly important period for the history of women generally, as many feminist historians have documented. If the war brought women into the work force and into public life with a vengeance, then the postwar period (really beginning midwar) attempted to shunt them back off into the domestic, familial world from which they had been recently liberated. As Mary Ann Doane argues: "'Rosie the Riveter'" was conceived from the beginning as a temporary phenomenon, active only for the duration, and throughout the war years the female spectator-consumer was sold a certain image of femininity which functioned to sustain the belief that women and work outside the home were basically incompatible."[1]

Women entered the labor force in unprecedented numbers during the war, often at the urging of an enormous government campaign that exhorted women to give their all for the war effort. But as the men began to return home from Europe and the Pacific, many women were also forced to return "home," literally: by 1946, four million fewer women were working than had been at the peak of the war.[2] In fact, the retrenchment started midwar: "Government propaganda, midwar, did an about-face. Because the original exhortations to women to do war work had never challenged the core of ideas about femininity, because no one had suggested that work was more than a sacrifice women had willingly made for the most motherly of reasons, the shift was an easy one. The message was clear: although women *could* do anything, authentic women would choose to be at home with their families."[3] Yet government officials and labor leaders alike began to realize that many women would not simply step down from their jobs and offer them up to the returning GIs. A 1944 Department of Labor survey showed that 80 percent of former working women, 75 percent of former students, and 50 percent of former homemakers hoped to continue working.[4] Clearly, the work of ousting women from the public sphere was going to be work indeed.

Numerous feminist historians have pointed out how the late 1940s and most especially the 1950s represented a period of regression for women when many of the gains and freedoms experienced during the war years were lost or, more accurately, wrenched from women in the name of a newly constructed familialism. As many historians have demonstrated, the familialism of the postwar years was not a "return" to a more "traditional" ethos but was instead a fundamentally new phenomenon: "The legendary family of the 1950s . . . represented something new. It was not, as common wisdom tells us, the last gasp of 'traditional' family life with roots deep in the past. Rather, it was the first wholehearted effort to create a home that would fulfill virtually all its members' personal needs through an energized and expressive personal life."[5]

It need not have turned out the way it did. Traditional gender roles had been challenged both by the depression and, much more extensively, by the experience of the war and women's work during those years. In addition, growing access to birth control and higher education could have encouraged a more progressive attitude toward the position of women in American society. The domestic containment of the postwar years was thus not a simple continuation, or even a resurgence, of an already existing ethos. It was a backlash of significant proportions related not only to establishing the nuclear home as the paradigmatic social/personal site, but also to establishing an ethic of consumerism as a vast bulwark against the threat of communism abroad and the internal "other" within. As Elaine Tyler May reveals, the famous 1959 Nixon-Khrushchev "kitchen debates" used women as central elements in their respective visions of the "good life." Anti-Communist writers in the United States ridiculed the "unfeminine" (working) Soviet women, implying "that self-supporting women were in some way un-American. Accordingly, anticommunist crusaders viewed women who did not conform to the domestic ideal with suspicion." The policy of containment was thus always something more than externally motivated. "In Nixon's vision, the suburban ideal of home ownership would diffuse two potentially disruptive forces: women and workers."[6]

The growth of the suburbs in the postwar expansion played no small part in this backlash, as women were ousted from their public, work environment and relocated in the relative isolation of the new suburban tract home, now itself symbolizing the changed ideal of the American Dream. As Cowan points out in her work on household technology, the relationship between the new home products, the suburbs, and the nuclear family ideal was close indeed: "The move to the suburbs carried with it the assumption that someone (surely mother) would be at home to do the requisite work that made it possible for someone else (surely father) to leave early in the morning and return late at night, without worrying either about the welfare of his family or the maintenance of his domicile."[7]

Warren Susman observes that the term "family" itself came to define not only a new media emphasis (the domestic sitcom) but a whole range of commodities and modes of existence: "The new medium of television found its function in domestic-centered television shows, from 'I Love Lucy' to 'I Remember Mama,' all seen in the 'family room.' (Indeed, think of all the family words enveloping the new suburban lifestyle: family-size carton, family room, family car, family film, family restaurant, family vacation.) In essence, one can represent the new affluent society collectively in the image of the happy suburban home."[8]

Certainly, the fifties are most often remembered as the period in which the ideal of the traditional nuclear family with 2.4 kids, a suburban tract home, station wagon, and assorted barbecue grills, pets, and home appliances restructured the social and cultural terrain. The mass media played a central role in this restructuring, for not only was the new medium of television filling up the "family room" and occupying a larger and larger space in the social body, but the images themselves were crucial to orienting both women and men to the new social and sexual order, which was organized to a great extent around the new consumerism born of the postwar economic boom.[9] As Lipsitz points out, early television production was an influential addition to the more "official" discourses of domesticity and consumerism: "Commercial network television emerged as the primary discursive medium in American society at the precise historical moment that the isolated nuclear family and its concerns eclipsed previous ethnic, class, and political forces as the crucible of personal identity. Television programs both reflected and shaped that translation, defining the good life in family-centric, asocial, and commodity-oriented ways."[10]

If women had previously been targeted by the mass media as potential workers, "Rosie the Riveters" hammering away at the hulls of fighter planes while their noble menfolk were off fighting fascism, they now were targeted as "happy homemakers," suburban wives and mothers keenly attuned to the newest home products, eagerly reading their Dr. Spock, and supporting their husbands' climb up the company ladder.

A sample from an episode of the classic fifties sitcom, "Father Knows Best," typifies the explicit ideological work of popular culture in orienting men and women toward traditional sex roles. In this episode, teenage daughter Betty hears a lecture from a vocational counselor in her high school and decides she wants to be an engineer. When she gets a summer job working on a highway surveying team, her family is appalled at the idea of a girl doing that sort of work. Betty goes ahead, citing a "changing world," and meets up with a sexist (but handsome) foreman on her first day. He constantly berates her ("Why are you doing this?" "What are you running away from?"), and Betty runs home in frustration. The young man comes to the house that evening, gives a passionate speech about the need for women to be in the home, and wins over the chastened and enamored Betty.

The ideological impetus of this episode is forthright and explicit. Betty's mother plays the part of a rather passive sex-role socializer while her father plays the central role of arbiter of values and morality. The running joke throughout the episode centers around Betty's refusal to be interested in the new dress her mother has purchased for her now that she is concerned with her career. The mother continually tries to entice her with the dress, to lure Betty away from her egalitarian fantasies and toward the replication of her mother's life. The episode ends with a newly coquettish Betty running upstairs and slipping on the new dress to entice the young male engineer who has come to woo her away from work and toward romantic love and domesticity.

The engineer's speech is filled with references to the new expanding world of the fifties (the new highway system, the housing boom) and the desire to have a lovely "sweet girl" to come home to. The sainted image of the wife and mother is here clearly depicted as the legitimation of postwar growth ("We do it all for her"). Betty, overhearing the speech (made to the father, of course), runs upstairs to transform herself from strident girl-engineer in jeans and boots to beguiling teen angel in dress and bows. Father looks on happily. By the show's end, the realities of a "changing world" are safely contained within the rhetoric of both essential differences and romantic love. The idea of the working woman is put down firmly and vigorously.

During this period, social messages became vehement in opposition to the enhancement and development of work opportunities for women, pervading all areas of popular culture: "A survey of women's roles as portrayed in magazine fiction in 1945 showed careers for women depicted more unsympathetically than since the turn of the century."[11] Yet the contradictions of this period are legion. The recuperation of women as primarily domestic was facilitated by playing up the images of "hearth and home" and celebrating the virtues of motherhood and family, particularly as the decade came to a close and the domestic ideologies of the fifties began in earnest. The old language of biology as destiny often merged with the new language of functionalist social science to provide ample evidence for the ineluctability of rigid gender positionings. In a 1956 article in *Parents' Magazine,* the well-known psychiatrist Bruno Bettelheim echoes his Parsonian colleagues in arguing for a "thinking based on . . . inherent function" in which "the completion of womanhood is largely through motherhood, but fulfillment of manhood is not achieved largely through fatherhood."[12]

This image of the fifties, as a period of happy and fulfilled homemakers waxing freshly washed floors and beaming brightly at their brood through their suburban picture windows, is one we strongly identify with the TV sitcoms of that period, particularly such shows as the hugely popular "Father Knows Best" and "Leave It to Beaver." If any one TV image says fifties, it is that of June Cleaver, ever patient mother, loving wife, and cheerful consumer, dispensing love and cookies to husband and madcap sons alike.

This concerted effort to regain a sense of stability about women and their place was clearly motivated by a felt concern over the realities of change, struggle, and confusion:

Despite its adoption of historical conditions from the 1950s, the suburban family sitcom did not greatly proliferate until the late 1950s and early 1960s . . . while the women's movement was seeking to release homemakers from this social and economic gender definition. This "nostalgic" lag between the historical specificity of the social formation and the popularity of the suburban family sitcom on the prime-time schedule underscores its ability to mask social contradictions and to naturalize woman's place in the home. [13]

In many senses, the postwar years were marked first and foremost by the reorganization and restructuring of sexual roles and ideologies. The anger and moralism of popular antiwoman texts such as Lundberg and Farnham's *Modern Woman: The Lost Sex* only attest to the extreme unease of these years, the sense that something had begun that could not wholly be kept under wraps, not entirely contained under the happy mask of hearth and home.

At the same time these ideologies of maternal beneficence were blossoming, the specter of Philip Wylie's malevolent mom reared her ugly head. Wylie's description of a society gone soft, ruined and shriveled by hordes of devouring, emasculating moms, is as much a part of the familial discourse of the forties and fifties as are the happy homemakers and cake-baking mothers.

These two aspects of postwar ideology—the glorification of motherhood and its simultaneous denigration by the exponents of "momism"—may seem to be in contradiction. But this double message, this insoluble paradox, is itself the defining discourse of mothering in the fifties, most especially of mothering daughters. The images of the devouring mother and the virtuous mother are part of the same double bind. Both are mystifications, both the haloed idealization and the vicious demonization, that further distance mothers and daughters from their own complex, lived reality. The fear, anger, and misogyny found in popular texts such as Wylie's *Generation of Vipers* and in many of the melodramas of the period are not an aberration, minor, or inconsequential. Rather, the attempt to erase mom, to find her guilty and responsible not only for her children's miserable failures, but for the failures of society as well, is part of the same ideological moment that locates June Cleaver and Mrs. Anderson as the ultimate examples of virtuous motherhood. As Ann Kaplan notes, this pattern was already beginning by the thirties:

But 30s filmic narratives already show increased attention to the Mother's responsibility for the child's psychic, as against social, health. The emphasis shifts in an interesting way from the 20s focus . . . on the mother as moral (Christian) teacher, to the greater burden of creating happy, well-adjusted and fulfilled human beings. Instead of being the agent for shaping the public, external figure (the man/citizen) the Mother is now to shape the internal, psychic self. By the 40s, aberrations in the grown-up child are her fault. [14]

This theory cannot simply be reduced to "two sides of the same coin." Rather, the more appropriate metaphor might be a mirror: but this time not Lacan's mirror, into which the male child gazes, signifying his own reality and his own otherness, but the funhouse mirror into which the anxious mother stares. This mirror splits and fractures her image, distorts it, bends it. There is no single image, no reflection of the self she believes herself to be. All images are freakish, all contorted, yet unified by their shared abstraction, joined by their fictiveness.

Many of the critiques of motherhood that emerged during the 1940s and 1950s (and reemerged with the new right/moral majority of the 1980s) draw a very firm connection between the evils of mothers and the evils of the developing mass society. Mass culture (and most writers include in this concept the new home technologies) is here seen as replacing the intimate familial environment in which a mother's love and nurture provided the sustenance and growth for the entire community. Women have lost their place in the world and now, having been made redundant by the new technologies, are looking for gratification in all the wrong places: "With the coming of an industrial civilization, woman lost her sphere of creative nurture and either was catapulted out into the world to seek for achievement in the masculine sphere of exploit or was driven in upon herself as a lesser being. In either case she suffered psychologically." [15]

This almost preindustrial yearning for a return to a time when men were men and women were mothers manifests itself in the attacks on working women made in films like *Mildred Pierce*. Mildred has tried to be "both a mother and a father" (a line echoed later by Faye Dunaway in her portrayal of Joan Crawford in *Mommie Dearest*) and, in so doing, has created a monster child.

As we move into the 1950s and firmly into a postwar world, many themes from the malevolent mother era of the 1940s remain the same, but the specific depiction and narrative resolution change significantly. There were two primary and simultaneous responses to the changing roles of women. The first can be seen in such films as *I Remember Mama* and *Little Women* and such TV shows as "Father Knows Best," "Mama," and "The Donna Reed Show." These images yearned for the (always fictional) good old days when mothers were all-tolerant and all-sacrificing. In many ways, these nostalgic images of traditional family life refer back to depression era films such as *Stella Dallas* in that they posit a benign and loving mother who is unproblematically governed by a maternal instinct of sacrifice and familial devotion. These images were often set in either a pseudo-Victorian past or a new suburban idyll, thus alluding not only to the benign vision of maternal sacrifice, but also to nineteenth-century ideals of true womanhood: "With their stress on manipulative femininity and the importance of purchasing marital harmony at the cost of a woman's individuality, the postwar themes closely resembled those of the nineteenth-century cult of domesticity."[16] Women's magazines consistently advocated not only the psychological dictum of maternal responsibility for the growth and development of husband and children, but the social doctrine of maternal responsibility for the growth and development of Western civilization:

They hold human happiness in their hands. Theirs is the power to make or mar human personalities, to supply a core of warmth and security for husband and children, or to withhold this. Theirs is the responsibility, as homemakers, to see that the same values are found throughout the community . . . a mother's responsibility for human living does not end with her home. Her home is not a desert island. It is part of a larger community, responsible for it and dependent on it. As members of this larger group, mothers must see to it that all the children of the community have good schools, good recreation, good training in democratic living.[17]

In these nostalgic representations, mothers and daughters are seen as united in their domestic orientation as well as in their position within the family. In both "Father Knows Best" and "The Donna Reed Show," the teenage daughters are seen as extensions of the mother—they help out in the kitchen, participate in mother's household chores, and laugh knowingly along with mother when dad and the boys act up.

The second response was far more interesting in that it obliquely acknowledged that women were not solely domestic and set out to explore the issues that arose from this "new paradigm" of work and family for women. This would include such films as *Imitation of Life* and *Peyton Place* and, surprisingly, many articles in women's magazines that began to discuss the new working mother and often (tentatively) supported women in their desire to remain in the labor force after the war had ended. More significantly, this second line of response continued the often vitriolic attacks against working mothers found in such 1940s films as *Mildred Pierce*, referring back to these complex wartime representations. Popular texts helped exacerbate this distress over the working woman.

This tension between the nostalgic image of the domestic mother and daughter and the tormented image of the working mother and neglected daughter characterizes this period. Yet these seemingly disparate representations are united not only by their shared hyperbole but also by their insistent emphasis on domesticity as the happiest possible route for women. Both sets of representations convey the feeling of a familial world in crisis. Both the nostalgic response and the angry response are so widely drawn, almost comical in their outlandishness, that the answers they propose are almost always fractured, unsteady, and not quite believable.

## I Remember Who? Nostalgic Domesticity

Two films of the early fifties explicitly harken back to an earlier era when ideologies of the companionate marriage and scientific management merged in the public consciousness. Both *Cheaper by the Dozen* and *Belles on Their Toes* tell the story (based on fact) of the rather large Gilbreth family, ruled with engineering efficiency by the pioneer of industrial management, Frank Gilbreth, who dies suddenly toward the end of *Cheaper by the Dozen*. The mother, a "lady engineer" herself, vows to carry on Frank's pioneering work; thus there is a 1952 sequel, *Belles on Their Toes*.

Opening with a grayed mother attending her last child's college graduation, *Belles on Their Toes* then goes entirely into flashback, beginning where the first film left off, with mother trying to keep the family together despite financial woes and the sexism of potential employers. In a portrait typical of the romanticized fifties images (even those set in an earlier period, as is this film), young adult daughter is depicted as her mother's confidante, a "little mother" to her younger siblings. But for all the lightness and cheery aspect of this breezy comedy, the underlying fear of daughter's "spinster-hood" and the desire to reconcile her to her femininity cannot be completely evaded. Eldest daughter Ann (Jeanne Crain) finally meets the man of her dreams, the brash young doctor, Bob. Bob, in true fifties fashion, wants them to get married right away. Ann at first agrees, but then she puts Bob off to allow her mother to take a teaching position at Purdue, vowing she'll care for the younger children. But mother will have none of this sacrificial nonsense. Upon discovering the source of discontent between Ann and Bob, she sets out to confront Ann:

| | |
|---|---|
| *Mother:* | "Why do you have to wait?" |
| *Ann:* | "Oh mother, it's just that you have this wonderful opportunity to go to Purdue and I ought to stay home so the others can have the chance I've had." |
| *Mother:* | "And how long did you figure that would take?" |
| *Ann:* | "I don't know. A year, two." |
| *Mother:* | "Why not 15 or even 20? By that time we may have Jane married off. Or maybe she'll decide never to get married. And you'll both be old maids and live with me forever. Is that why I've kept this family together? So I can have spinster daughters around the house? Is that why?" |

Thus the intersection of this problematic double bind for mothers of daughters is how to empower them to think that life is not only wife and motherhood, yet make them fully understand that they will be somehow freakish or pitiful if they do not become wives and mothers.

Nostalgic representations of mothers and daughters continued in a variety of media throughout the decade. An interesting case is that of *I Remember Mama,* noted for both its warm invocation of "old-time" family values and its negotiation of ethnicity in an age of consumerism. As Serafina Bathrick notes, *I Remember Mama* has a long and unusual media history: "*I Remember Mama* was originally written as a novel. It was serialized in a popular magazine, and was soon adapted for Broadway. It played a long and successful run during the late war years, and was finally bought for the screen rights to a high-budget movie released in 1948. The RKO film was not the end, for "I Remember Mama" was among the most successful early TV series, and was again revived on Broadway in 1979 as a musical."[18] Told from the point of view of Katrin Hansen, the young writer who lovingly details the trials and tribulations of an immigrant family in the city, *I Remember Mama* proposes the sturdy and no-nonsense Old World mother as muse to the developing daughter of modernity. Mama Hansen is here the mediator between the Old World and the New World, reconciling emerging adult daughter Katrin to the ways of the new mass society without propelling her into a world wholly nondomestic:

Within the discourse of the day, *I Remember Mama* steered a middle way between hysterical anti-feminist tirades (like Philip Wylie's *Generation of Vipers*) that charged domineering mothers with destroying the independence of American children, and the emerging war and postwar feminist consciousness stimulated by women's success in securing and maintaining war production jobs. The film featured Mama as a source for reconciliation, as a means of proving that threatening changes could be resisted while one accommodated to progress.[19]

The TV series, "Mama," which ran from 1949 to 1956 on CBS, replicated the essentially nonconfrontational relationship between mother and daughter, albeit with a greater focus on consumerism and the nuclear ideal. As Lipsitz notes: "Over two decades and five forms of media, the Hansens changed from an ethnic, working-class family deeply enmeshed in family, class, and ethnic associations, to a modern nuclear family confronting consumption decisions as the key to group and individual identity."[20] What is stressed in representations like these is the essential continuity of mother and daughter, not far from the continuity assumed in nineteenth-century representations and writings. Although daughter might move out of the maternal orbit by choosing different work, her way there is paved by her mother's skills and the preeminent values of home and family: "Mama's old-fashioned female identity provides the key breakthrough for Katrin's aspirations to become a professional writer. When Katrin despairs because her stories have been rejected and complains that she needs the critiques of an expert, Mama uses her traditional skills to launch her daughter's career."[21] Here, as in the film *Little Women* and the TV series "The Donna

Reed Show," is a world unlike that of the tortured melodramas of the 1940s, one in which mothers and daughters seemingly exist in carefree harmony, disrupted only occasionally by the angst of adolescence. But this nostalgic move was itself contradictory, for even classic fifties happy-family sitcoms such as "Father Knows Best," while ostensibly benign in their depiction of the mother/daughter relationship, created in no uncertain terms an ideological context in which the attempts of either mother or daughter to escape the confines of suburban domesticity were soundly put down. The tendency toward a more refined and glitzy version of "momism" was stronger than its nostalgic counterpart.

## Momism Revisited: "Be a Real Woman and Like It"

The publication in 1942 (before America had entered the war and thus before large numbers of women had entered the wartime work force) of Philip Wylie's classic attack on American women, *Generation of Vipers*, signaled the beginning of one of the darkest periods in the history of ideologies of motherhood. Wylie's thesis, that American women had become omnipotent "moms" damaging the psyches of their offspring, the masculinity of their mates, and the vitality of their country, was the initial salvo in a barrage of mom bashing that took hold of the popular imagination, soon followed by the publication in 1943 of David Levy's *Maternal Overprotection* and in 1947 of Ferdinand Lundberg and Marynia Farnham's popular and vicious *Modern Woman: The Lost Sex*. Although written in the forties, these texts provided the backdrop to the continued psychologization of the mother/daughter relationship. The language of both overprotection (Levy) and neglect and malevolence (Wylie and Lundberg and Farnham) continued into the fifties, albeit with less rancor and vehemence.

Nina Leibman has argued that fifties films continued the evil mother motif from the forties, presenting a very different version of motherhood than is typically associated with the period. She sees a much less rosy discourse, one, in fact, in which mothers represented a quite malevolent force in their children's lives: "The cinematic family melodramas of the 1950s, then, seem to exhibit an attachment to Wylie's Momism. Mothers are accused of being too smothering and are then relegated to a marginalized existence within the narrative, where they can witness (with admiration) the blossoming of the crucial familial bond, that between father and son." Leibman argues that this erasure, this marginalization, links fifties television to its filmic counterpart: "Both media depend on a systematic erasure of the mother in order to ensure an emphasis on the father's role in raising his children."[22]

This erasure is certainly apparent in the television sitcoms of the period, as "Father Knows Best" amply illustrates. Sitcom mothers seem absent, anonymous, or inconsequential: "It is possible to discern in domestic comedy programming of the period a concerted effort to deemphasize the mother's importance in the lives of her children; indeed, she is presented primarily as a domestic servant."[23] Interestingly, in an era that both celebrated and derided the mother, it was the *father* (or often the symbolic father figure in film melodramas such as 1959's *Imitation of Life*) who reigned as head of household and pivotal figure in his children's lives. The father/child interaction also proved the most substantive, in terms of both narrative structure and ideological weight.

Fathers seem to have been brought back into the picture as a result of the "realization" (promoted by Wylie, et al.) that mothers were ruining their children. If maternal instinct was now aggressive and predatory, if moms ruled the earth and made their children rue the day, then fathers needed to reenter the family fray and set things straight. "Father Knows Best," for all its innocuousness, implied in its very title that Moms may be cute and addle-brained (or mean and malevolent), but when it really comes down to the important issues of child rearing and family life, father really *does* know best. As many critics have noted, the father-centered family sitcoms of the late 1950s and early 1960s were perhaps a concerted response to what was seen to be a surfeit of "bumbling dads" in the media:

"Father Knows Best" and "Leave it to Beaver" . . . shifted the source of comedy to the ensemble of the nuclear family as it realigned the roles within the family. "Father Knows Best" was praised by the *Saturday Evening Post* for its "outright defiance" of "one of the more persistent cliches of television and scriptwriting about the typical American family . . . the mother as the iron-fisted ruler of the nest, the father as a blustering chowderhead and the children as being one crack removed from juvenile delinquency." Similarly, *Cosmopolitan* cited the program for overturning television programming's "message . . . that the American father is a weak-willed, predicament-inclined clown [who is] saved from his doltishness by a beautiful and intelligent wife and his beautiful and intelligent children."[24]

The title of the popular 1950s melodrama, *Imitation of Life*, implies that the life of a career woman (Lana Turner's character, in this case) is only an "imitation" of the real thing, presumably Mrs. Anderson's life. Directed by Douglas Sirk, one of the great melodrama *auteurs*, the film exemplifies the double bind mothers in the fifties faced in both the narratives of popular culture and, I would venture, the experience of their everyday lives. *Imitation of Life* was a 1959 remake of a popular Fannie Hurst novel originally produced in 1934, starring Claudette Colbert. It is the story of two mother/daughter couples: one black and one white. This racial theme is vitally important here, not only for what it reveals about the racial dynamics of American society in the 1950s but for the part it plays in this specific narrative and in the melodrama genre in general. If in the 1930s films such as *Stella Dallas* played out class conflict through the mother/daughter relationship as metaphor, then in the 1950s, in a film like *Imitation of Life*, the racial "issue" was refracted through familial interactions. Under the booming, "happy days" exterior of 1950s life, beneath the contemporary surge of rose-colored nostalgia, life was much more fraught, much more complex and disturbing, than popular memory would have it constructed.

The impact of McCarthyism on all areas of popular culture has been well documented.[25] Not only were producers, screenwriters, actors, and directors blacklisted, but the culture industry itself initiated anti-Communist imagery and narratives. These films and TV shows were often overtly anti-Communist, portraying an FBI agent or U.S. spy engaged in a holy war against the Eastern European infidels or a brave scientist battling invaders from another planet. But more often than not the ideology of anticommunism manifested itself in more subtle and oblique ways and was implicitly connected to other ideological agendas, particularly ones concerning the family, with which the red scare found common ground. As Elaine Tyler May notes, the relationship between the cold war and domesticity was close indeed: "With security as the common thread, the cold war ideology and the domestic revival reinforced each other. The powerful political consensus that supported cold war policies abroad and anticommunism at home fueled conformity to the suburban family ideal. In turn, the domestic ideology encouraged private solutions to social problems and further weakened the potential for challenge to the cold war consensus."[26]

As usual, the melodrama was a central site for the production of domestic ideologies. *Imitation of Life* is an exceedingly complex and contradictory melodrama, its overpowering, glitzy style often drowning out the more explicit ideological implications. Although the role of Lora Meredith is certainly similar in many ways to the career woman equals maternal deprivation theme of earlier films like *Mildred Pierce*, the presence of another mother/daughter couplet and the racial theme complicates this otherwise routine story of a mother's climb up the ladder of success and the havoc it wreaks on her home life. Fundamentally, this is another film highly critical of career women, particularly as seen in the context of them as parents. The very title and theme song, *Imitation of Life*, attest to the "falseness" of a working woman's life ("What is love without the giving? Without love, you're only living . . . an imitation, an imitation of life").[27]

There are two central narrative strands—two parallel stories— in this film that unify around the core issue of "mothering." Lana Turner plays Lora Meredith, a widow recently moved to New York who is trying to make it in the theater and raise her daughter, Susie. The story of Lora's rise is joined early on with that of another mother and daughter, Annie and Sara Jane Johnson (played by Juanita Moore and Susan Kohner), who come to live with/work for "Miss Lora" before she has made it and stay on with her through her success.

Certainly, this success and its repercussions construct a central ideological moment of the film. Lora, like Mildred, wants to give her daughter everything; and it backfires, as Annie lets Lora know after they've moved into a glamorous new house and Susie has been sent to boarding school:

Annie:    "Did you see those bills from Susie's new school?"

Lora:    "Uh huh. And it doesn't matter."

Annie:    "But Miss Lora—"

Fig. 11. Guess who's the good mother in *this* film? Lana Turner as Lora Meredith chastises little Susie while good mother Annie Johnson (Juanita Moore) looks knowingly on in the 1959 Douglas Sirk remake of *Imitation of Life*. (Universal Pictures, 1959; photo courtesy of Photofest)

Lora:   "No matter what it costs, Susie's going to have everything I missed."

Annie:   "From her letters, she misses you more than she'd ever miss Latin. . . ."

As in *Mildred Pierce* and even *Stella Dallas*, upward mobility is the province of fathers, not mothers. Later Annie reveals to Lora that Susie is in love with Steve, Lora's own hardworking but unglamorous lover. Lora, in shock, says, "Why didn't I know about this, why didn't she come to me?" Annie replies, "Maybe you weren't around." Lora, of course, gets the message: "You mean I haven't been a good mother." The next scene reiterates the evil career-mother theme, with an angry and love-struck daughter, Susie (played with a sort of wide-eyed adolescent glee by Sandra Dee), further condemning the mom who "gave me everything, but herself." Even Lora's dramatic attempt to make amends with her daughter by sacrificing Steve for the sake of their relationship backfires, as Susie pleads with her not to "act" because "I'm not one of your fans." Quite early in the film, when Lora is still living in near poverty and trying to break into the theater, Steve also tells her "not to act" in a fight they were having over her relationship to her work life. The repetition here reinforces the alignment of the daughter with the current patriarchal position on women's labor (its destructiveness and falseness—"acting") and places the mother on the receiving end of their scorn. Lora soon enough sees the light and settles down with the decent, hardworking Steve.

This narrative is contrasted with the story of Annie Johnson and her daughter, Sara Jane, whose desire to be white—and the "passing" that accompanies it—is the other central narrative element in the film. One way to understand this film is that it sets up a good mother/bad mother, good daughter/bad daughter split, with the white daughter and the black mother paired as the virtuous couple. Numerous scenes depict Susie's reliance on Annie as surrogate mother, just as Sara Jane's "passing" is witnessed through her running away to become a dance hall girl, narratively linking her to the white actress mother, whose career is just a sort of "passing" as well. The strange aspect of the film is that, in this case, the daughter who "goes bad" (Sara Jane) is the product of some obviously devoted and healthy mothering. *Mildred Pierce* blames Mildred for her daughter's badness, but no such blame can possibly be attached to Annie's mothering in *Imitation of Life*.[28] Rather, Sara Jane's rejection of her mother seems to be the result of a combination of factors: first, the rebellious/alienated teenager theme beloved of fifties filmmakers, second, and more to the point, the effects of a real and present racism. Sara Jane is the way she is not because of Annie's failures as a mother, but because of social failures. Because of the "naturalization" of black maternity (the "mammy" image beloved of Hollywood filmmakers), Annie cannot be condemned as a "bad mother"; that would bring into the narrative the mother/woman dichotomy reserved for white women.

Indeed, both Lora and her daughter are presented as enmeshed within that racist system. Although Lora is depicted as essentially good and loving to both Annie and Sara Jane, there are several significant moments in which the unthinking insensitivity of a white person toward a black person emerges and is critically examined. In one scene, Lora realizes Annie has a life outside her employ and

Fig. 12. A lovestruck Sandra Dee is less than pleased with mom's an-
nouncement of her engagement to old boyfriend Steve Archer in *Imitation of Life*. (Universal Pictures, 1959; photo courtesy of Museum of Modern Art Film Stills Archive)

says, "I didn't know you have friends," to which Annie gently replies, "Miss Lora, you never asked." Even Sara Jane's complacent
mother recognizes this insensitivity at one point, and the brutal
beating Sara Jane receives from a white boyfriend reinforces the
social construction of her rebellion rather than the psychological
construction via the mother.

This narrative of maternal beneficence and social injustice places
the more traditional narrative of maternal neglect and deprivation
on shaky ground because it then sets up two separate rule systems
for each mother/daughter pair. If Sara Jane is "bad" because of the
way a racist society has treated her, it becomes more difficult to
validate Susie's anger and resentment toward her career mother. It
almost appears as if Sirk didn't really have his heart in it: the confrontation scene between mother and daughter is mild compared
to *Mildred Pierce,* and after speaking harsh words, the daughter
immediately falls into the mother's arms and begs her forgiveness.

The prodigal daughter, Sara Jane, returns to the (white) fold after breaking down at the funeral of her heartbroken mother.

The fact that Lora has decided to give up her career and marry Steve *before* this confrontation scene reverses the traditional cause and effect narrative movement (bad mother realizes her neglect and repents). If Lora "repents" and settles down *prior* to the confrontation with the daughter (and thus prior to the full realization of her supposed negligence as a mother), then perhaps this resolution can be read as somewhat self-determined, not wholly in response to her guilt feelings. Thus for many reasons, *Imitation of Life* is not completely believable as a melodrama of maternal neglect.

The difference between the original version and the 1959 remake is instructive. In the original, Claudette Colbert plays a working mother, carrying on her dead husband's syrup business in a valiant attempt to support her daughter. Her rise to success is predicated on the pancake recipe of Delilah, the obsequious black maid who pleads to work for "Miss Bea" and stays with her until her own death, many years later. The work that propels Miss Bea to the top is thus domestic in origin, beginning in a do-it-yourself diner and moving up to a nationally famous pancake recipe (with Delilah's "Aunt Jemima" picture on the box).

This plot in itself places the film on radically different ground because the 1959 version turns the white mother into a glamorous actress whose neglectfulness as a mother is linked to her own ostentation and narcissism as a (sexualized) "star." Claudette Colbert, as Bea Pullman, is a paragon of virtue; never do we doubt her motherliness or compassion. Even when her daughter unwittingly falls for mother's intended (fish researcher Steven Archer), this is seen less as mother's neglect than as benign circumstance; indeed, they are thrown together when Bea has accompanied Delilah on her search for her runaway daughter.

The differences between the two films can be understood as exemplifying precisely that shift away from discourses centered on extrafamilial realities (race, class) to a psychologically centered melodramatic crisis. Although the racial theme is certainly more vividly and candidly expressed (and, one could argue, more socially responsive) in the 1959 version, it is narratively in the service of the repetitious discourse of bad working mothers. The 1934 version, although more explicitly racist in its blatant and appalling use of stereotyped images of black women, refuses to indict the working (white) mother and rather foregrounds her working classness (as in *Stella*) and her motherly devotion. The figure of the male savior, so crucial to the reconstruction of the domestic unit in the 1959 version (particularly in his alliance with the black mother), is almost incidental in 1934, peripheral to the narrative and, really, to the women's lives.

The 1959 version ends with a soundly reconstructed nuclear family after the tragic death of Annie, but the 1934 film continues past that moment and ends with the white mother giving up the lover (at least temporarily) and remaining bonded with the daughter. The wayward daughter, Peola, whose denial of her blackness and "passing" breaks her mother's heart and causes her death, is returned to the fold and reenrolled in a black college. Both mothers have (successfully) sacrificed for their daughters.

The beginnings are significantly different as well. The earlier version opens with a beneficent image of Bea Pullman lovingly washing and dressing her daughter; the 1959 version opens with Lora Meredith searching wildly for the daughter she has "lost" at Coney Island. It is Annie who "finds" little Susie, thus early on establishing her as the "good (sacrificial) mother" to Lora's self-involved actress/mom. As different as these two versions are, certain aspects remain the same. For instance, all the names of the characters change except that of the male figure, Steven Archer. More important, both films completely occlude the possibility of representing the black woman: she is either a stereotyped, sacrificial mother (sacrificing for her own daughter as well as playing surrogate mother and surrogate husband to the white women) or a stereotyped "tragic mulatto" whose desire to "pass" for white is rarely placed in a context that affords it any real meaning. Although white motherhood becomes problematized with the onslaught of popular psychology and the postwar rush to domesticity, black motherhood remains completely "natural" and assumed to be inevitably beneficent. Lora Meredith plays out the mother/woman split in the narrative, but Annie Johnson is denied one side of this admittedly limited dichotomy. Her sexualized daughter can play it out, although only on the basis of her "whiteness," itself made more complex by the fact that a white actress actually played that part (unlike in the earlier version).

Susan Hayward, another tortured actress similar in both style and substance to Lana Turner, tried her hand at another mother/ daughter melodrama about the theatrical life as one of sin and decadence keeping wayward women from their hardworking husbands. *I'll Cry Tomorrow* is the rags to riches to rags saga of Lillian Roth, poor daughter of immigrants who is pushed by her striving mother (Jo Van Fleet) to acquire fame and fortune as a stage singer. The film begins by firmly establishing the stage mother theme as mother accompanies young Lillian to an audition, then beats her viciously on the street when she fails to butter up the director as mama instructed. Lillian moves to semistardom (not quite as ostentatious as Lana Turner, but then this film was black and white and directed by Daniel Mann, not melodrama magician Douglas Sirk), and mama is always close by her side, pushing her reluctant daughter forward.

When childhood friend David Tredman shows up in Hollywood, Lillian's thoughts turn to romance, and marriage plans are in the wings. Mother, of course, tries to disrupt the happy couple and invites David over for a little chat. As she tries subtly to get him away from her daughter, he calls her bluff and thereby sets himself up as the voice of male-defined integrity against self-interested (s)mothering in a way reminiscent of Dr. Jacquith's homilies of independence. David says, "You and I want Lillian to be happy. And she wants us to be happy. But we're three different people. Each of us has the right to decide where we belong. Or if we belong at all. Without that there's nothing. Now you may want one thing and she may want another and I may want a third."

David knows what he wants: a "wife who will bawl him out for not being ambitious enough." When Lily walks in, she falls right into place after a brief moment of anguished ambivalence: "Whatever David wants . . . is what I want. Whatever makes David happy makes me happy. You see Mama, I want to be David's wife." As mama pleads with her not to throw it all away, Lily rhapsodizes on the joys of wifedom, the plenitude of her future with David, her desire to be a "real wife."

But it is not to be, and poor Lillian doesn't regain love until the end of the film. David dies, sending Lily into a bout of depression and mother-blame: "You always know what's good for me. How to dance, where to sing, what to wear, who to go out with. So what I'm doing now it's not for my own good. And I'm doing it!" Her anger builds, and her mother leaves in a defeated, martyred sort of way ("All I ever wanted was for you to be happy . . . that's what I want now so maybe it's better . . . if I'm not here for a while").

Lily starts on a downward spiral of booze and parties and ends up marrying a man while drunk, then divorcing him after a year of boozy nights. The next man, who looks to be her savior, ends up marrying her for her money and keeping her hostage as he beats and robs her. After escaping from her tyrant husband, Lily hits bottom, then finally finds her way back to mother. Now a frantic alcoholic, Lily plays cards in her mother's house, begging for booze and flying into rages when it is not immediately forthcoming. The requisite confrontation scene between overinvolved/underinvolved mother and victimized daughter is now played out in its full melodramatic potential. Mother, reluctant to go out and buy more liquor, has been stalling an ever more hysterical daughter. As she finally heads for the door, she breaks and gives her version of their relationship:

*Mother:* "All right, it's my fault huh? I made you become an actress. You didn't want to. All right. I've been a bad mother. You had to support me. All right, all right, all right—everything! (shaking Lily now) But just this and for once in your life you're going to hear it! You know at all why I did it, do you? No you don't. Do you know what kind of a life I had? Do you know what it was like to live with your father, put up with his mistakes and afterwards to be left with nothing. No money, no career, not young anymore, nothing to fall back on. No you don't. You don't know *at all* what I tried to save you from. The kind of *freedom* I *never* had I tried to give to you by making you Lillian Roth."

*Lillian:* "So you admit it. You invented Lillian Roth. All right. Now look at me! *I said look at me!* Don't turn your face away. I'm the looking glass you created to see yourself in. All right, all right see yourself now in me. Look at this ugly picture and

Figs. 13 and 14. Susan Hayward gets to play yet another drunken ruin in
*I'll Cry Tomorrow* (1955). This time she plays Lillian Roth, the victimized
daughter of a stage mother who plots to keep her from the man she loves
and, predictably, turns her into a needy wreck living back at home with
dear old mom. (MGM, 1955; photos courtesy of Museum of Modern Art
Film Stills Archives)

|  | then get out of here. But keep this ugly picture before your face as long as you live!" |
|---|---|
| *Mother:* | "It's true. Oh god help me. I owe you this. Every single word of it is true." |

Now that the evil done to daughter is out in the open and mother
has owned up to it, the prodigal daughter can reclaim the broken
mother. She holds her on the couch, saying she didn't mean it, and
gets rather apologetic, in a brisk sort of way. Lily leaves the apartment, contemplates suicide in a hotel room, and finds her way to
Alcoholics Anonymous and the strong arms of Eddie Arnold, a "sur-
vivor" like her. She dries herself out, starts singing again, falls
in love with Eddie, and culminates her reclamation with an appearance on "This Is Your Life," telling the world her tortured
tale.

Another guilty mom—doomed by her desire to give her all for her little girl—popped up several years earlier in a rather sporty twist on the overinvolved mother paradigm. Ida Lupino's 1951 film, *Hard, Fast and Beautiful,* is yet one more cinematic rendering of the talented but benighted daughter manipulated by the climbing, striving "stage mother." The film opens with the mother's voice narrating as the tennis whiz daughter steadfastly bangs a ball against a garage door: "From the moment you were born, I knew you were different. . . . I always wanted something better for you and I made up my mind to get it, no matter what I had to do." What she has to do is scheme dishonestly with a rather unscrupulous tennis promoter to propel her innocent daughter to the top, leaving behind the well-intentioned but hapless and weak father and the daughter's honest, working-class boyfriend.

Conniving mom, in a manner reminiscent of later *Mommie Dearest* scenarios, frames her obviously self-serving martyrdom in terms of giving her daughter all that she never had. In a crucial scene where mom's evil is clearly established, she is in the bedroom she shares with her hopelessly kind husband and informs him, "My

Fig. 15. Mom may hold the pursestrings of daughter's tennis career, but it's daddy who holds her heartstrings in Ida Lupino's *Hard, Fast and Beautiful*. (RKO, 1951; photo courtesy of Museum of Modern Art Film Stills Archive)

daughter's going to have everything, everything I missed. She's going to go places." As she speaks with her husband, they are literally separated by one of the strangest twin bed arrangements to hit the silver screen: the beds are placed head to head so that the supposedly intimate couple does not actually look at each other while they speak. Mother does her nails on one bed, and father first tries to stick up for the daughter and then falls into a pathetic plea: "Every year she was growing up, you were growing away from me. Why, Millie? Can't you love us both?" But in these representations, the love for the daughter must always be at the expense of the love for the father.

After the daughter's predictable rise up the ladder of women's sports, she becomes (predictably) hard and self-serving like her mother. As boyfriend Gordon tells her, "Your mother's done a first class job on you, honey. You're getting to be more like her every day." When Gordon leaves her, she becomes harder and faster (hence the title) and confronts her mother with her duplicity and unsportsmanlike pursuit of fame and fortune. The daughter briefly tries to emulate the mother's ruthlessness, but she is brought back to life by the efforts of a dying dad and a firm boyfriend who comes to take her away from the high-powered, sleazy world of women's tennis and into the haven of suburban domestic bliss. As she leaves in victory from center court at Forest Hills, she gives the victory cup to mom ("This is yours, you've earned it") and goes off with Gordon. The last shot shows mom alone, at night, watching the garbage blow over the darkened tennis court.

Six years later Lana Turner did a warm-up for her performance in *Imitation of Life* by playing another working mother neglecting the emotional/sexual life of both herself and her teenage daughter. The notorious melodrama *Peyton Place* (later to be followed by a television soap opera version) included two mother/daughter pairs—the virtuous Salina (Hope Lange) living in squalor with her mother, who works as a maid for Mrs. MacKenzie (Lana Turner) and her daughter Alison (Diane Varsi). In an early scene (the first between Alison and her mother), the existence of the absent father rears its ugly head. Supposedly, he is dead (a war hero); but because this is a soap opera, he turns out to be a married man with whom Mrs. MacKenzie had an affair. The daughter worships the father she has never seen. When the mother objects to the daughter kissing his picture before she goes off to school, Alison replies, "It's not my fault that he died before I was two." Alison lacks a father—a male presence—and it is this lack that motivates the mother/daughter conflict, as the mother replies angrily, "Stop talking about fathers and husbands and marriage." So an opposition is set up between careerist, unloving, perfectionist, cold mother and daughter's desires for male attention and approval. This is spelled out in a later scene in which mom catches the daughter kissing at a party held in their house:

*Mother:*    "I don't want you to be like everyone else in this town. I want you to rise above Peyton Place."

*Daughter:*    "I don't want to be perfect like you, Mother. I don't want to live in a test tube. I just want to be me. . . . I'd rather be liked than be perfect."

In the ensuing battle, the mother tries to make up by saying that she wants the daughter to fall in love, to meet the right man, and so forth; but the daughter will have none of it, "*You* want! Is that all you can say? Well if any man would seriously ask me I'd run away and become his mistress." The daughter's need to be sexually desired is thrown in the face of the mother's fear and denial of her own sexuality. This is reiterated in a later scene where mother accuses daughter of having been swimming nude with a boy:

*Alison:* "Mother, if you keep this up someday I will do what you keep accusing me of."

*Mother:* "I wouldn't doubt it. You're just like your father when it comes to sex."

The daughter is again identified with sexuality, freedom, and father, and the mother is clearly the force of repression.

The claustrophobia of the suburban idyll, the endless repetition of actions and reactions, is expressed through the mother/daughter relationship. Alison confides in the maid Nellie after a fight with her mother in much the way Susie confided in the maid Annie when her working mother was "unavailable":

*Alison:* "Nellie, you've been both a daughter and a mother, which one is worse?"

*Nellie:* "Being a mother."

*Alison:* "Why?"

*Nellie:* "You find yourself doing the same thing you hated your own mother and father doing."

*Alison:* "That's very interesting. Somewhere along the line doesn't somebody get intelligent and realize that the children have to grow up their own way?"

Here are shades of Dr. Jacquith's theme of "growing free and blossoming." Yet these ideas of letting children grow up "their own way" emerge in the context of a society in which the professionalization of motherhood and the rise of the expert have inserted themselves into every nook and cranny of social life: "Whether or not all Americans read or believed the professionals, there can be little doubt that postwar America was the era of the expert. . . . Science and technology seemed to have invaded virtually every aspect of life, from the most public to the most private. Whether in medicine, child rearing, or even the intimate areas of sex and marriage, expertise gained legitimacy as familiar, 'old-fashioned' ways were called into question."[29]

As Clifford Clark and others have noted, there existed in the fifties competing discourses of maternal incompetence and natural maternal functioning that make it difficult to decipher the dominant ideology of maternal behavior: "The tension between self-sufficiency and ineptitude which was expressed in Dr. Spock's contradictory emphasis on both personal self-reliance and professional expertise, placed women in an ambivalent position."[30] Indeed, the venerable town doctor in *Peyton Place* is the voice of professional authority: he advises the victimized Salina, reveals the truth of her rape by her stepfather, and informs Mrs. MacKenzie that it isn't healthy to have only one child.[31]

The mother eventually blurts out her confession (the daughter's illegitimacy), and the daughter leaves Peyton Place and moves to "The City," only to be reunited with her mother when mom proves her "goodness" at Salina's trial for accidentally killing her drunk stepfather. The reunion, though, occurs only after a man (the handsome new schoolteacher) has broken down mom's icy reserve, and she becomes an available object of the gaze. The ending is thus similar to *Imitation of Life* in that the mother and daughter can be brought back together only when a man enters the picture and "balances it out," thus legitimating the connection, now safely ensconced in a nuclear-family context, and eliminating any suggestion of self-defined mother/daughter intimacy.

## Containing the Crisis, Domesticating Dissent

In many of the films of the late fifties, in contrast to the dominant images of mothers and daughters in the forties, the women are reunited by film's end. Whereas Veda is arrested and Charlotte gets rid of her mother by a convenient death, these later films leave us with the sense of a relationship maintained, albeit with chastened mothers. This should not be surprising, given the dominance of family ideologies in the fifties. The drastic separation entailed in a film like *Mildred Pierce* implied trouble in the domestic nest. But the vision of familial harmony produced by the culture industry and

Fig. 16. Lana Turner stars as the repressed working mother who fears
that her acting-out daughter will repeat her own (sexual) mistakes in the
suburban potboiler *Peyton Place*. (20th Century-Fox, 1957; photo courtesy
of Photofest)

supported by government policies simply could not tolerate so
drastic a rift in the domestic landscape.[32] In both *Now, Voyager* and
*Mildred Pierce*, the families we are left with at film's end are
strange and fractured: Charlotte becomes the keeper of her lover's
daughter, suppressing her own sexuality in the service of this awkward arrangement. Mildred is reunited with her first husband,
Burt, but is rendered childless—one daughter lost to her neglect
and another to her obsessiveness. Neither is a simple vision of a
domestic idyll.

Although *Peyton Place* revealed the underside of the suburban
paradise (tellingly set right at the beginning of the U.S. entry into
World War II), it ended up arguing that the family can be internally
cleansed. By film's end, mother and daughter walk into their beautiful bourgeois home together as father/lover figure (the schoolteacher) and Alison's boyfriend look on proudly. You can almost

hear them saying, "Gosh, it's good to have our girls back together again!"

Images of mothers and daughters in the forties, for all their meanness, expressed and explored the turmoil of a world in crisis, a world amazed at the horrors of fascism and unsure of what the future would bring. But in the fifties, popular culture was passionately enjoined in the effort to acclimate and orient Americans to the "brave new world" of mass consumption, tract housing, and ideological homogeneity. *Peyton Place* could expose the contradictions, but it could not let them exist. *Imitation of Life* could present mother/daughter conflict, but it had to reestablish a familial harmony by film's end.

Even the conflicts between mothers and daughters that went on in both films of the fifties seem more like a rather benign generational struggle than a profound psychological disharmony, reflecting perhaps the popularization of "youth rebellion" as a legitimate social category. When Alison threatens to run off with a lover, we can picture the mothers in the audience smiling gently at her youthful naiveté, sure that, as the psychologists say, this is only a stage she is going through. And Susie's "you've given me everything but yourself" speech is shot through with a sort of humor, as when she asks her mother pertly if she has worded her college application correctly.

The rifts between mothers and daughters could now be managed, worked out, rectified. But this working out was intimately tied to the reconstruction of the harmonious (patriarchal) nuclear family. Representations of the mother/daughter relationship in the postwar years presented a vision of an endlessly malleable nuclear family, able to withstand problems and disagreements, secure in the knowledge that everything can be worked out eventually. Although conflict between mother and daughter remained central to the narratives, it was interpreted not so much as the imposition of the neurotic mother on the victim/daughter, but rather as part of a "life stage" or even generational rebellion. As in the films of the mid and late forties (*Mildred Pierce, Now, Voyager*), psychology eclipses class as a mediating theme. But the type of psychological offering here is a bit different, a psychology now searching for continuity and conformity, resolution and adjustment.

So the mother and daughter are reunited in many of these fifties images; yet it is a problematic reunion. Without acknowledgment of class and history, the reunion is rather sterile. More important, the reunion in both films discussed here depends on the reconstruction of the nuclear family and the reestablishment of a dominant male presence, a reestablishing that is also performed in terms of genre. Perhaps this return of the male presence signals the end to the female-centered "women's films" and a resurgence of more male-defined generic formulas, particularly in the "rebel" films of the fifties and early sixties.

The fifties and early sixties remain marked by the rigorous attention of popular culture to an explicit and rarely wavering ideological agenda of familial harmony and feminine containment. Turning again to "Father Knows Best" we see how an unambiguous ideology permeates the very fabric of cultural design. In a 1958 episode entitled "Medal for Margaret," the subject is trophies and medals. As father and the kids busy themselves building a case to hold their symbols of achievement, mother, who has none, is made to feel lacking, yet assures her concerned brood that she is "perfectly happy cooking all of the meals to keep all you champions hale and hearty."

But, to keep the family happy, Margaret secretly takes up fly casting in order to compete in a women's contest and thus win the admiration of her husband and progeny. True to sitcom logic, Margaret breaks her arm and is unable to compete in the contest. Finding out her plan, her touched family entertains her with a "This Is Your Life, Margaret Anderson" ceremony. Each member of the family recounts an event in which resourceful and reliable mother/wife Margaret has exhibited exemplary maternal behavior. Eldest daughter Betty begins by recalling the time when she was nine years old and her mother valiantly dashed off a new, prize-winning costume after she had fallen and ruined hers on her way to a party: "I thought that she was the greatest, smartest mother in the whole world. Of course now that I'm older I'm sure of it. And so, Mrs. Anderson, I award you this plaque for most valuable mother," giving her a frying pan with "Most Valuable Mother" written on it. Each child continues—"Boy's best friend," and so forth—and father finally pops in with a medal for "being the best darn wife I ever had."

First Margaret is mocked for her lack of achievement. Then, when she does try to learn a skill, she is terrible at it and, finally, taken out of the running. Ultimately, Margaret is compensated for her lack of official recognition by the recognition of her family: her maternal/wifely nurture and caretaking have allowed her family to excel. This vicarious success, the show implies, is all that she should ever need or want.

But mother's caretaking and functioning (as the positivist sociologists would have it) is at the same time presented as inadequate to the task of preparing her children for the major moral and social issues that will confront them in their adult years: "Philip Wylie's presence in Fifties television is felt not in a preponderance of violent or evil mothers; rather, the programs 'solve' the 'problem' of mother's all-powerful and harmful influence within the family by decisively reconfiguring the father as *the* crucial molder of his children's psyches, while simultaneously suggesting that the mother is fundamentally inadequate to this and other familial and household tasks."[33] "Father Knows Best" is quite literally what it says it is: mother *is* the family (she is intimately aligned with the domestic) yet she is strangely insignificant. Here again is that double message of the fifties: extolling the virtues of motherhood and domestic femininity while promoting fathers as primary socializers. The background to this seemingly antinomous message is the lingering scent of the rabid misogynists, Wylie, Strecker, Lundberg and Farnham, and others.

In a 1959 episode entitled "Kathy Becomes a Girl," the role of the father as both the figure of knowledge and moral guidance and the educator into appropriate femininity is made explicit. In a reversal of what would typically have been a dialogue between mother and daughter, father now supplants mother as the one most able to educate their daughter in the realities of adult femininity. The episode begins with mother's concern about youngest daughter's tomboyish behavior ("Kathy, don't you think you're getting a little old to be wrestling boys and playing football?"). Kathy's initial resistance ("What else is there to do?") quickly turns into concern over her lack of girlfriends and her status as "oddball." Mother informs her that "there comes a time when girls like girls who act more, well, more like girls." Kathy continues, objecting, "You mean I should act the way they do and be a stuffed shirt?" Mother replies,

"No! Just be a normal, average girl." Kathy replies, "I don't think I'm the type." Mother here is able to express the desire for conformity but has not the power to create it; that job is left to father.

The inculcation of appropriate femininity into Kathy is painful to watch. Kathy's inappropriate behavior is signified by her physicality: roughhousing with boys and swinging and hugging her girlfriends. Part of the breaking of Kathy, of constructing the feminine in a little girl, involves restricting the body and producing a repertoire of "feminine" deceit and manipulation.

This episode of "Father Knows Best" puts to rest any doubts concerning the authenticity of Simone de Beauvoir's comment that "woman is made, not born." The entire family becomes engaged in making a woman out of Kathy. When Kathy is ignored by her girlfriends as a party is being planned, the tension heightens, and father legitimizes mother's exasperated (and rather comical) concern by pointing out the implications of this problem for Kathy's "development": "If she feels rejected at school this can become a big problem for her. We've got to find a solution." When sister Betty suggests that the solution lies in a gender switch, Kathy runs down the stairs to concur with her joking sister, "I wish I was a boy!"

Although mother buys Kathy a frilly dress in the hopes that it will "encourage her to be more careful and ladylike" and big sister initiates her into the world of feminine appearance ("I'll turn her into a girl if I have to black her eye doing it"), father finally gets through to the still reluctant Kathy in a little talk they have on the steps. The reference point in his pitch is mother; he's going to let Kathy in on the little tricks mother uses that make her so wonderful: "Oh, I mean cute things. Like, uhh, being dependent, a little helpless now and then, expecting me to take over. You see, men like to be gallant. All you have to do is give them the opportunity." He convinces Kathy that little tricks are a part of being a woman, and she concludes, "We girls have got it made. All we have to do is sit back and be waited on." But father is quick to point out (and here is the nod to the reality of women's lives, including participation in the labor force) that "it's very important for a girl to be capable and self-sufficient." But Kathy continues to get it wrong, and more work is needed to set her straight:

Kathy:    "I am! I can beat Eroll wrestling any day!"
Father:   "Worst thing you can do. Never try to beat a man at his own game. You just beat the women at theirs."

Fig. 17. All eyes (and hearts and minds) are on dad in that classic of domestic sitcoms, "Father Knows Best." (CBS; photo courtesy of Photofest)

*Kathy:*    "I'll remember Daddy. But are you sure it'll work?"

*Father:*    "Your mother's worked it on me for over twenty years."

In the end, Kathy accedes to her feminization. She successfully seduces the boys by acquiring the trappings of "girlness" and employing the "womanly" arts of deception. The final scenes show her rendered prone and helpless by a (false) broken ankle and thus rewarded by the attention of admiring boys. Kathy wins over the girls as well, who now find in her a successful sister who is finally able to attract the sought-after males.

This induction into appropriate femininity is also the subject of an appalling article written in 1956 by Constance Foster entitled "A Mother of Boys Says: Raise Your Girl To Be a Wife." The author here is clearly angry at the "confused" roles in contemporary society and wants to get wayward women back on the right path to wife and motherhood: "The one essential qualification for a satisfactory daughter-in-law is the ability to be a real woman and like it. For such a girl having children is the most natural thing in the world because it's what everything is all about." Foster cites Farnham and

Lundberg in stating her case against willful mothers who would lead their daughters into the never-never land of female independence: "Long before it's time for Mom to help plan the wedding or Dad to give the bride away, it's time to be raising a future wife in your home. Because wives aren't born—they are made. Your daughter is born a female, but she has to learn to be feminine." [34]

This strange twist on de Beauvoir, like its "Father Knows Best" counterpart, encourages mothers to be diligent in their education of their girl children. Bolstering dads seems to be a principal ingredient in the construction of a wife: "Sometimes a mother harms her daughter's chances of future happiness in marriage by deprecating men in general and the girl's father in particular. If she is the one who 'runs' the family she then gives her daughter the feeling that men need to be managed." Those important "inner patterns of femininity" are almost solely contingent on daughter's worship of father and mother's ability to access those for the daughter: "I hope my daughters-in-law are lucky enough to have Dads who rave over their first fumbling attempts to bake a cake and make dresses for their dolls. The fonder they are of their fathers, the better they will be someday for my sons." [35]

Mothers of daughters are not only urged to prepare them for the dubious distinction of wife/helpmate/mother but are also often informed of the intractability of generational struggle and the necessity of remaining forgiving and accessible throughout. In an article on how to be popular with your daughter (a very common theme in the fifties age of conformity), Marjorie Marks urges mothers to be endlessly malleable in relation to their daughters' teenage angst: "Never be too busy when Daughter talks or too pressing if she is reticent. It's normal procedure for her to prefer Friend Irma to yourself as confidante. This is proof that the apron strings are lengthening as they should be. Some day she will come back of her own free will. A girl's best friend is her mother—on request only." [36]

Yet Jo Wagner is not so sure that what goes around will, in fact, come around: "There is a theory that a teenage girl, once she herself has grown up and becomes the mother of a teenage girl, will say, 'Mother was right!' Comforting, that theory—if you can subscribe to it. I can't. I am sure that she will do no such thing. My daughter will look at *her* daughter in amazement and consternation. She'll wonder, What is the matter with kids these days? *She'll* be saying, 'Now when *I* was your age—' " [37]

One thing remains clear in both these statements and the issues previously discussed: the fifties continued the process of constructing the mother/daughter relationship as a series of double bind discourses. On the one hand, mothers are to be endlessly available and responsive to the caprices of their teenage daughters. Indeed, the inevitability of generational struggle (or, more accurately, "irritation") is produced here as a natural category and a prerequisite for development (lengthening of those apron strings as they should be). The theme in many women's magazine articles was one of a sort of benign tolerance toward rambunctious daughters. Yet mothers were simultaneously condemned for *not* being attentive and diligent enough with their kids and thus urged to exert a more substantial maternal influence on both their wayward youth and their wayward society.

The double binds continue. Mrs. Anderson is held up as the epitome of well-adjusted womanhood; yet she is not even deemed competent enough to teach her daughters the "necessary" lessons of womanhood. Mothers are to initiate their daughters into appropriate femininity (turn them into wives, as the article states), but how can Mrs. Anderson reproduce herself if dad has taken over that job as well? Mothers continue to be held responsible for their daughters' psyches and personalities yet are given little narrative power to make that responsibility meaningful.

These double binds help maintain a no-win situation for mothers and daughters in the postwar years, one that continues to plague contemporary representations and lived experience. The daughters of these fifties mothers are shown that mothers who work miss essential feminine experiences and deprive their families. The alternative image of the period—the Margaret Andersons and Mama Hansens and June Cleavers—offer daughters a model of sappy, happy serfdom and sacrifice, completely negating any path for these daughters other than an endless reproduction of the same. The closeness of some of these fifties mothers and daughters is not an intimacy built on the richness of human experience but a cloying attachment firmly anchored to the patriarchal constraints of female domesticity.

## Chapter Four

# The Turning Point

### Mothers and Daughters at
### the Birth of Second-Wave Feminism

Carol: *"I mean I know you're trying to help, but you can't be objective about this. You're my mother."*

Maude: *"Carol, I'm not only your mother. I'm your friend, Carol, your best friend."*

Carol: *"Well you can't be my mother and my best friend too."*

Maude: *"Yes I can!"*

Carol: *"No you can't!"*

Maude: *"Now don't contradict me, Carol. I'm your mother."*

Carol: *"Well I don't need a mother right now. You say you're my friend. Then be my friend."*

Maude: *"All right. I will speak to you as a friend. Listen to your mother, Carol!"*

—"Maude," 1975

In 1963, Betty Friedan published *The Feminine Mystique* and echoed torch singer Peggy Lee when she asked American women, "Is that all there is?" After over a decade spent amid the eerie cheerfulness of the domestic fantasy, the facade was beginning to crack. Friedan's book spoke of this domestic ideology as both illusion and entrapment. She grieved for the images of valiant heroines and independent women she had seen in the thirties and during the war years and tried to understand the "retreat to the home" that characterized the period in which she both lived and wrote. Because of her own work as a women's magazine writer, she articulated a familiarity and forcefulness that bespoke her intimate knowledge of what she termed "the problem that has no name."

Clearly, the women's movement, much less feminism, did not emerge full-blown the day after Friedan's tome hit the bookstores. Indeed, for a large part of the sixties, it was business as usual. "Oz-

zie and Harriet" ran until 1966, as did "The Donna Reed Show,"
even though June Cleaver of "Leave It to Beaver" and Margaret
Anderson of "Father Knows Best" had faded out by 1963. The lure
of an idyllic suburbia still exerted itself on the ever-expanding body
politic, and barbecues and home decorating remained favorite domestic activities. Yet the sixties saw the full development of the
significant social movements of our time: the civil rights movement, the antiwar and student movements, and, toward the end of
the decade, the women's movement. Indeed, as Sara Evans so
forcefully argues, the women's movement itself was in large part a
product of women's engagement both in civil rights struggles and
in the culture and politics of the New Left.[1] These years were saturated with a social upheaval made even more compelling in contrast
to the previous years of feminine containment and McCarthyite
repression. "The sixties" (really the late sixties and early seventies)
have come to represent America's own unique experience of internal dissonance and rebellion. They mark off a watershed of American history as distinctive as World War II, one that shaped and
structured the public consciousness in fundamentally new and
challenging ways.

What happens to the images of the mother/daughter relationship
in a world of televised napalm bombings and Woodstock, sit-ins and
marches on Washington? What happens to these images when the
women's movement really emerges, both as a cultural discourse
and as a vast panoply of experiences and practices? How does the
new language of feminism and the new location of women as media
subjects structure and shape the way we look at and think about the
mother/daughter relationship?

The shift from an ideology in the sixties that perpetuated a (left-
over from the fifties) maternal evil/maternal good dichotomy to the
emergence of full-blown feminism in the seventies can also be seen
specifically as a media shift. Television, and the sitcom in particular,
came into its own in the seventies as a medium that was something
more than a simple reinforcement of the status quo. Television exhibited a greater willingness than film to engage with the women's
movement and the new familial configurations. As TV critic Ella
Taylor notes: "The ubiquity of television and its intensely domestic
character make it an ideal form in which to observe changing ideas
about family. It is watched by a vast number of people in their

homes; its advertising is geared to both the parts and the whole of
the family unit; its images, in both news and entertainment, are
stamped with the familial."[2] One of the greatest surprises of this
research has been the realization of the vast difference between
television and film in the early years of the women's movement.
Typically thought of as an endless repetition of hackneyed clichés,
television in this feminist heyday of the seventies far outstripped
film in its intrepid adventures through a changing social terrain.
Except for a few notable exceptions, the "new Hollywood women's
cinema" of the seventies made only occasional inroads against the
hegemony of the alienated male/buddy films of the sixties and seventies. Thus I focus here more on television and women's magazines than on film because these media were engaged more closely
with the radical offerings of the women's movement.

## Rebel with a Bad Mother, or, the Case of
## the Missing Daughter

What is most striking about film in the sixties and seventies is the
almost complete absence of images—either "good" or "bad"—of
mothers and daughters. Aside from *Inside Daisy Clover* (1965), *The
Graduate* (1967), *Rachel, Rachel* (1968), *The Turning Point* (1977),
and a few others, one is hard-pressed to find any films dealing with
mothers and daughters in even the most remote and oblique fashion. Certainly the most popular films of the period were more engaged with themes of war, male bonding, rebellious (male) alienation, and the counterculture male antihero. In these narratives,
women were the less than secondary sexual objects serving as release or, alternately, frustration to the ever-present angst of the angry young man. If the backdrop to mainstream sixties culture was
the counterculture New Left, then the narratives provided by this
New Left were relentlessly male in subject and style, with women
occasionally grafted on as new products of a "sexual revolution" that
made them more available to the male (anti)heroes and less available as substantive subjects of the narrative itself.

Molly Haskell might be overstating the case when she claims,
"From a woman's point of view, the ten years from, say 1962 or 1963
to 1973 have been the most disheartening in screen history."[3]
Nevertheless, it does seem a period more notable for its absence of

significant female roles in film than for anything else. This absence is accentuated when we look for the more specific representation of mothers and daughters. Although mother/son relationships abounded in the sixties (*Sons and Lovers, Return to Peyton Place, Long Day's Journey into Night, All Fall Down, The Manchurian Candidate, The Stripper, Five Finger Exercise, The Loneliness of the Long Distance Runner*, etc.), mothers and daughters seem to be invisible in the ever-present dramas of rebellious male torment and ball-breaking momism.[4]

Sixties films introduced a new angle on the theme of the bad mother warping her children. Studiously ignoring the specificity of student protest, civil rights struggles, and the antiwar movement, the films of the sixties instead refracted social discord through the lens of domestic, intergenerational disharmony. No film could speak to this theme more eloquently than *Rebel Without a Cause*. Even though made in 1955, *Rebel* exemplified the sixties trend toward narratives of alienated young men, docile fathers, and overbearing and dominating mothers. Typically thought of as a classic and heartrending tale of youthful alienation and social/parental repression, it takes on a less valiant hue when viewed through the eyes of mothers. If ever there was a Wyliesque "mom" personified, it is in the figure of Jim Stark's (James Dean) mother—overpowering, smothering, aggressive, and, most important, denying her son the strong male model he needs through her dominance of the "hen-pecked" husband. In this saga of generational rebellion, mothers play the unfortunate role of the subjugator of youthful growth and development. As David Considine notes:

The image of the mother that dominated the sixties was a logical outgrowth of a trend that began in the forties and developed steadily throughout the 1950's. It was an image that seemed to obsess the industry. In the process, it served to obscure the issues of the day. While film families throughout the decade are strife-ridden and torn apart, the issues dividing them remain obscure. . . . What we find instead in these film families is domestic discord based on the possessiveness and aggression of wives and mothers.[5]

*Splendor in the Grass* (1961) similarly pairs overbearing mothers with weak fathers (Deenie's parents) and macho fathers with submissive mothers (Bud's parents). The echo of structural-functionalist theories of complementarity can be heard in this oft-repeated formula of familial patterns. Deenie's mother drives her daughter to the asylum by articulating her own Victorian ideas of sexuality to the desirous and suffering teenager ("Your father never laid a hand on me until we were married. And then I, I just gave in because a wife had to. A woman doesn't enjoy those things the way a man does. She just lets her husband . . . come near her in order to have children.").

*Inside Daisy Clover,* although primarily a film about the tawdry and manipulative construction of "the star" in the days of the studio system, allows a sympathetic mother figure, but one rendered likable only through her obvious insanity. Daisy's mother, played wonderfully by Ruth Gordon, is not used narratively as a maternal presence, but serves as the narrative ploy to return Daisy to her prestar "naturalness." As in so many earlier films, the mother must die for the daughter to "cleanse" herself and break out of the patterns of self-destruction.

The 1967 hit *The Graduate* (still understood as a "classic" film of the sixties, like *Easy Rider*) pitted the adulterous, cynical, almost grotesque Mrs. Robinson against her angelic daughter, who is the real object of Jonathan's affections. The generation gap is made manifest both in the relationship between the mother and daughter and in Jonathan's relationships with his egregiously middle-class parents. But it becomes embodied in the person of the demonized mother, as the final scene in the chapel indicates. As Jonathan comes to "save" Katherine from an unloving bourgeois marriage, the mother is literally silenced; we only see her lips furiously spewing forth her anger and resentment at her daughter and at Jonathan. The daughter is allowed the final words: "You had your chance, now let me have mine." The daughter's voice breaks through the imposed silence of maternal possessiveness and domestic pathos. But, more important, *both* women's voices are reduced to mere plot devices in the service of the male coming of age narrative.

Mother as grotesque was a popular theme in many other films, such as *Rachel, Rachel* (1968). Like her Bette Davis counterpart in *Now, Voyager,* the Joanne Woodward character is a slightly off-center "spinster" daughter living with her even more off-center and domineering mother. Once again (as in *Now, Voyager*) the father has died years ago, leaving the devoted but seething-inside daugh-

Fig. 18. Poor Katherine Ross is caught between the selfish desires of her lusty mom and the rebellious angst of her male savior in the 1960s classic *The Graduate*. (Embassy Pictures, 1967; photo courtesy of Photofest)

ter to take care of her demanding and dependent mother. Here, too, the daughter is kept a virtual prisoner by her Wyliesque mom and achieves an attenuated sort of freedom by leaving town and forcing her mother either to come with her or to stay on her own (the mother comes along). Given these options, one wonders whether absence (of mothers and daughters in film) isn't more desirable!

Sixties television was equally wanting when it came to representing mothers and daughters, indeed, when it came to substantial female characters at all. First, westerns had a resurgence with such popular shows as "Gunsmoke," "Wagon Train," and "Bonanza." These continued to receive high ratings throughout the sixties, even with the influx of the "wacky" comedies such as "Bewitched," "The Beverly Hillbillies," "Green Acres," "Hogan's Heroes," "Get Smart," "The Addams Family," and "The Flying Nun."[6] From 1960 to 1970, no shows with significant mother/daughter relationships achieved ratings in the top ten.[7] When it came to the serious exploration of mothers and daughters, the TV industry in the sixties was as uninterested as the film industry appeared to be. Not until the

1970 season, with the birth of "Mary Tyler Moore," and 1971, with "All in the Family," do adult mother/daughter relationships begin to peek forth from behind the ossified images of western macho men and countrified sex kittens. In 1972, with "Maude" and "The Waltons" joining the pack, mothers and their teenage or adult daughters emerge as a significant force in television narrative.[8]

## The Problem *Does* Have a Name: Slouching Toward Feminism

While the visual media of the sixties retained a resolutely male (albeit often alienated and rebellious) outlook, the women's magazines, in their implicit targeting of a gendered audience, continued to explore issues of relevance to women's lives, including the relationship of mother to daughter. The women's magazines present a microcosm of the contradictory images of mothering and the mother/daughter relationship during the sixties and seventies. Beginning in 1963 with Friedan's *The Feminine Mystique*, they engage in a series of highly truncated debates over the central challenges of Friedan's thesis. Importantly, Friedan was one of their own, not simply an outside expert who could be cited and then pushed aside to make way for a more homegrown editorial stance. As in the fifties, the women's magazines expressed a wider variety of responses to the changing social/sexual situation than did film and television. Not until the mid-seventies did the visual media explore "women's issues" with the same vigor the women's magazines had used earlier.

This is not to say the magazines gave their full and unfettered support to the growing women's movement. In fact, writers commented harshly on the "trend" toward liberation, a harshness magnified in other popular presses, such as *Time, Look,* and *Life.* For example, in *Look* of January 11, 1966, Patricia Coffin extols the virtues of "true womanhood" very explicitly in reaction to what she sees as a dangerous move toward the obliteration of sex distinctions. She quotes Friedan disdainfully and goes on to tell women, "It's time you woke up, because the joke is on you." In arguing for the intractability of gender difference, Coffin obliquely blames mothers for the "alienation" of modern (male) youth, a theme evident throughout the sixties and one that has been thoroughly echoed in film: "The boys grow their hair because the girls wear the pants. . . . The climate is phony. You don't really want to look like a tinker toy or a little boy. You are a gender apart and lucky to have a man to lean on. . . . You ought to go back to being a woman." She connects the return of the real woman with the return of the real man: "If you can find your way back to true womanhood . . . in the deep, beautifully illogical female sense, the American man will recover his pride and his manhood."[9]

An article by Eunice Kennedy Shriver in *McCall's* of June 1965 echoed this plea for a return to women's true destiny with an angry attack on abortion rights activists and those who would in any way impinge on the sanctity of motherhood: "I believe in motherhood as the nourishment of life. Women have been rearing children for fifty million years. It is what we do best. Only we can do it. It is the most wonderful, the most satisfying thing we could possibly do."[10]

A 1966 forum in *The PTA Magazine* that included pieces by Ann Landers and Mary S. Calderone specifically addressed the question, "Are Girls Getting Too Aggressive?" Again, the reference to the new women's movement is explicit, and, again, mothers are the sole referents for the cause of their daughters' putative aggressiveness. Here, as in so many articles, the inclusive language of "parent" is invoked; yet the specific example is always mother: "The solution lies with the parents of American girls. Girls need to be taught by their mothers that sex is not dirty or evil, that it is an important part of married love."[11] Yet this forum is symptomatic of the contradictory impulses within the women's magazine literature. On the one hand, Ann Landers is bemoaning, like Patricia Coffin, the sorry state of womanhood in the mid-sixties. Yet other articles contest this angry and nostalgic discourse of "return to true womanhood" and seem to tolerate, and at times even embrace, a critique of traditional gender hierarchy, as in Lester Kirkendall's piece in the same forum entitled "Away with Stereotypes."

As with films, women's magazines often interpreted social rebellion and "social problems" through the stern gaze of parental (again read "maternal") responsibility. In a 1961 piece in *Good Housekeeping*, David Lester asks, and answers, the question: "Are You Pushing Your Daughter Into Too-Early Marriage?" Lester identifies the rising rates of teenage pregnancy and marriage as a significant social problem and, not surprisingly, blames mothers for the precocious social/sexual behavior of their daughters: "Youngsters are pressured into dating by their own socially active parents, who urge them into a variety of social situations. Mothers are generally the prime movers; fathers, busy with the bread-winning, generally go along with the decision." [12] Notice again the discursive move from "parents" to "mothers," a trusty maneuver of almost every women's magazine article that concerns parents and their children.

This article has a double message in that it positions the girl as responsible for the social problems of early pregnancy and marriage and then further implicates women by positioning the mother as responsible for creating the situation of precociousness that led to daughter's downfall. After recounting the horror story of sixteen-year-old Clarissa's early marriage and subsequent suicide attempt, Lester clearly sees mom as responsible: "Let us look more closely at girls such as Clarissa who teeter to the altar on high heels they have barely learned to wear. What makes them rush so? Even more important, how are their parents, particularly mothers, actually forcing them into early matrimony without realizing it?" [13] Ironically, Lester completely overlooks another part of his own story— the fact that Clarissa's young husband "wished her dead" prior to her wrist slashing—and finds the origin of daughter's acting out in her mother's nostalgia for her own lost youth:

With the prospect of oncoming middle years too painful to contemplate, they look back, instead, where there is fun once again in dates—this time their daughters! . . . The young girl, knowing she has her mother's approval, finds her a willing listener and even an accomplice in her romantic problems. . . . The mother deludes herself into believing she has a confiding relationship with her daughter. Actually, it's a conspiratorial one, and one she enjoys hugely. The result, however, is to push her child deeper and deeper into an advanced social and sexual whirl. [14]

The author is here criticizing mothers for trying to "keep up with the times," but just a few years before the women's magazines had been filled with advice urging mothers to remain as hip and flexible as possible. This reversal needs to be seen in the context of a social environment that positioned youth as "dangerous" and thus initiated a discourse of parental (read "maternal") responsibility. This discourse of responsibility is not new, as shown in preceding chapters. Yet it changes its focus in the context of the student and anti-war movement in the sixties, for the student movement was certainly not equivalent to the juvenile-delinquency panic of the late forties and fifties, and the participants much more profoundly challenged the values of their parents and of society at large. Nevertheless, just as Wylie castigated mothers for being overbearing and producing weak sons, unprepared for manly military heroism, his sixties counterparts took mothers to task for creating rebellious youth, for raising children too "liberally" and with not enough discipline and authority. Many things remain constant about the two periods, but the most striking is the lack of concern for girls and their mothers and the overwhelming focus on the mother/son and sometimes the father/son relationship. Daughters are simply not considered actors in this new drama of generational and cultural rebellion. So the discourse on the mother/daughter relationship remains more firmly anchored to the "classic" psychological constructs that had begun in the forties and in many ways is little transformed by the social and political turmoil of the (prefeminist) sixties.

Mothers are generally taken to task in relation to more traditional complaints from daughters (e.g., maternal interference and the lack of separation). In the regular *Good Housekeeping* section called "My Problem and How I Solved It," a woman tells the story of how her mother came to live with her and her family, causing a breakdown in the daughter, who finally realizes (with the help of the friendly psychiatrist) that it's because she can't grow up with her overinvolved mother: "Most mothers know they must to some degree 'lose' their children as they grow up. The best mothers, even at pain to themselves, try to help them to be independent. But my mother, I came to realize, had never accepted this idea. She fought to keep me from growing up, from growing away from her." The good doctor explains the woman's "fatigue" completely in relation to her mother's presence and her own failings: "Dr. Harvey had been right. My fatigue had been a symptom of everything that had been bottled up inside me—resentment of Mother, a childish fear of her disapproval, anger at my own failings, and a lot of self-pity. Nowadays, I can do all the housework in half the time, with half the effort." Given the later "problem that has no name" interpretation of housewives' depression, this passage has particular poi-

gnancy, and the resolution reasserts rather than challenges her submission: "I'm still Mother's daughter, but I am even more Howard's
wife, and Jill's mother."[15]

Other authors insist on a mother's right to work, not merely to
maintain the family's level of consumption, but for "personal satisfaction." Norman Lobsenz, writing in a 1961 *Redbook* article, argues that because so many wives are working ("One out of every
three wives in the nation holds a job today."), it becomes important
to move away from guilt and toward an honest assessment of why
women desire to work: "What concerns the experts on family life
today is not that so many mothers are working, but that they are so
often confused about their reasons for working, and that by delud-
ing themselves and their families about their motives in taking a
job, they create a host of wholly unnecessary problems."[16] Although
he still sees the women and work question as precisely that—a
question (like child care and birth control) that is solely up to
women to resolve, as if male attitudes and male power didn't enter
into the equation—Lobsenz is careful to argue against the guilt
feelings of many mothers. He even discusses the possible benefits
working mothers might transmit to their children, a debate that
hasn't progressed much further since.

A specific discourse about the "problem that has no name" began
even before the phrase was coined. In 1961, *Parents' Magazine*
published an article by Elizabeth Schmidt entitled "The Best
Mothers Aren't Martyrs" in which the author expresses precisely
the frustrations of the feminine mystique: "I'm bored with the
housework, irritated by my children and tired—tired all the time.
I love my husband and my family, but what about my own needs
and wishes? I'm lost—nothing more than a machine for cleaning
furniture and scolding children. What's ahead of me? Nothing but
more of the same. I feel just awful feeling this way, but I can't
help it."[17]

After detailing her life before marriage, where she felt immense
satisfaction as an army nurse overseas, she has "to admit that when
I said all I wanted was to be a good wife and mother, I wasn't being
honest. I wanted something else besides—to be a person in my
own right." Several interactions with her young daughter push her
into this realization and force her to initiate change on her own
behalf: "One day . . . I watched six-year-old Jan . . . playing house.

'Oh, now I have to do the dishes,' Jan wailed. Then, shouting at the long suffering doll, 'How can I get anything done with you always in the way?' Her performance as a weary, sighing mother got better and better. I realized I was looking at an imitation of myself." This is precisely the process the mother wants to halt, brought home by yet another instance of the daughter's budding domesticity: "Another time, Jan was helping me dust. She rubbed listlessly at the dining room table, confiding to me with a long face, 'It's hard to be a mother, isn't it Mommy?'"[18]

Schmidt is able to break out only so far; her decision to take part-time work and be a less perfectionist housecleaner are predicated on a reading of her situation in completely individualistic terms (my fault, not society's) and in fact adopting as a rationale a resurrected version of the companionate marriage: "The aims I set for myself weren't conflicting at all—perhaps I could be a good wife and mother without sacrificing my own personal growth! Perhaps what was wrong was not my situation but myself—what was needed was not martyrdom but energy and determination. I decided to try for both worlds."[19] Little Jan's premature domesticity is thus understood solely in terms of her mother's modeling rather than as part of the socialization of young girls into "appropriate femininity."

A 1966 *Look* article entitled "The War Between Mother and Daughter" attempts to reassert both the language of biological determinism and the metaphors of war to describe the mother/daughter relationship. In this reading, mothers and daughters are drawn together through their biological destiny as mothers; yet, paradoxically, this sameness initiates what the authors tellingly call the "cold war": "And there is a rapport, an intimacy between women, which men can never achieve. Women are drawn together by a simple and complicated fact: Their bodies are designed to bear children, and they share an understanding of the physical changes and discomforts that accompany that privilege. The cold war starts when the little girl discovers she and her mother are of the same sex—and daddy is different." As penis envy creeps into the discourse of women's magazines, so does its ultimate Freudian purpose: the construction of an inevitable rift between women and the subsequent push toward an overriding male identification: "I believe that no girl can ever become a whole woman unless she understands and has made a mature acceptance of her mother. . . .

For if she still resents her mother and yearns for the kind of affection she thinks her mother denied her, she may have difficulty ever reaching a satisfactory relation with a man, leaning (consciously or unconsciously) toward women as mother substitutes."[20]

Coming to terms with mother is not yet understood in feminist terms (e.g., mother as another woman) but still in terms of how the mother/daughter relationship affects the "real" heart of our existence: our relationships with men. It is precisely these discourses —of biology as bonding and bonding as healthy heterosexuality— that begin to change as feminism enters the popular language of the women's magazines in the early seventies. Even more than in the sixties, women's magazines in the seventies continued to explore central issues of the mother/daughter relationship in the context of an ever-growing women's movement. In 1976, Janet Kole asked these very questions in an article she wrote for *Harper's Bazaar:*

Is it harder to raise a child these days? Has 1976 brought any revelations about mothers and daughters? Is it easier or harder for them to have a good relationship in this atmosphere of increasing awareness of what it means to be a woman? . . . The 70s and the Women's Movement have brought new dilemmas and new joys for women and one area in which dilemma and joy are particularly intermingled is the mother/daughter relationship. All the talk and thinking about ourselves as feminists has brought us back to our beginnings; we are examining the women who made us what we are and the daughters whom we will inevitably shape.[21]

Other writers became aware of the paucity of materials on mothers and daughters:

One could make a good case for there being no human relationship so dramatic and so rich in possibility as that between mother and daughter; and it is strange to me that so little literature—always excepting psychiatrists' notebooks and the literature of pathology—has attempted adequately to deal with it. One is hard-pressed to think of contemporary novels that focus on mother-daughter relationships. On the other hand, one has no trouble finding novels about Portnoy-mother-and-son relationships; and there is a surfeit of father-and-son novels.[22]

These are questions and concerns that could not be, and were not, asked by previous women's magazine writers.

The language of (maternal) separation and struggle still exists

("All children . . . must separate emotionally from their mothers before they can become healthy, independent adults").[23] However, it is now often couched in a discourse that not only stresses the commonalities between all women (not solely biologically based) but that (finally!) takes daughters to task for being emotionally responsible for the well-being of that relationship. As Sabert Basescu notes in a dialogue he had with a group of daughters: "You've complained that your mothers had plans for you, but it seems you had plans for your mothers too. If your mothers didn't fit certain molds that you'd like them to fit, you're disappointed. So you don't accept *them* for what they are either."[24]

The new concern about women's identity and sense of self produced a discussion of the possibility of mother as role model in a changing society. What was mother able to pass on to her daughter in the age of feminism? "We all know that fathers pass their names and sometimes their ambitions along to their sons. But what do mothers pass on to their daughters? 'My mother gave me recipes and the secret of how to endure,' a friend told me. But like so many other daughters, she also feels she inherited many negative things from her mother—feelings of guilt, a tendency to martyrdom, a mistrust of men."[25] Yet this aspect of the discussion—the inheritance of submission and domesticity—is more dormant in the seventies than in earlier periods. Unfortunately, it emerges again with real force in the feminist literature of the eighties. But the emphasis in the seventies was much more on understanding commonalities and, more important, understanding the reality of mother's life and mother's options. Fundamental to this was an insistence, after so many years of relative silence, on the simple importance of a daughter's relationship to her mother in forming her own identity, an importance that was now being addressed with language that went beyond the forties bond/separate dichotomies: "Your mother's role as model heightens the intimacy between you. For better or worse, she gives you many of your most important impressions of what it is like to be female."[26]

There was an explicit understanding being developed that, if we resented or even hated our mothers, there was a *social* context that helped construct these feelings: "Too often mothers fail to understand and daughters fail to explain that the anger comes, not from what our mothers did or failed to do, but from who they were, from the image of themselves that they passed along to the daughters they loved. In many instances, our mothers were the first generation of American women to feel trapped in their homes, frustrated in dead-end jobs, bitter about not finishing college. As a result, they expected more from their daughters." Teri Schultz continues to explore the power of this relationship using a new feminist language that recognizes the internalization not only of our mothers, but of sexist assumptions by implication. She explicitly moves away from the separation models by acknowledging the continuities between mothers and daughters in a very social sense: "Every woman wants to love her mother, and every mother wants to be loved by her daughter. Those daughters who say they hate their mothers usually realize at some point that they cannot truly hate them without hating some part of themselves, for each of us has internalized our mother to some extent. She is at the core of our identity, whether we like it or not."[27] It is hard to overestimate the importance of this shift. For the first time, the relationship between mother and daughter is placed within a social context that acknowledges the often painful reality of the "prefeminist" mother, that relieves her of some of the overwhelming responsibility for her daughter's psyche in the name of a more realistic appraisal of mother's life options and limitations.

This is not to say that the seventies were without their mother-blaming moments. Indeed, one of the unique aspects of women's magazines is the existence, side by side, of contradictory discourses about women in general and mothers and daughters in particular. Even such a conscientious writer as Signe Hammer, although careful to point out "both sides" of the mother/daughter "problem," still holds to the theme of inevitable struggle when she claims, "Some conflict between the generations is inevitable, and hostility between mothers and daughters can be a sign of health, a sign that a daughter is developing normally."[28] Nevertheless, this author does not resort to the more typical urgings to mothers to "let go." Rather, she speaks in the new voice of female independence, urging both mother and daughter to find their own identities and come to a new mutuality.

Themes of sexual rivalry and jealousy crop up frequently, as in a 1976 article, "Can You Ruin Your Daughter's Sex Life?" The author sees mother's jealousy of daughter arise because "Daughters reach their bloom just as mothers are beginning to fade, and a mother may well be jealous of her daughter."[29] One curious thing about this position is the assumption that a middle-aged mother would be jealous of her teenage daughter. This seems a resolutely male perception of female sexuality; it seems ludicrous to imagine that a mature woman would want to return to (or relive, as so many of the articles insist) those horrible and usually unsatisfying years of adolescent sexuality. As any woman knows, the sexuality of a forty-year-old woman is bound to be more developed and personally enhancing than that of a seventeen-year-old girl. The insistence on the mother's envy and jealousy seems a weak remnant of Freudian orthodoxy coupled with a denial of the mother as a sexual being.

Ann Landers joined the fray with a peculiar article, "What To Tell Your Daughter About Women's Lib," that is a mass of contradictions. Landers does acknowledge the changing status of women: "Daughters need help in deciding what they will be because it is no longer true that, like their mothers and grandmothers before them, the majority will grow up to be housewives without even considering alternate lifestyles. What's a mother to do?" Landers answers her own question with uncharacteristic ambiguity. On the one hand, she warns mothers not to encourage their daughters in certain "male" activities, lest "they come off as being terribly unattractive, excessively aggressive, and . . . really turn men off." On the other hand, she argues adamantly for abortion on demand. She rails against the "libbers" and for the ideal of woman as housewife/mother, yet simultaneously praises that central constituent of feminist activism, the pro-choice movement.[30]

Perhaps the ultimate moment of seventies revisionism comes when the venerable Dr. Spock proffers his apologia to American womanhood in a 1972 *Redbook* article:

I've been reproached for contributing to the prejudice. A number of years ago, before there was a Women's Liberation Movement, I wrote that girls should be brought up to think of child rearing as exciting and creative work. "Brainwashing!" said the feminists. Of course I *should* have said— as I honestly believe—"Girls *and* boys should be brought up to think of child rearing as exciting and creative work. . . . More positively and more importantly, parents should prepare girls for careers throughout their childhood—psychologically and educationally—as they prepare their sons. That's my belief now.[31]

## Sitcom Subversions: Working Daughters and Radical Mothers

One year after Spock bid farewell to his well-meaning paternalism, the wittiest matriarch ever to hit prime time emerged on CBS. The sitcom "Maude," a turning point for the representation of mothers and daughters on television, has not received the attention or the accolades it deserves.[32] It certainly has not achieved the near cult status of such classic seventies "quality" sitcoms as "All in the Family" (from which "Maude" was a spin-off), "The Mary Tyler Moore Show," and "M*A*S*H." This is not surprising, given the character Maude herself. If Mary Richards used traditional feminine qualities to rethink office politics and women and work questions and Edith Bunker was the stereotypical silly woman with a heart of gold, then Maude was the loud, brazen, brassy Bella Abzug of prime time. She was funny without being self-abnegating, smart without being coy, and contentious without being apologetic. She was, in other words, a radical woman.

"Maude" was also the first prime-time TV sitcom to portray an adult mother and daughter living together. In that, and in so many other ways, this was really a "social issue" sitcom with a sincerity and depth that surpassed that classic of social sitcoms, "All in the Family." There were no fools in "Maude," no buffoons, no sitting targets waiting to be dissected with a dose of Learian liberalism. Even the right-wing character, Arthur, though often buffoonish, was more often than not a relatively articulate spokesman for the small-minded Nixonian conservatism that Maude was always battling. The subject of Maude was not the single girl in the big city, working-class bigotry, or the hellishness of war, but rather the liberal, enlightened family itself. Maude represents the grand reversal of the "domesticoms" of the fifties, in that it locates itself in terms of genre within that trusted environment of the family home and then explores the new configurations and struggles engendered in that space since the late 1960s.

One of the significant dislocations of the traditional nuclear family has most certainly been the growing rates of divorce and single parenthood, two issues that provide narrative grist for the mill of the social sitcom.[33] Maude was obviously no exception here: she had been married four times before she settled on her current mate, the wry appliance salesman Walter Findlay; and her daughter was a divorced, twenty-seven-year-old mother of an eight-year-old son when she came to live with Maude and Walter.

The relationship between Maude and her daughter Carol is unlike any I have seen on TV shows. Unlike "Rhoda," which framed the mother/daughter relationship within the more traditional structure of old-fashioned, interfering Jewish mother and daughter struggling to be liberated, "Maude" shows both mother *and* daughter as feminists and "liberated women." This sets "Maude" apart and in some ways makes it more advanced than the times would suggest. Although Carol often plays the part of spokeswoman for the "new woman," she is by no means alone in this; it is this dialogue between mother and daughter that is so refreshing and enlightening. In one of the best (and most controversial) episodes, Maude has gotten pregnant at age forty-seven and faces the dilemma of whether to have this baby, which she clearly doesn't want, or to have an abortion (legal by this time in the state of New York). Carol urges her mother on: "There is no earthly reason for you to go through this at your age," and she is amazed at Maude's hesitancy, given her politics:

Carol:    "Mother, I don't understand your hesitancy. When they made it a law you were for it."

Maude:    "Of course, I wasn't pregnant then."

Carol:    "Mother, it's ridiculous, *my* saying this to *you*. We're free. We finally have the right to decide what we can do with our own bodies."

Maude does go on to have the abortion, with the support of her daughter and her husband.

Although struggle and conflict are openly and humorously acknowledged, they never entail a sense of the need for rift and permanent separation: these two women obviously love each other and, in many ways, are much alike. Several episodes point this out clearly. In "Like Mother, Like Daughter" (1972), Carol has begun dating a man many years her senior, and, importantly, a man Maude used to see before she met Walter. Maude is concerned that Carol will be jilted as she was and, after waiting up for Carol all night, confides her distress to Walter over breakfast:

Maude:    "Walter, I am going to put a stop to this right now!"

Walter:   "Now look Maude, if you break this up Carol's going to think you're an interfering mother. You want that?"

Figs. 19, 20, 21. Bea Arthur is the liberal doyenne of East Coast suburbia and Adrienne Barbeau is her equally feisty/feminist daughter in the complex, challenging, and always funny "Maude." (CBS, photos courtesy of Columbia Pictures and CBS Stills Archive)

*Maude:*    "It's a hazard of the trade Walter. I didn't interfere when she eloped with Pete and it ended in divorce. I've never forgiven myself."

*Walter:*    "Then why didn't you interfere?"

*Maude:*    "I was in Reno at the time divorcing Albert."

First, as in many such scenes, the explicit and humorous discourse of "the interfering mother" helps make it less deadly, less *prescrip*tive and pathologizing. In addition, Maude's statement about her own divorce not only links the experience of mother and daughter but gives the mother a life, so her interference is put in perspective.

In the next scene, Carol has come down the stairs and into the kitchen, clearly not eager to talk. Yet Maude persists, putting her hand on Carol's shoulders and facing her, a stance that is repeated time and time again between mother and daughter throughout the series: "I know you're going to tell me again to mind my own business. But look at it this way: God couldn't be everywhere, that's why he invented mothers." But Carol is having none of it, telling Maude she doesn't intend to see him again anyway because he called her "Maude" last night. Maude assumes it was during lovemaking and is flattered, but it turns out it was during an argument in which Russell (the lover) accused Carol of sounding just like her mother. When Russell emerges to make amends, he is placed physically between the two women, who proceed to demolish him (as an egocentric jerk) and send him out the door. As Maude returns from the doorway, she walks over to Carol: "Good morning honey," "Good morning mother," and they smile, hug, and kiss.

However, the scene doesn't end on that note. Maude continues to tell Carol of her experience with Russell, and Carol comforts her. When Walter walks in to apologize for his jealousy, Carol and Maude are seated on the edge of the couch, one slightly behind the other in a "matching" shot (similar clothes, hairstyles, position on couch, etc.) that is accentuated by the identical warm smile they give Walter during his speech. The women are brought together by a sense of wry sisterhood refracted through the egocentric man they both slept with and by a sense of mutual nurturing and caretaking.

In a 1976 episode entitled "The Election," both Maude and her daughter are working for the Carter campaign. This shared work, although typically providing material for discourses of "enmeshment" and "lack of separation," here is expressed in terms of mutual pride and, always, humor:

*Maude:*    "Oh you know Carol, I just think you're wonderful. The way you have *thrown* yourself into this presidential campaign."

*Carol:*    "Well, after all, I am your daughter. You know what they say: the acorn doesn't fall far from the political nut."

*Maude:*    "Carol, you know you're getting to be more like me all the time. And some day we're both going to pay for it."

It sounds banal, but the simple statement from a mother to a daughter, "I think you're wonderful," and its response, "I am your daughter," moves us decades away from the agonizing ideologies of separation and struggle. To acknowledge love, closeness, and sameness without being stamped as "overinvolved," "enmeshed," and "immature" is a major step in a feminist direction for the image of the mother/daughter relationship.

Another 1972 episode also depathologizes the stereotype of the interfering mother. Carol has just announced, after being unemployed and suffering sexual harassment while looking for work, that she intends to get married. Maude is understandably upset because Carol has discussed none of this with her.

*Walter:*    "Maude, I don't want Carol to make a mistake any more than you do. But I got a pretty good feeling that you're beginning to lead her life again."

*Maude:*    "Will you do me a favor with your feelings Walter? Save them, and then someday give them all to me together in a lump. In my old age maybe I'll browse through them and find out who you were."

If this event had occurred, say, in "Father Knows Best," the father would have gently showed the mother the error of her meddling ways and led the family into complete harmony. But here, in the 1970s, Maude's humor undercuts Walter's attempt at paternalism (the man who knows best about how to handle both mother and daughter) and implies that, in this universe, *mother* knows best. Walter continues to play the role of mediator, but it is a role without the ideological power it had previously. When he calmly tells Maude that "Carol's a grown woman. You're her mother but you can't talk to her like her mother," Maude swiftly dispatches him with a biting remark and proceeds to deal with her daughter in her own way, which clearly does not include enacting this cloying psychological dictum of "loving and letting go," as she illustrates when she comes up to Carol's room:

| Maude: | "Honey do you mind if I come in? If I promise . . . ." |
| Carol: | "Promise what?" |
| Maude: | "If I promise not to talk like a mother?" |
| Carol: | "All right." |
| Maude | (strides over to Carol): "If I promise not to talk about the way you're wrecking your life." |

When Carol reproaches her, Maude asks, "Would it disturb you terribly if I cried? Very quietly?" Then she gives a delightful speech, pleading for her daughter's attention: "Carol! I've been your mother for 27 years. I carried you for nine months before then. I lived with your father for 2 years longer than I wanted to because I thought you needed him . . . so don't try to keep me to some promise I made a few minutes ago when I was half out of my mind with grief." Here Maude undercuts the traditional maternal martyr theme by introducing her own humorous note regarding Carol's father and the overstatement of the grief. The issues in their discussion of Carol's impending marriage are important: Maude doesn't want her daughter to "settle"—to marry for anything less than love, even though they both acknowledge the hardships of single parenthood. Ironically, the reversal here is complete: in contrast to images of earlier years, the *mother* is arguing for love and integrity while the daughter is arguing for compliance and compromise. But in the mother's victory (Carol doesn't marry) is a victory for all women, both mother and daughter.

"Maude" remains unique in that it acknowledges the scripts already written for mothers and daughters (as Maude says to Carol, "Children resent and mothers interfere. That comes with the territory.") while implicitly challenging their authenticity. The traditional scripts, with their emphasis on separation and the inevitability of discord, certainly have no narrative space for an adult mother and her adult daughter living and thriving together. "Maude" takes on June and Margaret and Donna and, in doing so, challenges not only the mythology of the perfect mother (who knows that father really does know best), but the mythology of the demon mother, too. Maude insists on being involved in her daughter's life, and her daughter insists on being involved in Maude's life.

Although Rhoda and her mother do not live together, as Maude and Carol do, Ida Morgenstern is nevertheless a persistent presence in "Rhoda." In many ways, "Rhoda" is a much more conservative and traditional series than "Maude." I would have expected otherwise because one show depicts the classic feminist subject of the seventies (single working girl on her own in the big city), and the other is located firmly in the heartland of domestic sitcoms: the suburban family home. Yet the centrality in "Rhoda" of the "search" for a male partner (indeed, just look how quickly a husband is found for her, placing her sister Brenda in the role of perpetually dateless man seeker) effectively devalues and limits the exploration of either the mother/daughter or the sister/sister relationship in a meaningful way. Even numerically speaking, "Rhoda" has very few episodes devoted to exploring this relationship in a narratively significant way, especially when compared to "Maude." In addition, the choice to make Ida so stereotypically "the Jewish mother" often took the possible depth and poignancy out of the interactions between the two women.

In the early episodes, Rhoda and her mother are largely sparring partners (indeed, the battle metaphors abound when Rhoda and Brenda describe their mother) competing in a lightweight battle of goodhearted and warm generational boxing. In later episodes, there are signs that the relationship is being depicted for something more than knowing and guaranteed chuckles. Perhaps it was in response to the declining ratings after the incredibly boring marriage to the uninteresting character of Joe, but for whatever reasons, several 1976 and 1977 episodes begin to get beyond the obvious.

Generally, the interactions between Rhoda and her mother center on the mother arriving unexpectedly at Rhoda and Brenda's apartment building and making a variety of critical remarks about their apartment, their clothes, the men in their lives, their weight, and so forth. There is usually a bit of playful banter, and everyone ends up laughing and cheery at the end. The mother/daughter relationship is typically defined within the narrow terms of loud, interfering, guilt-making but well-meaning mother and loving and tolerant but often exasperated daughters. While "Maude" overturns Donna and Margaret, "Rhoda" departs from the familial setting but, in many ways, recaptures the spirit of working girl in the big city series such as "Our Miss Brooks" and "That Girl."

Yet "Rhoda" occasionally slipped outside this generic straitjacket, allowing for a richer interaction between mother and

Fig. 22. One of several spinoffs from the highly innovative "Mary Tyler Moore Show," "Rhoda" was a peculiar cross between "That Girl" and "The Goldbergs." (CBS; photo courtesy of Photofest)

daughter than the usual faintly humorous generational and ethnic repartee. In the episode where Rhoda is getting separated from Joe, Ida is allowed to emerge as more than a caricature. Rhoda, afraid of her mother's disappointment, does not immediately tell her, but Ida finds out anyway from Joe. She immediately goes over to Rhoda's to try and help, and Rhoda resists, insisting that she's fine:

*Rhoda:*   "I'm telling you that I'm fine. Can't you see that I'm fine?"

*Ida*       (tremulously, with an atypically small and quiet voice): "Rhoda . . . I love you . . . don't lock me out."

*Rhoda*     (long pause): "I'm terrified. I have never been so scared in my entire life."

*Ida*       (moving over to her, she takes her in her arms and holds her while talking): "No, no sweetheart, no, don't be scared. I'm here, I'm here." (Rhoda is now sitting on the edge of the couch so that they are the same height.)

*Rhoda:*    "Don't you be scared either, OK?"

Ida:    "Yeah, right, listen. There has to be something that I can do for you. You know in my day my mother would have said do anything to save the marriage, make any kind of adjustments, put up with anything. I, I guess that doesn't go now anymore, does it?"

Rhoda:    "No Ma, no, it doesn't."

Ida then goes to call her husband to say she's staying with Rhoda for a few days, and Rhoda protests loudly:

Ida:    "That's no good huh? (She looks at Rhoda, who gently shakes her head.) Right. (She puts down the phone.) That would have been good for me but, uh, that's no good for you, huh? OK, well, uh, I guess the best thing I can do then is to uh leave you alone."

Rhoda:    "That's right ma."

Ida gets ready to leave, they kiss goodnight, and, as she is halfway out the door, Rhoda calls to her, "Ma?" Ida turns back, "Yeah?" Rhoda says, "Stick around?" Ida comes back in to her ("Oh yeah"), they embrace, and the image fades out.

This scene is interesting on a number of levels. First, it is definitely atypical of the series as a whole, which generally tended toward the more secure sitcom laughs via the caricatured mother. Nevertheless, this scene references both Ida's needs (e.g., to reframe "interfering" in terms of love and caring) and the new feminist era ("You know in my day. . . ."). This signifies a theme common to many of the "new woman" series in 1970s TV: the daughter's life as fundamentally different from the mother's. The interaction between mother and daughter is thus framed through this one historical disjuncture.

In "One Day at a Time," we get this two ways—divorced single parent Ann's life is different from her mother's, but her own girls extend this trajectory of liberation. Much of the narrative of this series centers on the trials and tribulations of raising two adolescent daughters, and the series was quick to feature the context of single parenthood. In a 1976 episode entitled "Ann's First Decision," the reality of Ann's status as single mother becomes the subject of the episode. Daughter Julie has assumed that her "liberated mother" would allow her to go on a camping trip with a group of girls and boys. When mom refuses, hysterical teenage Julie runs off to be with her father, and mom feels like she made a mistake: "It's really something. For the first seventeen years of my life, my father made the decisions. And the next seventeen, my husband made the decisions. The first time in my life I make a decision on my own and I blow it." This statement surely had enormous resonance for a whole generation of women undergoing divorces, sustaining the inevitable drop in income, and suddenly being faced with responsibilities and positions that had formerly been closed to them. Yet the resolution of this mother's dilemma comes from a sadly obvious source: her boyfriend. Boyfriend and divorce lawyer David gently points out to her the error of her ways, and only then is she able to sit down with her girls and give a speech that sounds more like a team pep rally than a family dialogue ("Stick with me, huh? We'll make it . . .").

Although generally an uninspired show, "One Day at a Time" was innovative simply for what it was: a single-parent family with an unrepentant working mother. By existing at all, it must have given validation to the thousands of women and children going through that experience and fighting against the ideologies of "broken homes" and "latchkey children."[34] Daughters Barbara and Julie were shown engaged in the responsibilities familiar to children of single parents (cooking, cleaning, watching out for each other) and were not summarily identified as "overly responsible" or "parentified" children. Indeed, "One Day at a Time" went out of its way to portray them as "normal" American teenagers, not in any way "afflicted" by the stigma of living in a single-parent family.

A made-for-TV movie, "Like Mom, Like Me" (1978), also deals positively with single-parent families. As in "One Day at a Time," mother's feminist coming of age is paralleled with that of her adolescent daughter. As mother searches to "discover herself" and explore her sexual independence, her young daughter simultaneously works out her own developing sexuality in a social terrain new to both women. Linda Lavin plays a woman who has come to a new city to take a job as an English professor at the local college after her husband has run off with one of his students. The intimacy and mutual support between mother and daughter is apparent, as is the importance of the absent (and much loved by daughter) father. Although mom initially gets "punished" for her independent sexuality when she spends a late evening with a visiting professor (leaving her worried daughter to eat her dinner alone and subsequently call the police), she nevertheless refuses to reunite with her husband: "I don't ever want to be so dependent upon anybody, that I feel that my life is lost without him. . . . I *do* have someone else finally. . . . I have me." Daughter is joined with mother in this early feminist quest for independence by a remarkable speech extolling the virtues of single parenthood and the mutuality of mother/daughter nurturing. Although problematic in its identification of female independence with sexuality (we see very little of mom's new teaching career), this TV movie nevertheless refuses the bond/separate motif, instead opting for an inscription of both mother and daughter within the new discourses of female self-identity and familial change. In so doing, the film ends not with a rupture between mother and daughter, but with a continuation of a genuine and reciprocal bond of care and concern.

The difference with a series like "Maude" is that feminism and the women's movement are *active* signifiers in the overall narrative, whereas neither "Rhoda" nor "One Day at a Time" gives us a sense of these women's involvement in the women's movement or that they have been influenced by it in any significant way. Indeed, Rhoda seems to have left much of her sisterhood behind when she left Minneapolis and moved back to New York, and Ann Romano seems rather like a hipper version of the "perfect moms" of the 1950s like Donna and June. As Ella Taylor notes, feminism was active in defining the new features of Ann's life, but so too was the newly resurgent language of psychology: "Ann learns to be an adult, a new woman, and a new kind of parent. If feminism helps her to redefine the terms of her life, so too does a highly contemporary psychological sensibility, which comes to usurp the language of ethics as a basis for action." [35]

Although Carol's life *is* different from mother Maude's, it is a difference that they share rather than a difference one owns at the other's expense (either humorous expense or otherwise). In one episode, when Maude first starts seeing Walter, they contemplate living together. Importantly, Walter voices the traditional love and marriage ideology. Maude and her daughter are represented equally as women warriors in the same suburban battlefield, turning over the last remnants of charred domesticity in their march toward a feminist future.

## Brave New Movies and Rehashed Reruns

If "Maude" was a turning point for the representation of mothers and daughters in television, then the 1978 hit, *An Unmarried Woman*, starring Jill Clayburgh, Alan Bates, and Lisa Lucas and directed by Paul Mazursky, was similarly a turning point in the medium of film. It has come to be regarded as the archetype of the "new women's cinema" of the 1970s, which included films such as *Girlfriends, The Turning Point*, and *Alice Doesn't Live Here Anymore*. What marked these films as different from their cinematic predecessors was their explicit attention to the emergent women's movement and the issues it provoked.

*An Unmarried Woman*, typically understood in terms of its primary narrative of marriage, divorce, and reconstitution of life as "liberated" woman, is quite instructive in its parallel narrative of the relationship between the central character, Jill, and her smart-aleck teenage daughter, Patty. Importantly, this film does parallel the lives of the mother and the daughter, an unusual strategy for narrating the mother/daughter relationship. In earlier films, this relationship is rarely analyzed synchronically: the daughter is shown either to surpass the bad and denying mother (i.e., not repeat her life) or not and therefore to be her victim in some way. *An Unmarried Woman* allows us to see the emotional and political development of mother and daughter simultaneously, placing neither as victim or victimizer and firmly anchoring the ins and outs of their own relationship to the new social milieu of feminism.

Although certainly not the first film to discuss a woman's struggle for self-definition or to show a loving, mature relationship between a mother and daughter (although there are remarkably few examples of this), this film nevertheless does these things with an explicit referencing of the women's movement. If ever there was a "grand signifier" in a film, it must certainly be feminism in *An Unmarried Woman*. Indeed, we witness consciousness-raising sessions, separation and divorce, feminist psychotherapy, women and work questions, and a host of other issues deemed of concern to the new women's movement.

The daughter's sophistication is not simply the product of liberal, seventies parents, but is precisely concerned with a new sense of what it means to be a woman, particularly with regard to sexuality.

In one scene, mother and daughter are discussing the daughter's relationship with her boyfriend, and the dialogue expresses not only the daughter's new choices (e.g., not to marry, to be actively sexual), but also the reality of a familial world increasingly being redefined around divorce and single parenthood:

| | |
|---|---|
| *Mother:* | "I think you're serious about Phil." |
| *Daughter:* | "Mom, I'm still a virgin, if that's what you meant." |
| *Mother:* | "That's not what I meant. I'm glad you told me. I just meant that you like Phil." |
| *Daughter:* | "I like Phil. I'm not going to marry him. I'm never getting married." |
| *Mother:* | "You will." |
| *Daughter:* | "Don't be so sure." |
| *Mother:* | "Why not?" |
| *Daughter:* | "Why should I? I mean, everybody I know that's married is either miserable or divorced. I don't want that." |
| *Mother:* | "Oh Patty, that's ridiculous. There's lots of happily married couples." |
| *Daughter:* | "Name three." |
| *Mother:* | "Uhh, I'll have to think about it." |

The mother cannot respond with the traditional pat answer, and the next scene reveals the mother's marital problems and her abandonment by her husband. This reinforces the daughter's perceptions of love and marriage.

In a later scene, the mother has come home to see Patty locked in a passionate embrace with her boyfriend. Her response is out of control, as she quickly admits to Patty after she has settled down:

| | |
|---|---|
| *Daughter:* | "God, what is it with you?" |
| *Mother:* | "I'm sorry. God. Oh, God. It's just confusing. I'm sorry I screamed at you Patty. I'm sorry." |
| *Daughter:* | "It's all right. I just don't understand why you get so upset." |
| *Mother:* | "I just can't be your father." |
| *Daughter:* | "So just be my mother." |

Tied up in this exchange is an acknowledgment of the mother's confusion not only about her daughter's sexuality and how to be a single parent, but her own confusion about how to be an "unmarried woman."[36] The scene ends with both women checking out each other's "OK-ness." By explicitly discussing this "confusion," the mother and daughter simultaneously depathologize and demystify the mother's outburst.

In *An Unmarried Woman*, the ideologies of angst, separation, and generational dislocation cease to exert themselves on this mother and daughter. Mother is *not* punished for being sexual; she does not lose or ruin her daughter as a result of her assertion of a sexual self. Indeed, in the scene where Erica brings her lover Saul home to dinner, the final moment is between mother and daughter, as they play the piano and sing "Maybe I'm Amazed." The two women are locked in the frame together in a medium close-up two-shot that excludes the unseen Saul. As the camera pulls back, they burst into laughter, and the image fades to black. Thus is the sexual woman reunited with the loving mother.

One year before *An Unmarried Woman*, another film—this one more explicitly about mothers and daughters—was made that was as melodramatic and cloying as *Woman* was low-keyed and engaging. Herbert Ross's *The Turning Point*, about two women friends whose lives diverge when one (Anne Bancroft) continues her dancing career and the other (Shirley MacLaine) marries and has kids, may be most remembered for its grotesque "catfight" between the two central characters. The thrashing, kicking brawl between these women on the roof of Lincoln Center sets the general tone for this film. Much more than *An Unmarried Woman*, *The Turning Point* expresses a reading of "woman's situation" in the seventies that is clearly patriarchal and, not surprisingly, remains with us today, albeit in somewhat different language. The new generation daughter is positioned in the middle of what is here constructed as "the female dilemma": family versus work, domestic happiness and professional disappointment versus personal loneliness and occupational accomplishment.[37] The narrative structure thus catches her between these dichotomies.

In so many ways, this film recapitulates the dichotomies it sets out to explore and reproduces the more traditional dichotomies of mother/woman that films like *An Unmarried Woman* more successfully challenged. For example, the tension between Deedee (MacLaine) and both her daughter Amelia and her friend Emma is

Fig. 23. Mother and daughter mellow out in early feminist togetherness in *An Unmarried Woman*. (20th Century-Fox, 1978; photo courtesy of Movie Star News)

initiated when Deedee accompanies daughter Amelia to New York to study dance. Parallel love stories emerge, Amelia falling for the smooth Russian ballet star (played by Mikhail Baryshnikov) and Deedee rekindling an old affair. When Amelia returns home devastated one evening after witnessing her lover with another woman, she finds her mother absent, as loyal father calls to check in. From this moment on, the daughter becomes infatuated with Emma (Bancroft) as pseudomom, thus leading us narratively to associate Deedee's infidelity (her womanness) with her decline as a maternal figure for the daughter. The narrative plays out perfectly in accordance with this grand script: Deedee is able to win back her daughter's affection only after she begs her forgiveness for the affair and, as if that wasn't enough, has a poignant reunion with steadfast hubby, a reunion the daughter looks on, literally, with approval.

*The Turning Point* recapitulates yet another traditional theme of mother/daughter narratives, one that has found much currency in recent feminist writing. Not only is daughter Amelia placed synchronically as the figure of new woman (career versus family), but she is located diachronically as the person who will successfully redeem her mother's lost and neglected dreams, as Emma says to Deedee during an argument: "I don't want to be anybody's mother. I think of Amelia as a friend. And one reason I tried to help, stupid me, I thought it would make you happy if your daughter became what you wanted to be and never could be!"

With the onset of feminism in the late sixties and early seventies, mothers and daughters began to emerge as having a relationship worthy of public discussion and representation. For the first time in television, for example, the relationship itself begins to demand narrative attention, rather than just being part of the background of the domestic bliss sitcoms of the fifties. For the first time, there is something to look at, something to analyze, a relationship that becomes socially imprinted as important and vital.

Although both television and women's magazines were relatively quick to pick up on the specifically familial aspects of changing sexual politics, film of the sixties and seventies seemed almost to ignore completely the importance of the mother/daughter relationship. Not until the late seventies and early eighties does film once again explore mothers and daughters.

Clearly, the media have had quite different responses to the development of the women's movement and are certainly not, as many critics are quick to assume, monolithic entities that simply reinforce each other with a shared ideological stance. Although this discrepancy between the different media cannot be easily explained, several reasons come to mind. First, TV was, and is, primarily a domestic medium. It is viewed in the home, and the subject matter of television itself is often domestic and/or familial. Therefore, given that the mother/daughter relationship has been primarily understood as a domestic and familial one, it stands to reason that the medium of television could perhaps explore this relationship in greater depth than did film.

With the development of the contemporary women's movement, it seems that television and film explored different aspects of the social/sexual transformations and dislocations emerging in the late sixties and seventies. Film primarily chose to explore the implications of changing gender positions via an examination of single independent women. Although the "new woman" was also a subject of the TV formulation of feminism, television was much more apt to delve into the familial changes engendered in and through the women's movement.

With the maturation of television as a medium in the sixties and the sitcom as a genre in the seventies, television to a certain extent replaced film as the epitome of popular entertainment. As film costs rose and film became more and more specialized (film as art, on the one hand, and film as special effects/teen love, on the other), television emerged as a medium more attuned to the diverse tenors of the times. The immediacy of television and its lower production costs (via the subsidizing by advertisers) allowed television, contrary to the critics who rail against its banalities, not only to be closer to the contemporary conditions of its diverse audience, but also to enact narratives that were more responsive to the prevailing social conditions than film.

Women's magazines, as we have seen, played out in their pages the dialectical drama of feminism and the resistance to it by allowing these contradictory voices to permeate the discussion. The same old debates often continued (Should mother work? Why do mothers and daughters quarrel? How should the difficult adolescent years be handled?), but the women's magazines began to shift the discourse to one specifically engaged with the women's movement. For example, although Ann Landers addresses the traditional subject of how to communicate with your daughter, she does so under the more specific aegis of how to speak of this new liberation movement. Very few magazines could afford to ignore a social/sexual movement that was occupying the minds and bodies of many of their educated, middle-class readers.

It is more than coincidental that the book that broke the waters, *The Feminine Mystique*, was written by a women's magazine writer, for the issues that the women's movement focused on (beyond that of economic justice)—issues of family life, marital happiness, how to be a mother and what motherhood means, the "trapped" housewife, sexual pleasure, personal relationships—had all been central aspects of the women's magazine gestalt for years. So the extent to which the magazines included such a wide and diverse range of opinions, positions, and arguments on the emerging "woman question" of the late 1960s and 1970s is not surprising. Indeed, the genre that would have explored this relationship most in film—the melodrama—had declined by the late 1950s and had virtually disappeared by the 1960s, being replaced with genres less available to the representation of a female subject, much less one in relation to another female subject.

## Chapter Five

# Terms of Enmeshment

## Feminist Discourses of Mothers
## and Daughters

*The girl's relationship to the mother, emphasizing merging
and continuity at the expense of individuality and independence, provides fertile ground for submission.*
—Jessica Benjamin

*Probably there is nothing in human nature more resonant
with charges than the flow of energy between two biologically
alike bodies, one of which has lain in amniotic bliss inside the
other, one of which has labored to give birth to the other. The
materials are here for the deepest mutuality and the most
painful estrangement.*
—Adrienne Rich

If the dominant culture only reluctantly took up a rethinking of the
relationship of mothers and daughters, then the women's movement—and women's culture in particular—engaged with this issue
as central to the feminist project. For many feminist critics, the
topic of "motherhood," with all its associated themes, has proved to
be one of the most fruitful avenues for research and analysis. Not until
the contemporary feminist movement does any serious and sus-
tained theoretical discussion of mothering and the mother/daugh-
ter relationship begin to emerge. As Ann Kaplan argues, this omission is hardly innocent: "The absence of concern with the Mother
as subject, not only in dominant literature but also in intellectual
and scholarly pursuits, cannot be an accident. Significantly, until
the work produced by the recent women's movement, there has
been no history of Motherhood analogous to the work done on
childhood, the family and sexuality."[1]

For feminists, redressing this absence and beginning to formu-
late alternative histories and theories of motherhood were vital

tasks because women's position and location as mother were seen as central to understanding women's situation in broader terms. Motherhood as ideology, institution, and experience has been a central aspect of the feminist rethinking of the family. Although there is much variety in the feminist analysis of mothering, most would agree on its centrality to the overall project of feminist theorizing. The mother/daughter relationship has taken on exceptional importance as young feminists seek to identify with their mothers in more mutually affirming ways, to explore their mothers' lives in the effort to find positive meaning for their own. Many feminists have acknowledged the importance of rethinking the mother/daughter relationship: "There is perhaps no subject of more significance to the women's movement than this one: it raises historically and psychologically important questions about . . . women's roles, and more importantly about the kinds of family bonds that are traditionally maintained through these relationships."[2] The myths and images of motherhood and the "maternal" remain some of the most compelling within the vast lexicon of masculinist popular culture.

Part of the difficulty in writing about these feminist discourses is that feminist work is more generally about "mothering" and "motherhood" than specifically about mother/daughter relationships. Clearly, I cannot review all the various feminist theories on mothering because this literature has become rather enormous in recent years, and I cannot begin to do it justice here. This task of examining the feminist perspectives on the mother/daughter relationship is thus a difficult one because most feminist work on this subject is itself embedded within a larger discourse on the family, motherhood or psychological development, and the construction of gender identity. Significantly, there is a dearth of *theoretical* work that focuses solely on the mother/daughter relationship, although it is a prevalent theme in feminist culture—from poetry and novels to art, film, and video. The feminist discourses discussed here are often implicit in other practices, particularly within film criticism, feminist fiction, and the growing concern with women's autobiography and "everyday life."

Although feminist discourses on mothers and daughters are many and varied, two broad trends within this area of research are discernible. As is typical with feminist scholarship, these trends are difficult to categorize neatly because they overlap at crucial points, blurring what one would like to believe are analytically clear lines. However, the feminist discourses discussed here have much in common with each other and with those elaborated in the previous chapters. Although these feminist theories are not "popular" in the way films and other mass media are, certain underlying elements of them have entered into our commonsense understandings of what it means to be mothers and daughters. Thus "naturalized," they have largely escaped rigorous feminist criticism. A central task of this chapter is to "denaturalize" these feminist assumptions and the political positions they provoke. The fundamental question is again one of change: Have feminists successfully mapped out alternative theories to those of the dominant culture?

## The Daughter's Legacy

A central approach to the feminist analysis of mothers and daughters coheres around Adrienne Rich's important book, *Of Woman Born*, but it can be found in other studies as well, including Judith Arcana's *Our Mother's Daughters*. To a great extent, this approach (if one can really call such a diverse range of texts an "approach") needs to be seen as a response to both the "mother bashing" that was and is so essential a part of mainstream ideologies of motherhood and the avoidance of the topic of mothers and daughters altogether by mainstream scholarship.[3] As Rich notes:

This relationship has been minimized and trivialized in the annals of patriarchy. Whether in theological doctrine or art or sociology or psychoanalytic theory, it is the mother and son who appear as the eternal, determinative dyad. Small wonder, since theology, art, and social theory have been produced by sons. Like intense relationships between women in general, the relationship between mother and daughter has been profoundly threatening to men.[4]

Appalled at the extent to which the mother/daughter relationship had been either denigrated or ignored, many feminist scholars sought to "reclaim" motherhood and the mother/daughter relationship from its patriarchal heritage. There was an important utopian moment to much of this early criticism, particularly as found in the work of Carroll Smith-Rosenberg. If contemporary (patriarchal) images of mothers and daughters focused mostly on conflict or struggle, then perhaps feminist historians could unearth earlier models of female bonding that suggest more benign—and even more sisterly—forms of interaction:

> The functional bonds that held mothers and daughters together in a world that permitted few alternatives to domesticity might well have created a source of mutuality and trust absent in societies where greater options were available for daughters than for mothers. Furthermore, the extended female network . . . may well have permitted a diffusion and a relaxation of mother-daughter identification and so have aided a daughter in her struggle for identity and autonomy.[5]

This strand of feminist history, with its harkening back to a brighter past, has its "spiritualist" counterpart in the work of writers like Briffault and Bachofen (and even Jung), who theorized an original "mother right" that was overthrown by the forces of patriarchal religion and culture.[6] Patently utopian, this work has been heavily criticized by other feminists. One significant criticism centers on Smith-Rosenberg's inability to theorize adequately the possible reasons for this purported closeness. It seems clear that at least some of that intimacy was related less to some sort of "protofeminist" bonding than to the real lack of an enabling vision of female activity outside the maternal home. A parallel might be made here to the intimate, nonconflictual images in films such as *Stella Dallas*, where the closeness must in some ways be tied to a shared female world made so, at least in part, by the strictures of dominant social relations. Nevertheless, female closeness can never be described mechanistically as simply a reflection of the limitations imposed by male dominance.

This work is also important in its suggestion that things were not always (and thus need not be) the way they are now. Smith-Rosenberg, by providing evidence for a less conflictual and more supportive mother/daughter relationship, opens the door to a historicizing of the whole "culture of conflict" that even the most enlightened thinkers have come to see as inevitable. By historically analyzing mothering itself, feminist historians have implicitly challenged one of the primary mythologies about motherhood: its timelessness.

Adrienne Rich's passionate and ground-breaking book, *Of*

*Woman Born*, is not solely about mother/daughter relationships; it is about the totality of mothering and motherhood. First and foremost, Rich attempts to distinguish between the *institution* of motherhood under patriarchy and all the distortion and pain that has wrought for women and the *experience* of mothering that implies new and feminist possibilities. This split between the patriarchal framing of an experience (and therefore the institutionalization of that experience) and the possibilities of that same experience freed from male control and domination is central to Rich's rethinking of the mother/daughter relationship. For Rich, patriarchy has imprisoned motherhood, turned it into a form of oppression and exploitation that alienates women from their own bodies. This alienation and distortion are extended to the mother/daughter relationship, as they are to every relationship between women under patriarchy. The victimization of the mother is carried over onto the daughter: "Many daughters live in rage at their mothers for having accepted, too readily and passively, 'whatever comes.' A mother's victimization does not merely humiliate her, it mutilates the daughter who watches her for clues as to what it means to be a woman. . . . The mother's self-hatred and low expectations are the binding rags for the psyche of the daughter."[7] Rich thus eloquently depicts the double binds mothers and daughters live through under patriarchy, as does Judith Arcana when she declares, "The oppression of women has created a breach among us, especially between mothers and daughters. Women cannot respect their mothers in a society which degrades them; women cannot respect themselves."[8]

Neither Rich nor Arcana is a Pollyanna about the mother/daughter relationship. Neither rhapsodizes to any great extent about its joys or triumphs. Both are explicit about the distortions of this relationship under patriarchy, but, significantly, they see them as just that, distortions that occur under and because of patriarchal social relations. Although Rich may argue, "Few women growing up in a patriarchal society can feel mothered enough," behind this statement lies the belief that this relationship can be rediscovered, reconstructed, and rejuvenated once freed of its patriarchal baggage.[9] "What we need is not to break the tie, but to make it healthy—to wrest it from its patriarchal context, to allow for its full impact on us, strengthening the line of women."[10] The message is therefore one of an "essential" bond that has been mangled by years of male domination and medicalization of women's bodies but that can and must be recovered by active feminist intervention.

The most troubling assumption behind this schema is the implication that there is something "real" and "original" in the mother/daughter relationship outside the context of patriarchal relations. DuPlessis asks Rich: "Is everything good about motherhood generated by the 'real' woman's self, and everything bad about motherhood generated by patriarchy? Is there a 'pure' self which exists beyond the system in which it is immersed? How has it gotten there; what sustains it?"[11] This is the central question. Like Rich and so many others, I too believe that the relationship between mother and daughter can be rediscovered and rejuvenated to empower both women. What must be avoided, however, is a dangerous slip toward essentialism, as if there were a true maternal essence underlying the falseness of patriarchal constructions. This idea of "essence" leads down the pitted path of a biologically rooted identity, a path feminists have fought so hard to escape.

Although Rich does not exactly idealize the mother (as many feminists have done), she does place a sort of "essential" weight on mothering and on the mother/daughter relationship in particular. She does this in two ways. First, drawing on theorists of matriarchy such as Bachofen, Briffault, and feminist scholar Elizabeth Gould Davis, Rich attempts to claim historical—or at least symbolic—space for a different understanding of women, mothering, and, by extension, the mother/daughter relationship. If, during matriarchal periods, mothers were revered and respected and were not alienated from their bodies, then contemporary women can envision new possibilities for their own mother/daughter relationships.

Second, and following the first point, Rich repeatedly emphasizes the primacy of the mother/child bond: "The mother-child relationship is the essential human relationship." In this view, mother/daughter relationships take on an almost spiritual and primordial quality, signified largely by their shared "femaleness": "Mothers and daughters have always exchanged with each other—beyond the verbally transmitted lore of female survival—a knowledge that is subliminal, subversive, preverbal: the knowledge flowing between two alike bodies, one of which has spent nine months inside the other."[12] The basis for the mother/daughter bond thus appears here to be both spiritual and biological, tied in as they are to each other through the experience of pregnancy and birth and through their shared physical attributes. Rich thus poses (but does not resolve) a central dilemma in rethinking the mother/daughter relationship: how to acknowledge the real and embodied sameness between mothers and daughters—the fact that we inhabit the same bodies in a world in which women's bodies are a primary site for the reproduction of male dominance—without lapsing into a sort of feminist biological determinism that locates our impetus for woman identification solely in our physiological likenesses.

This argument for the special bond between mothers and daughters is tied in with Rich's conception of woman identification and the lesbian continuum. For Rich, there is a deep connection between coming to terms with the mother/daughter relationship and coming to terms with sexual love for another woman. She portrays the loss of the mother as the grand metaphor for the loss of all women to each other, a loss predicated on compulsory heterosexuality and a fear and hatred of intimacy between women. Interestingly, it is at this juncture of lesbianism and mothering that American radical feminism meets certain forms of French feminism. Luce Irigaray's work in particular (but also Julia Kristeva's, in a rather different way) concerns itself with the double binds of the mother/daughter relationship under patriarchy and finds a positive and erotic potential in a "return to the mother."[13] This equation of a "merger with the mother" with lesbian identity (a version of which is to be found in the psychoanalytic discourses as well) remains a highly problematic aspect of these discourses. It does a disservice to the specificity of both lesbian identity and the mother/daughter relationship. If lesbianism is seen as a "return" to the mother, that can be understood only as a regressive form of sexuality in our psychologized society because separation from the mother supposedly marks a person as adult. It also confuses the myriad reasons for the adoption of a lesbian sexuality (among them, political choice) and thus blurs and limits the multiplicity of lesbian experience. Clearly, too, it can also fit into more general heterosexist assumptions concerning the "regressive" and "narcissistic" character of homosexuality.

So although in one sense *Of Woman Born* is a eulogy for the

mother/daughter relationship as it exists under patriarchy, it is simultaneously a celebration of this "most essential" bond. Rich, like
Judith Arcana in *Our Mother's Daughters*, finds fault with mothering and the mother/daughter relationship but is at pains to place
the "blame" for mother's role in maintaining patriarchy firmly on
the side of men in power, especially the male medical profession.
In this feminist version, Mama has done us wrong, but it really ain't
her fault: "Thousands of daughters see their mothers as having
taught a compromise and self-hatred they are struggling to win free
of, the one through whom the restrictions and degradations of a
female existence were perforce transmitted. Easier by far to hate
and reject a mother outright than to see beyond her to the forces
acting upon her." [14]

## The Law of the Mother

Perhaps the primary way feminist scholarship has tackled the
mother/daughter relationship is through some version of psychoanalysis. This is not surprising, as the psychology of the mother/
daughter relationship has been the central focus for mainstream
scholarship, even when analyzed sociologically. The influence and
impact of Nancy Chodorow's *The Reproduction of Mothering* cannot be overestimated. The appeal of Kleinian object relations
theory to feminists is in some ways quite obvious. More than any
other psychoanalytic theorist, Melanie Klein and her followers
brought the mother back into psychoanalysis, where the reign of
the Oedipus complex had kept her in a rather passive and secondary position. Object relations, with its focus on the preoedipal years
and on the active position of the mother as the first "object" the
infant encounters, has been eagerly taken up by feminists as a key
to unlocking the process of gender formation.

With the feminist inflection Chodorow gives object relations, the
daughter as well as the mother assumes a new importance and centrality. No longer is the drama of the daughter's development playing second fiddle to the "genderless" (male) child. This psychological development is seen in the social context of parenting practices
that locate the mother as the primary parent of both female and
male children. Nevertheless, this social context is more often than

not given mere lip service rather than integrated thoroughly into the object relations analysis.

Chodorow's arguments are by now well known, so I will simply review them here. Indeed, I want to avoid arguing with the "truth value" of her claims because that is always a fruitless project when engaging with psychoanalysis, which clearly involves a certain leap of faith. Central to this leap of faith is a belief that early childhood experience is fundamentally determining. Gender formation in this context is understood as being formed primarily in the child's earliest years. From this basic psychoanalytic assertion, issues for *adult* women can be understood as having their origin in early childhood experiences and structures. I would want to hold on to an idea of gender formation that sees the construction of femininity, for example, as a much more contradictory and drawn out process that does not begin and end before age three but evolves throughout our lifetimes. Indeed, I would want to maintain an understanding of gender formation and the replication of patriarchy generally as a contradictory process in which the paradigm of female parenting is but one instance in a plethora of structured relationships and formations.

However, my major interest in Chodorow's work—and that of other psychoanalytic feminists—is as it informs both popular and feminist representations of mothers and daughters. How does it relate to the paradigm exemplified by the work of Adrienne Rich? What other discourses (about parenting, psychology, women) intersect with it? Most important, what are the implications of this discourse for the construction of ideologies of mothers and daughters?

Starting from the basic fact that only women mother, Chodorow argues that the experience of being mothered has different psychological consequences for boys and girls. For both boys and girls, the first object choice is the mother. But in order for boys to differentiate, to understand themselves as "subject," they must assume a gender identity that is not female (not mother). For girls, the process of individuation is quite different. Built on a primary sense of unity and continuity with the mother, a girl's gender identity is formed not in opposition to her first object choice, but in continuity with it. The results of this differential process of psychological development should be quite familiar to feminists who know Carol

Gilligan's work on moral development. Chodorow sees women's psychology as more relational and with less firm ego boundaries because of the continuity with the mother. In her view, and that of others such as Jane Flax, women therefore have problems with autonomy and differentiation, with a sense of separate "selfhood" arising out of the patterns of child rearing. As Iris Young says in summarizing Chodorow:

> Because of her own gender identity, the mother identifies with her girl child more than with her boy child. In relating to her daughter she unconsciously replays many of the ambiguities and identifications she experiences with her own mother. The mother thus often tends to relate to her daughter more as an extension of herself than as a separate person. . . . The mutually reinforcing identification of mother and daughter results in the girl's acquiring a sense of separate identity later than boys, and never acquiring a sense of separation from others as strong as the boys.[15]

Clearly, Chodorow is not only addressing the question of how mothering is reproduced but how, through this reproduction, patriarchy itself (or at least the psychological "types" needed to maintain it) is reproduced. Women's mothering provides the grist for the mill of unequal gender relations, and the mother/daughter relationship proves particularly helpful in reproducing the psychological patterns that maintain patriarchy. It follows, then, that Chodorow's "solution" (as well as that of Dorothy Dinnerstein, author of another influential text on mothering, *The Mermaid and the Minotaur*) is shared parenting. Only when "mothering" becomes a task performed by both sexes will we be able to break this cycle that assures a masculine identity formed in opposition to mother/woman and a feminine identity formed in continuity with that very same mother.

The heterosexism of this "solution" should be obvious in that it assumes a parenting couple that is heterosexual. If "dual parenting" is advocated so that the child receives a "balance" of parents of both genders, what would we make of a homosexual couple for which no such "balance" exists? Here, too, the dual parenting answer can unwittingly participate in the social condemnation of single parents as they become defined by the absence of this "ideal" model of egalitarian heterosexuality. In addition, "dual parenting" has severe limitations as an answer to patriarchal social relations in which real questions of power, coercion, and male violence cannot be simply "parented" away.

Both Dorothy Dinnerstein and Jane Flax take up the same line of argument concerning the negative effects of women's mothering on social life as a whole (Dinnerstein) and on daughter's sense of selfhood specifically (Flax). For Dinnerstein, the results of women's exclusive mothering has been that men are compelled to control themselves, women, nature, and culture in order to contain symbolically the fear of the all-powerful and terrifying mother. Dinnerstein attributes all the oppressive relations of the modern world to mother-dominated children.[16] So long as mothers "rule" the cradle, they will create fundamentally warped human psyches, individuals whose fear and terror of that awesome maternal power lead them on a path of destructiveness and consent to violence. The prevailing conditions of gender inequality are just one aspect of the larger and more profound malaise.

Jane Flax's work, dealing much more specifically with mother/daughter relationships, takes both the Chodorow and Dinnerstein positions to their logical conclusion. Jane Flax is also an object relations theorist, but (like Dinnerstein) she generalizes these psychic foundations further than Chodorow in claiming: "The repression of early infantile experience is reflected in and provides the grounding for our relationship with nature. This is true, as well, of our political life, especially the separation of public and private, the obsession with power and domination, and the consequent impoverishment both of political life and of theories about it." Flax here, in quite orthodox psychoanalytic fashion, moves outward from the repression of infantile experience to the panorama of social ills. The agency for this repression is the mother. Flax thus *pathologizes* Chodorow's description of the mother/daughter relationship: "The development of women's core identity is threatened and impeded by an inability to differentiate from the mother. I see as a central problematic in female development the very continuity of identity with the mother." Flax sees an "endless chain of women tied ambivalently to their mothers, who replicate this relation with their daughters" because of their inability to deal with their anger at their mothers and their inability to fully separate from them.[17] Separation for the daughter is more difficult because, as Flax sees it, the important "symbiotic" experience is never "enough":

The feeling that women often report of not having had enough of something, of being cheated, is also related to the inadequacies of the symbiotic phase. It is not that women lack the experience of being nurtured; but it is rather that their experience takes place within a context in which the mother's conflicts render the experience less than optimal. . . . If the symbiotic experience has not been adequate, the process of separation and individuation that follows is also more difficult.[18]

Kim Chernin, writing in this object relations tradition but focusing more specifically on women and eating disorders, starkly reinforces the belief that the key to women's emotional and psychological problems can be found in their relationship with their mothers: "If we are to understand the contemporary struggle for female identity, we must place it in relation to this fateful encounter between a mother whose life has not been fulfilled and a daughter now presented with this opportunity for fulfillment." Chernin's book is an endless cataloguing of the mother's failed life and how it impinges on the budding independence of the daughter to such an extent that the daughter is forced to engage in self-destructive behavior (anorexia and bulimia) in order to call attention to it: "Because her mother cannot give her what she needs—cannot enter with full understanding into her struggle, cannot model for her its potential resolution—she reaches for food in place of the mother and thereby incurs the terrible danger of becoming everything she most fears to be: a human being for whom the question of rightful development has not yet been formulated."[19]

Flax and Chernin, too, by implication, see women as faced with a dilemma: "To be loved and nurtured, and remain tied to the mother, or to be autonomous and externally successful, to be like a man."[20] All the contradictions of Flax's position are wrapped up in this sentence, for the options are to be *tied* to mother versus to be *like* a man. In her choice of words, Flax betrays her inheritance of patriarchal ideologies of apronstrings and clinging, dependent mothers. One is either tied to mother, bound to her, or "like" a man. But how is this dilemma any different from the dilemma splashed across the pages of the women's magazines? Mainstream culture has always depicted those options and dilemmas for "today's woman": she can either be homebound and mired in the dependent domesticity of motherhood and mother's life or join the man's world of work and autonomy but risk losing her "femininity" and becoming an unloved and unloving "career woman." Why should feminists help maintain this false polarity?

Jessica Benjamin's fascinating and erudite book, *The Bonds of Love*, takes up where Chodorow left off. In what is an attempt in many ways to break free of the acultural limitations of Chodorow's analysis, Benjamin presents a compelling argument for the relationship between gendered patterns of domination and submission and the vicissitudes of the modern "administered society" of capitalist patriarchy. Although a significant advance from Chodorow's early work, Benjamin nevertheless replicates many of its fundamental assumptions. First, she engages in what I can only call the "great psychoanalytic leap." That is, Benjamin starts out by expressing her dismay at the persistence of the sorry state of gender polarity and then jumps from there to the necessity for a psychoanalytic interpretation: "The fundamental question we must consider is why these positions continue to shape the relationship between the sexes despite our society's formal commitment to equality; what explains their psychological persistence?"[21] In the first place, it is doubtful that the United States (for example) really has a formal commitment to equality between the sexes. But even if it did, formal commitment can by no means be equated with socially/politically enacted commitment. Benjamin does her own argument a disservice with this sort of tendentious logic and seriously downplays an analysis of the political persistence of patriarchy (a word she herself rarely uses).

Benjamin is, at least, honest about her psychoanalytic commitment to the determining quality of early childhood experience. Like Dinnerstein, she wants explicitly to locate the generative moment of the culture of domination in the culture of the cradle: "I will show how the structure of domination can be traced from the relationship between mother and infant into adult eroticism, from the earliest awareness of the difference between mother and father to the global images of male and female in our culture. We will begin with the conflict between dependence and independence in infant life, and move outward toward the opposites of power and surrender in adult sexual life." Thus, once again, woman's mothering (albeit constructed not entirely by her) is seen as the great thief that steals away male nurturance and, most important for this study, female independence: "The female difficulty in differentiation can be described almost as the mirror image of the male's: not the denial of the other, but the denial of the self. Thus the fact of women's mothering not only explains masculine sadism, it also reveals a "fault line" in female development that leads to maso-chism."[22]

This model of complementarity and this insistence upon a dual-istic framework for understanding psychological development is it-self problematic. Fundamentally, this reasoning can't allow for the active reality of male power to enter into its equation because that would disrupt the complementarity in her logical apparatus. More to the point, we are once again faced with the insistence (this time a feminist one) that daddy may make the world go round, but it's mommy who makes our heads spin. Even very well meaning femi-nist therapists like Susie Orbach, although careful to note that mothers are not consciously out to "get" their poor daughters when they oppress them with their own repressed desires and dreams, still understand mothers as nothing more than the willing accom-plices to the act of constructing a subordinate female psyche:

The mother-daughter relationship is the site in which the preconditions are established for the taking up of this sex role. At the same time it pre-figures future relationships. In other words, within this relationship, the mother exercises restraint about meeting the needs of her daughter. . . . At the same time, she may thwart her daughter's initiatives, supporting instead aspects of her behaviour that conform with appropriate notions of 'feminine' activity.[23]

Benjamin herself is very explicit about the deleterious effects of mother/daughter togetherness on the daughter's psyche:

Mothers tend to identify more strongly with their daughters; whereas they push their sons out of the nest, they have greater difficulty separat-ing from daughters. Thus it is more likely that girls would fear separate-ness and tend to sustain the tie to mother through compliance and self-denial. If not acute, this tendency would be unremarkable. But the girl's relationship to the mother, emphasizing merging and continuity at the expense of individuality and independence, provides fertile ground for submission.[24]

Benjamin returns once again to what has now become a familiar theme in the literature on divorce and single-parent families: the restoration of the missing father. Although she is quick to point out that male identification is not the whole answer for women ("fail-ures in the struggle for recognition cannot be fully repaired by using a male identification to revolt against the mother"), she comes perilously close to just such a position, not coincidentally echoing Flax's limited options for women: "Lucy had unequivocally made the choice to beat back maternal power with paternal power, to find liberation in the father. But to do this, she was always having to struggle against her father—his command of and contempt for her, her mother, and women in general. Lucy's choice had led her to a common daughter's dilemma: How to be a subject in relation to her father (or any man like her father)? How to be like her father and still be a woman?"[25] In the choices the patient "Lucy" is offered by the feminist psychiatrist, the mother as a subject in her own right (and therefore as an option for identification with the daughter) is completely absent. "Maternal power" here is ever present, but the specific mother as subject seems once again to have receded in favor of the more tantalizing possibilities of identifying with the contemptuous father (while still remaining, of course, a "woman"). Identification with the mother (and implicitly with other women) can here be understood only as a regressive move back into the bonds of (maternal) love.

## Surpassing the Mother

Certain polarizations and dichotomies such as those previously mentioned run through almost all feminist work on mothers and daughters. An opposition is often set up between the mother trapped in "old" ways, whose life has not been fulfilled, and the "new" and "modern" daughter who is liberated or at least sees the possibilities for liberation and growth: "We are a generation who, with every act of self-assertion as women, with every movement into self-development and fulfillment, call into question the values by which our mothers have tried to live. . . . For the daughter . . . the confrontation with the despairs and failures of the mother's life must inevitably produce a feeling of profound dismay."[26]

This easy opposition is problematic in a number of ways. It posits an overly simplistic and coherent view of women's history as a progressive and linear movement from ignorance and oppression to enlightenment and liberation. This not only denies the long history of women's struggles for equality and recognition, but also overlays historical categories with psychological "truths." For Chernin, this historical move from oppression to liberation is paralleled by a psychological move from unfulfillment to fulfillment. This monolithic view of "prefeminist" mothers assumes a unitary march toward self-fulfillment that is very questionable historically and assumes a single "institution" of motherhood to which all mothers unambivalently ascribed. But "motherhood"—and patriarchy as well—are hardly that monolithic and uncontradictory:

> But we should resist the temptation to present conflict and tension as wholly characteristic of mother-daughter relationships when the latter were at the adolescent stage, nor should we stray into representing mothers as the main agents of their daughters' oppression. Certainly, mothers tended to provide their daughters with the latter's earliest models of "femininity." But one cannot assume that mothers themselves possessed simple, unambiguous personalities wholly at ease with their social roles, nor that daughters learned from their mothers passively, like blotting paper simply absorbing impressions.[27]

In addition, there is a certain arrogance in this position. Contemporary feminists, identifying as the daughter rebelling against the outmoded mother, often assume a position of superiority when it comes to reflecting on their mothers' situations. Although it is vitally important for us to understand the real changes that have occurred with this second wave of feminism, it is equally important to avoid the sort of sweeping generalizations about our mothers' lives that so many feminist historians have warned against. We need to be much more historically circumspect and much more specific in terms of racial, ethnic, and class differences to avoid this view of history that places modern daughters in an omniscient position vis-à-vis their mothers' lives.

If the mother's life is consistently depicted as one of despair and frustration (as Chernin certainly presents it), then Chernin's notion of "surpassing the mother" becomes a necessity. But although real despair and real frustration are part of most women's lives under patriarchy, ours included, feminist historians have consistently unearthed and rediscovered evidence of all sorts of struggle and opposition that occurred in the everyday lives of "prefeminist" women and girls. To "surpass the mother" is to lose the continuity with that history, which is often the history of the victims and the violated but is one that (like any legacy) we "surpass" at our peril.

Behind this glib opposition of oppressed, unfulfilled mother and liberated daughter struggling for fulfillment lies a larger question about the relevant object of analysis for mother/daughter relationships. Much feminist scholarship on the mother/daughter The mother's "secret" is that she has an "illness" and is going to die. relationship discounts or ignores new developments in the real social relations of mothers and daughters. In speaking of the new daughter attempting to break free of the depressed mother, one makes the assumption of a heterosexual, nuclear family with dad at work and mom at home, tied to her kitchen and her children. The reality is that most women, most mothers, work outside the home. We now have an entire generation of young women whose mothers came to maturity alongside the development of the feminist movement. Many of these mothers were that first wave of feminists who responded to Friedan's call and started to transform their lives and those of their daughters.

Many daughters of the postwar industrial world grew up with mothers who "fit the bill" of the dependent, clinging, homebound wife and mother. But we can no longer assume that image of mother when we do research on mothers and daughters today. Feminist discourses of mothers and daughters need to respond to new historical situations and to specify and locate shifts that occur in the relationship as it defines itself against a new social formation and new ways of seeing women's lives.

For many groups in our society, particularly black women, the vision of a homebound and dependent mother simply does not accord with their history or their lived experience. Gloria Joseph and Jill Lewis have written of the real differences between black and white women's lives, including other ways of mother/daughter relating and of conceptualizing that relationship. They argue, as others have, that the current feminist fear of "becoming like your mother" is a particularly white and middle-class phenomenon and cannot simply be extended to the black female population. In fact, their research on black mother/daughter relationships reveals quite different patterns and issues arising from the experience of being black women in a society that is both racist and patriarchal: "Societal conditions intensified Black mother/daughter relationships. While social factors had a tendency to fracture the European mother/daughter relationships, in an ironical way they forced the role of the Black mother in her family to persevere."[28] Research such as Carol Stack's on black extended family kinship structures also points to different sorts of familial arrangements and conceptions of "family" that in turn help organize mother/daughter interactions.[29] Of course, this concern for specificity does not affect the psychoanalytic work because it presents itself as a universal and timeless description of human psychological development.

Unfortunately, feminist theories of the mother/daughter relationship leave intact much mainstream scholarship and many popular ideologies. This is particularly a problem in the psychoanalytic work, which, while claiming to be critically psychoanalytic, never really problematizes the basic terms upon which that psychoanalytic account rests: "separation," "individuation," "autonomy," and "differentiation." Mother/daughter relationships are almost always described using these concepts. There is a clear line from Melanie Klein to John Bowlby's "maternal deprivation" and D. W. Winnicott's "good enough mother" right down to feminists such as Chodorow, Dinnerstein, and Flax. How far from Bowlby's regressive theory of "maternal deprivation" is Flax's concern over the daughter's identity if the "symbiosis phase" has been "inadequate"? That Bowlby's work was central to the concerted postwar attempt to press women back into the domestic roles of wife and mother should itself point to the ideological nature of concepts such as bonding, separation, and symbiosis. Moynihan's racist thesis of black matriarchy illustrated once again that theories of mothering are never value-free or nonpolitical and that they can be continually reformulated in new (racist, patriarchal) discourses. Feminists who treat these concepts as if they had no ideological history run the risk of coming to the same dichotomous and disempowering conclusions: too much mother or too little mother.

But these terms should not be taken as pure, natural, psychological givens. Sound feminist methodology insists that we look at the history of these concepts and search for ways in which they have a gendered meaning. Feminist scholarship revealed early on that no term, no idea, no concept is gender neutral, not even in the natural sciences, where the much vaunted "objectivity" of masculinist science has recently come under fire from feminists. Then why, when it comes to mothers and daughters, do we drop that critical and questioning gaze? One wouldn't have to dig deep to realize that all the concepts mentioned previously are deeply gendered. Rather than ask why women have trouble with differentiation and separation (and then ascribe it to their continuity with their mothers, as do Chodorow and Flax), perhaps we should first question the concepts themselves and trace the intersections between their gender, class, and racial moments. We should critically examine how "autonomy" and "differentiation" have always been placed on the valued side of an artificial dichotomy between reason and emotion, selfhood and symbiosis. The identification of the mother/daughter relationship with that web of values and practices mired firmly on the "emotion" side only reinforces a dichotomy that has traditionally been used to oppress all women, both mothers and daughters. To attempt to wrench the daughter over to the "masculine" side of reason, autonomy, separateness, and the public world is to give up on the much larger struggle of challenging those very dichotomies and their gendered status.

The choices offered us by feminists such as Flax are as limited as their patriarchal predecessors: "The successful woman in our society must choose between autonomy and self-fulfillment in the external world, and her mother."[30] But this is certainly not the only choice women have; posing this as *the* choice is deeply ideological and buys into deterministic models of women's possibilities under patriarchy.

Perhaps we will find those terms useful for examining the mother/daughter relationship. But their usefulness can be revealed only after they have been subjected to a thorough, historical, feminist critique. We might then want to revise our thinking about terms like "separation" (the most prevalent term in any discussion of mothers and daughters) and begin to speak of the "ideology of separation."

We also need to think more carefully of the implications of our theories about mothers and daughters. And here there are important insights to be gained from thinkers such as Adrienne Rich and Nancy Chodorow. Rich's work—as well as that of Ann Oakley, Sheila Kitzinger, and others—helps us recognize the extent to which motherhood has become an institution under patriarchy and, as such, has been used with great effect to reproduce the conditions of women's inequality. Chodorow has forced us to recognize the depth and range of gender inequality. All these feminist writers have played an important part in showing how the mother/daughter relationship is constructed within patriarchy and must be understood in that context.

Less contextual is the psychoanalytic work. Additionally, there is a problem with a theory that locates the root causes of the reproduction of sexual inequality firmly in the mother's lap. Fathers, both in the literal and familial sense and in the more metaphorical sense of representatives of male culture, are let off the hook too easily. Both Dinnerstein and Flax are more explicit in their identification of patterns of domination as rooted in mothering practices, but these implications are there in Chodorow's work as well.

If the mother is seen as the root of asymmetrical gender formation, which in turn constitutes the building blocks of patriarchy, then the *activeness* of male domination gets lost. Male hegemony and dominance loses its conceptual and political vitality as it becomes a mere "result" of women's mothering. Questions of male power, ideology, and coercion recede in this psychoanalytic version except as they relate to the seemingly all-powerful mother. The important political question of interest is obscured in the almost automatic version of the acquisition of gender identity. In whose interest is it to maintain certain systems of child care and to reproduce ideologies that legitimize those systems?

This trajectory in feminist thought has been somewhat inevitable. In the early, heady days, all energies were focused on detailing, describing, and analyzing male dominance. Deconstructing patriarchy and the myriad ways it shaped and organized our lives was the central project. Then, as in any movement that matures, we began to look inward, to examine the more complex and painful ways we were implicated in the reproduction of patriarchy. The more we discovered the depth and range of male dominance, the more we realized its complex and contradictory nature and the real difficulties of overcoming it. This larger feminist shift (by no means linear and still continuing)—from an emphasis on our shared experience as women, our commonality and similarity, to a new recognition of the "differences" (class, race, sexual preference) that made identification as women so problematic—has its corollary in studies of mothering and the mother/daughter relationship.

There was also another shift from an early emphasis on the oppressiveness of motherhood, its centrality to the maintenance of male domination, to a more positive and ambiguous sense of motherhood. Rich's work is located firmly in this shift, trying to affirm the positive aspects of mothering while understanding its location within patriarchy. This was a shift from a focus on victimization to a new concern with women's agency. Too often, though, mothers are seen to be either passive victims of patriarchy, guilty by omission, or controlling agents of patriarchy, inculcating their daughters into femininity, and thus guilty by commission. We seem to oscillate between these twin poles of similarity and difference, extolling the transcendent bond between mother and daughter or declaring the need to be free, to maintain one's difference.

Although feminist theory has opened up a new and exciting range of study on mothers and daughters, much of it repeats these same old dichotomous stories. The relationship between mother and daughter is either valorized as a transcendent bond of almost sexual plenitude or pilloried as the "bond" that keeps women tied to self-destructive behaviors and patterns of submission. Once again mothers are either victims or agents, pawns in the game of male domination or sneaky operators in their own psychic power plays. And daughters are, as always, the passive respondents to these maternal machinations. In the following chapter, we see how these theoretical dichotomies often emerge in feminist cultural work. But it is in the feminist cultural imagination that we begin to discover interesting and empowering departures from these limited and limiting paradigms.

## Chapter Six

# Parting Glances

### Feminist Images of Mothers and Daughters

*In the Oedipus myth, the son murders his father in order to replace him. Contrastingly, in the new woman's myth, the daughter "kills" her mother in order not to have to take her place.*

—Judith Kegan Gardiner

The subject of mothers and daughters has not only been a central topic for feminist scholarship but has played an important part in feminist cultural practice as well. Not surprisingly, most feminist cultural work on mothers and daughters emerges out of contemporary women's fiction. The mother/daughter relationship has become one of the central themes of women's writing, enough to warrant several books of criticism and a host of articles.[1] Given the realities of the world of film and video production and its increasingly corporate nature, it is no wonder that most images of mothers and daughters are to be found in a medium that, at least at the outset, does not require a substantial infusion of finance capital. Nevertheless, feminists have produced work on mothers and daughters in other media, including film, video, and photography.[2]

Although this explosion of mother/daughter imagery, much of it from an explicitly feminist perspective, is undoubtedly a welcome development, serious questions remain for those of us still deeply concerned with the prevalence of "mother-blame" in our culture. As I have argued in previous chapters, the women's movement has forced this long-submerged relationship out into the full glare of the cultural spotlight, but this excursion into visibility and analysis is not unambiguously positive if the fundamental (male-defined) modes of analysis remain unchallenged and are simply replicated. I argued in the preceding chapter that feminist theory has all too often allowed itself to remain largely within the dominant categories of psychological thinking on mothers and daughters.

The question of whether feminist *cultural* work has moved beyond these limiting frames of reference now arises. Has the feminist movement attempted to develop self-consciously oppositional forms of imagining this relationship? Or has this literary work, albeit with more grace and artistry, fallen into the same traps of bond and separate, love and let go? The verdict on this tough issue is a mixed one. The most up-to-date feminist text analyzing fiction on mothers and daughters (*Mother Puzzles: Daughters and Mothers in Contemporary American Literature*) proclaims in its introduction the all too familiar refrain: "The reality of the mother-daughter experience (at least in the writing examined here) is that mothers are often more disabling than enabling, that daughters are often more attached to (or detached from) their mothers in ways that are disturbing and disheartening." Mickey Pearlman, the editor of this volume, goes on to identify an almost transcendent imperative that these writers have in searching to understand the mother/daughter relationship, once again placing on this relationship a sort of either/or, life/death kind of emotional and psychological weight. Pearlman argues that these novelists "must finally understand their own relationships with their mothers or be condemned to a lifetime of daughterhood, to a 'girl's' angle of vision, to a dependent emotional space within a mother's parameters." Yet the ambivalence of the new feminist writing on mothers and daughters is neatly expressed in the editor's closing lines, where she echoes the romance of separation endlessly found in mainstream literature while simultaneously evoking the pleasure of maternal love: "And every mother-daughter story is also finally the story of how we find ourselves in leaving, or in being left, in excoriating the past or beatifying it, about finding the missing connections or losing the infantilizing ones, and most centrally about being loved, being loving, and what daughters do in solving mother puzzles."[3] Thus we see once again the dichotomous framing, where "loving" and "letting go" are two sides of the coin of adult development.

Nevertheless, feminist cultural work on mothers and daughters
has produced a wide range of diverse and complex texts, by no
means as easily characterized as the more explicitly theoretical
work. This realization forces me now to engage in a bit of self-
criticism regarding my own approach to this particular chapter. I
approached this work in an attempt to prove what I perceived to be
a sharp divide between the cultural production of white women
writers and fiction by women of color. Angered at the incipient
mother-blame and double binding of much white feminist work, I
sought to translate my critique of the theoretical material in Chapter 5 to a critique of the cultural material in the present one, this
time including an analysis of women writers of color as an antidote
to the white feminist propensity for buying into the dominant psychological frameworks.

But representations do not lend themselves to easy oppositions,
and ambiguous and contradictory meanings often slip out from
under the closed door of a simple critical distinction: no such pat
and fixed distinction could be drawn. This is not to say that serious
and profound differences in content, form, genre, and such could
not be found in comparing several texts in this way. There is no
question that the lived experience of black and ethnic writers must,
by necessity, produce at least a somewhat different reading of this
particular relationship. Instead, what emerges for me here in examining the cultural writings of both women of color and white
writers is that the axes along which distinctions can be made need
to be multiplied and diversified. In other words, although race (and
class and ethnicity) do structure these representations, perhaps the
specific representational choices also structure the final ideological
moment of the text. The central issue seemed to settle around the
extent to which the author located her mother (either literally *her*
mother or the fictional mother of the novel) in a set of complex
social relations—in a world, a culture, a class, an ethnicity, a politics, in short, in history. As was true in my analysis of films of the
thirties and forties, this location of the mother and the daughter in
a real and social world lies at the heart of creating complex and
thoughtful representations of the mother/daughter relationship.
When this relationship is seen solely through the lens of psychology, through the double bind of the paradigmatic dichotomy of
"bond/separate," it gets further mired in that selfsame double bind.

So I will not argue here that writers who are women of color some-how "like" their mothers more than white women writers but rather that they locate this relationship to an extent that mitigates against the purely psychological interpretation.

Rather than closely read feminist literary texts, I focus on what I see to be the central issue that determines whether these represen-tations fall inside the dominant psychological frameworks or offer up alternative and empowering visions for both mothers and daughters. The novels examined in this chapter are paradigmatic examples of recent women's writing that help me elaborate my con-tinuing discussion of the problems in the narrowly psychological representation. This is not an exhaustive comparative survey of white and nonwhite writers. Indeed, I do not give these literary texts their full analytic due in what follows. Most of these texts are quite well known and have received extensive critical attention elsewhere. In place of the detailed and delicate literary critical approach, I focus more narrowly on the continuation of the psycho-logical theme examined in the discussion of feminist theories of mothers and daughters and how this theme is subverted and actively negated by both women of color and ethnically conscious writers.

I initially concentrate on the work of three well-known white feminist writers: Kim Chernin, Robin Morgan, and Vivian Gornick. I pick these three for specific reasons. First, all are well known as both scholars and novelists, so their fictional work is always some-thing more—or other—than that. Second, each has written a bio-graphical/autobiographical story of her and her mother's life. In other words, they have chosen a similar generic form to explore the mother/daughter relationship. A myriad of other texts abound but these seem emblematic of a very common—and troublesome—trend in contemporary feminist writing, a trend paralleled in the theoretical work discussed in the previous chapter.

## Writing a Mother's Life: The Omniscient Repository and the Interested Chronicler

Kim Chernin's popular and critically acclaimed 1983 memoir, *In My Mother's House: A Daughter's Story,* constructs just the loca-tion mentioned previously. In telling the story of her mother's life and her own entry into it, Chernin contextualizes both their experiences through the rich specificity of left-wing Jewish culture. But Chernin must struggle to resist constructing her mother as the grand floating signifier of her daughter's angst. The two voices in this memoir are not simply those of mother and daughter but of two different approaches to a relationship. Nevertheless, Chernin's mother's Marxism, her lifelong commitment to political struggle (however Stalinist), produces a voice that militates against the daughter's tendency to turn specific lived experience into great and transcendent pronouncements on the mother/daughter relationship.

For all of Chernin's deep love and care, too often she seems to slip into the easy oppositions, the grand theorizing that dislocates the complex specificity of the memoir. When faced with her mother's proposal to write her life story, Kim writes: "I am torn by contradiction. I love this woman. She was my first great aching love. All my life I have wanted to do whatever she asked of me, in spite of our quarreling. . . . But it is not so easy to turn from the path I have imagined for myself. . . . I fear, as any daughter would, losing myself back into the mother."[4] By transposing her own ambivalence into pronouncements that signify eternal "truths" about mothers and daughters ("I fear, as any daughter would . . ."), Chernin invokes a whole set of ideological discourses that only further serves to separate those discourses from the richness of her mother's story. Such pronouncements detract from the textures of everyday life between a mother and a daughter in an attempt to draw from this life and these events eternal truths about the mother/daughter relationship.

Yet the daughter Chernin, in agreeing to tell her mother's story, allows this maternal voice to emerge most completely. A beautiful passage toward the end places the love of mother and daughter firmly in the realm of a shared experience that is stronger than any sort of mythical bonding:

I can feel from my own love for her the certainty that nothing can destroy the bond between us. It is stronger than ideology, unshakable in its binding. It is not the birth bond which made us a mother and daughter; that we could have trampled down, in our impatience and confusion. This bond is a comradeship, won from the work we have done together. It comes so rarely to a mother and daughter, but once it is achieved it tangles itself in with all the nature and shared flesh. And then even they, if they wished, could no longer pull it down.[5]

What is clear about this memoir and so many others is that the daughters writing them are passionate in their belief that, by telling their mothers' stories, they are also uncovering the truth of their own: "With the resurgence of women's fiction in the twentieth century, many autobiographical or confessional novels by women trace the coming to adulthood, that is, to individual identity, of a daughter who must define herself in terms of her mother."[6] As Rose Chernin says in speaking of her granddaughter, Kim's daughter: "My whole life will be in the story. And then we'll have to start all over again. But this time you will do the telling. . . . These stories are also for Larissa. Who her grandmother is, who her mother is, for a fifteen-year-old girl, what could be more important?"[7] This is, paradoxically, both the feminist moment in these writings and the patriarchal.

For the hard question with all these memoirs is this: How does a daughter write the story of her mother's life? Can she, in narrating the elusive experiences of past events, do justice to the felt realities of her mother's existence? Or does the mother's story as told by the daughter become merely a vehicle for detailing the daughter's life or a lengthy compendium of a mother's mismothering? This terrain is most assuredly a difficult one. To write the story of our mother's lives is indeed a precarious and problematic project that raises a crucial narrative distinction in the telling of these tales: the difference between constructing oneself as a repository of one's mother's life or as an interested chronicler.

A writer who constructs herself as the repository of another's life assumes a unitary grandness to her own narrative expertise (for who can speak another's life with such surety?). If Gornick, for example, must be the repository for her mother's life, then what does that say about her mother's own ability to speak her own story, safeguard her own existence? But the dialogic chronicler realizes that one cannot be a repository for another's life, that the sifting through the complex meanings of generations of women is about a dialogue, a multitude of voices, a dialectic of mothers and daughters. To be a repository is to say your history ends here with me: I am the result of your life, and I can speak the truth of it. To be a chronicler is to perhaps be more modest, more local, more wary of any claims to truth, aware that there are many chroniclers, many ways of telling a story.

Alice Walker deals directly with this issue in an interview with Mary Helen Washington for *Ms.* in the early eighties. When Washington asks her the final question, "Do you actually speak with your mother's voice in your writing?" Walker thoughtfully replies: "Just as you have certain physical characteristics of your mother's—her laughter or her toes or her grade of hair—you also internalize certain emotional characteristics that are like hers. That is part of your legacy. They are internalized, merged with your own, transformed through the stories. When you're compelled to write her stories, it's because you recognize and prize those qualities of her in yourself."[8]

Chernin manages, I think, to be a chronicler. Never denying her investment in this project, she nevertheless allows her mother her own reality, her own subjectivity, her own history. Chernin's own entry into the story is, appropriately, at the end, therefore granting legitimacy to her mother's life, a life that most assuredly had meaning and sustenance before her daughter entered into it.

Vivian Gornick's *Fierce Attachments* locates itself on the other side of this repository/chronicler fence. Whereas Chernin's book is filled with the richness and detail of Jewish left-wing life, Vivian Gornick chooses to locate her mother almost completely outside of time, place, politics, and history. In so doing, she makes the text of the world a mere extraneous background to the text of this mother's mismothering. Indeed, she explicitly says, "I am the repository of your life now, Ma." It is less a memoir of a mother, or even of a relationship, than of an adult daughter's anger, unhappiness, and confusion. The jacket blurb is telling: "Vivian Gornick's brave and deeply moving memoir is a tour de force, a book that dissects one of life's most complex, maddening and closely entwined alliances— the relationship between mother and daughter. Heralded as a landmark in American autobiography, *Fierce Attachments* probes the intimate, sometimes destructive family passions that can shape a woman's childhood—and change her life forever."[9] Here is the familiar language that formulates the mother as all powerful, all impacting, potentially destructive.

Now, granted, this book constructs itself in an autobiographical mode rather than the more mixed biography/autobiography of Chernin. Yet, by making the relationship between mother and daughter the focus, the recurring narrative core of the text, Gornick attempts to tell us not only of her own life, but of her mother's as well. Like Chernin, Gornick acknowledges right off the difficulty in the relationship ("My relationship with my mother is not good"), but, unlike Chernin, she never socially locates this anger and disappointment. Thus she leaves us with the evil simplicity of the mother in *Now, Voyager*.[10] Even the rare moments of self-criticism that emerge in the book are couched in a discourse that locates her mother as the ultimate cause of her own callous behavior.

When her mother does speak of her own experience of past events (events that, after all, happened to her), the narrator/daughter Gornick is unable to resist her own interpretation, her own intervention, as in this scene early in the book where Gornick and her mother are walking (as they are in all their dialogues) and her mother is repeating a story from her childhood, a disturbing story about her molestation by a young uncle:

The third time she told the story I was nearly forty. We were walking up Eighth Avenue, and as we neared Forty-second Street I said to her, "Ma, did it ever occur to you to ask yourself why you remained silent when Sol made his move?" She looked quickly at me. But this time she was wise to me. "What are you getting at?" she asked angrily. "Are you trying to say I *liked* it? Is that what you're getting at?" I laughed nervously, gleefully. "No, Ma, I'm not saying that. I'm just saying it's *odd* that you didn't make a sound." Again, she repeated that she had been very frightened. "Come off it," I said sharply.[11]

This scene is horrifying on a number of levels. First and most obvious is the sad irony of a feminist activist (here the daughter) questioning the silencing terror that accompanies sexual assault and male brutality. But just as important here, we have a daughter disallowing the feelings of the mother about her own experience and exhibiting almost no empathy, either sisterly or filial, toward another woman victimized by sexual violence. Gornick repeats this lack of empathy in her account of her father's death, where her depiction of her mother's grief is a sarcastic parody of what she perceives to be her self-serving histrionics. The point is not whether the grief was self-serving or histrionic—it might very well have been. But if one attempts to speak of another's grief, perhaps the voice of the griever ought to be accorded some modicum of space for articulation. To say this text is solely from the daughter's point of view is too simplistic, although that is true as well. But a daughter's point of view need not demean and negate the felt reality of the mother at the same time, as Chernin has amply demonstrated.

Robin Morgan's *Dry Your Smile* is yet another (feminist) tale of a daughter produced and victimized by bad mothering. You could literally open this book to any page and be assailed by a catalogue of vicious mothering techniques that make Joan Crawford look like Stella Dallas. Unlike Chernin and Gornick, Morgan has written her memoir as a novel (or a novel within a novel), but there is no question that this is a memoir, the story of a child actress (Morgan was the child star of an early TV series called "Mama") smothered and curtailed by an overbearing and obsessively controlling mother. The daughter grows up, becomes a feminist leader/writer (like Morgan), and is finally liberated by her mother's death. This circularity (daughter reborn as mother dies) is central to the conception of the daughter as repository for her mother's (failed) life.

Morgan's book directly addresses the problem inherent in writing a memoir that is at once both a telling of your own life and a telling of the life of your mother: How do you give power back to the mother and to the mother/daughter relationship without falling into the trap constructed by the patriarchal psychology of singular blame? How does the daughter speak of her mother's impact on her without locating mother as sole and essential creator of the daughter's psyche (and usually her neuroses as well)? Morgan expresses this ambivalence when her alter ego, Julian, considers writing about her life with her mother: "*Why* would you write it? To justify yourself? Poor beleaguered Jule, beset by evil nonstepmother and then by wicked nonprince and finally by starving masses of enthralled women? Come *on*." Yet that is precisely what she does. Every time the character Julian acts, every interaction she has with her husband, her female lover, and her interior self, is referenced through the mother, to the extent where, in her dreams, her mother and her husband seem to merge. The desire to write this story is not, she claims, "some sophomoric catharsis," not "another act of vengeance against her," and certainly not "an expression of love." It is rather the pressing need to explain her own identity through the realization that she had never "committed an act pure of her." To tell the truth of their shared life is here to tell a narrative where one partner is most assuredly the total victim, the other the total victimizer: "This time, *this* time to *really* write about it, her wardrobe of faces and the faces she bequeathed me, lies appliqued with the skill of a needleworker, possession and terror and hunger so interthreaded and unacknowledged as to become inseparable from the fabric of living itself. *Fool, you'd have to dare become her even more than you fear you already have.*"[12]

In using the metaphor of rebirth at the end of the book, after the mother has died, Morgan falls (perhaps unwittingly) into the stance of perpetual child, and ultimately into a feminist form of mother-blame.[13] In an earlier scene, Julian has come to visit her mother and suggests she read to her. When the mother responds, "We'll see," adult woman Julian says, "Momma, 'we'll see' are the two words a child of any age most dreads hearing from a parent."[14] The point is that Julian/Morgan is no longer a child; she is a grown-up woman. Yet, like Gornick, she is unable to relate to her mother as such and, importantly, refuses to take much responsibility for that inability. In the context of this narrative, which insistently details the mother's controlling, infantilizing behavior toward the daughter, the only possible reading is to legitimate Julian's childishness as the result of the kind of mothering she had.

This mother-blame is not limited to feminist novels. As Madonna Miner has pointed out, twentieth-century women's best-sellers elaborate the daughter's angst with equal fervor:

Daughter-heroines voice complaints shared by daughter-readers: it is mothers who condemn daughters to inhabit bodies capable of mothering . . . , it is mothers who leave, failing to provide adequate nourishment, it is mothers who remain, exacting compensation for nourishment not provided. The story told in the bestsellers, then, is built on a bisexual triangle, with tremendous psychic tension marking the relationship between mother and daughter.[15]

## Situated Relationships: Roots and Branches

Much of the fiction of women of color avoids the perils of the repository narratives so prevalent in white women's fiction. If these white feminist representations of mothers and daughters have been characterized by their dichotomous framing (good versus evil mothers, etc.) with an emphasis on conflict, literary images produced by women of color have tended to be more nuanced, more complex, less starkly defined. As many black critics have argued, mother-blame is less the issue than is the role of the mother (or often the surrogate mother) as healer to the daughter wounded by the vagaries of racism.[16]

In the most general terms, the relationship is depicted differently because the experience of mothers and daughters of color in a racist culture is so patently different from that of white mothers and daughters. Central here is the role of work outside the home in defining daughters' relationships to their mothers. Most black and ethnic daughters have been witness to the labor of their mothers, labor that they knew—even in an unspoken way—supported them, made their very existence possible. Thus the anger that so many white daughters feel toward their mothers, largely provoked by the limitations of a mother trapped in the domestic role, is not perhaps as prevalent among black daughters, who have had to develop a certain respect for their mothers as competent and active women. In a study of black mothers and daughters conducted by Gloria Joseph and Jill Lewis that included extensive interviews, the authors report a very positive sense of respect between mother and daughter: "The reason for this . . . seems to be located in the Black daughters' familiarity with the circumstances within which their mothers existed and raised their children and an empathy caused by understanding these situations."[17] Indeed, even black women's magazines such as *Ebony* and *Essence,* although not completely outside the psychological frameworks that encase the magazines of the dominant white culture, speak in voices suffused less with blame and resentment and more with gratitude and respect.

This respect born of familiarity and social consciousness is true not only for black writers, but also for many daughters of mothers who worked. Chernin's witnessing of her mother's political work, however distressing it often was in the McCarthy years, enables her to experience her mother as something other than, or something besides, her mother. The competency and skill the mother exhibits cannot help but place her in a more complex light.

The same authors also note the importance of extended kinship systems in defining the black mother/daughter relationship. The presence of other emotional supports for the daughter—aunts, siblings, grandmothers, fictive kin—may play a role in defusing the "overwhelmingness" of the mother/daughter relation:

The presence of othermothers in Black extended families and the modeling symbolized by community othermothers offer powerful support for the task of teaching girls to resist white perceptions of Black womanhood while appearing to conform to them. In contrast to the isolation of middle class white mother/daughter dyads, Black woman-centered extended family networks foster an early identification with a much wider range of models of Black womanhood which can lead to a greater sense of empowerment in young Black girls.[18]

Similar patterns of closeness and mutuality have been found by sociologists studying the working-class family, where the mother/ daughter relationship is often the most enduring familial relation.

The existence of such different patterns of mother/daughter relating and such different representations of that relating should point to the "constructedness" of that relationship. What we assume to be *the* issues for mothers and daughters (separation, autonomy, etc.) are themselves products of particular historical times and specific social and cultural groupings: they are not transhistorical or transcultural. Perhaps the whole notion of this relationship as one constructed in conflict is itself a phenomenon limited to white, bourgeois society.

The implications of acknowledging this "constructedness" are critical for the elaboration of a more positive and mutually affirming rendering of the mother/daughter relationship. For example, if a black daughter seems more respectful and appreciative of her mother because she recognizes her strength and competency, then we need to think of how to enhance every mother's sense of competency. In addition, a media world of greater cultural diversity might present a wider and more complex array of representational offerings.

Women writers of color have consistently acknowledged the importance of their maternal heritage, a heritage that refuses the easy oppositions so characteristic of less located tales:

Black women writers acknowledge the need to "recite our matrilineage, to find a ritual to both get back there and preserve it." They testify, explains Mary Helen Washington, "to the existence of a generational conti-

nuity between themselves and their mothers, and they write that continuity into their texts." Imbued as daughters with an inside vision, they
write of complex mother-daughter relationships that have no simple
equation for friendship, no fail-safe formula for bonding.[19]

In the fiction of women of color, mothers and daughters bond and
break up, love and hate each other (like everyone else in the
world), but the writing tends to avoid the pitfalls of an essentialist
discourse where the all-powerful mother wreaks havoc on her all-
victimized daughter or (less frequently) the beneficent mother
gently guides her adoring daughter into the pristine fields of adult
femininity. As Alice Walker (and many others) have so eloquently
articulated, the "search for our mothers' gardens" is central to the
reconstruction of a tradition long repressed by the powers of dominant white culture and thus central not simply to the daughters'
understanding of "herself" in a strictly psychological sense, but to
the understanding of a history and the vibrant female desires that
often are the lone voices of resistance in the wilderness of racism
and oppression.

This attention to the maternal voice as historical memory crops
up in an early (1973) short story by Alice Walker called "Everyday
Use," in which the prodigal daughter comes home to visit her poor,
country family. As in much of black women's fiction, the generational conflict in this story is analyzed through the lens of black
identity and culture. The eldest daughter has come back from college with a new African identity/name and a similarly politicized
boyfriend. This mother/daughter story contains two daughters, and
the differences between them—as much as the differences between the mother and daughter—are the subject. In many ways, it
is a good daughter/bad daughter story, but the difference from most
white fiction is that the good daughter is the one who remains tied
to the ways of her mother and her mothers before her, who remains
identified with the patterns of "everyday use." The title itself refers
to a quilt made by women in the family that the eldest daughter
now wants to take back with her to hang on the wall as a "sign" of
"authentic" black culture and identity. But the mother has prom-
ised it to the younger woman, Maggie, for her wedding, and she
will submit it only to everyday use; it will not be a decoration or a
sign.

The story begins with the mother waiting for her daughter to arrive and immediately refers to TV images of families reuniting and the unreality of those images, as the mother indicates in this internal narrative:

You've no doubt seen those TV shows where the child who has "made it" is confronted, as a surprise, by her own mother and father, tottering in weakly from backstage. (A pleasant surprise, of course: What would they do if parent and child came on the show only to curse out and insult each other?) On TV mother and child embrace and smile into each other's faces. Sometimes the mother and father weep, the child wraps them in her arms and leans across the table to tell how she would not have made it without their help. I have seen these programs.

Sometimes I dream a dream in which Dee and I are suddenly brought together on a TV program of this sort. Out of a dark and soft-seated limousine I am ushered into a bright room filled with many people. There I meet a smiling, grey, sporty man like Johnny Carson who shakes my hand and tells me what a fine girl I have. Then we are on the stage and Dee is embracing me with tears in her eyes. She pins on my dress a large orchid, even though she has told me once that she thinks orchids are tacky flowers.

In real life I am a large, big-boned woman with rough, man-working hands. . . . But of course all this does not show on television. I am the way my daughter would want me to be: a hundred pounds lighter, my skin like an uncooked barley pancake. My hair glistens in the hot bright lights. Johnny Carson has much to do to keep up with my quick and witty tongue.[20]

The presence of the white (distorting) media is significant here because it intrudes on the reality of the mother's life and helps move her daughter away from her, as when Dee/Wangero takes posed Polaroids of her "authentic" poor black family.

When Dee announces that she now calls herself Wangero, her mother accommodates the change, although she keeps using the other name in the narration. She ends up giving the quilt to Maggie, and Dee leaves after telling them they should "do something with themselves." The story ends with mother and Maggie settling in on the porch with snuff, reinforcing the continuity of female presence both in the face of the "radicalized" daughter and in the white media, of which the daughter's presence conjures up images.

A story by Gloria Naylor from her novel *The Women of Brewster Place* is similar to Walker's "Everyday Use" in its account of a young woman dedicated to her newly found black radicalism, her African identity, as it comes in conflict with a mother she considers either anachronistic or downright counterrevolutionary. Like the daughter in Walker's story, Kiswana has changed her name to an African one, and that in itself is a source of conflict. Kiswana's mother has married an "educated man" and is living a very middle-class life that Kiswana has left in defiance. She now refuses to take money from her mother and lives in relative poverty in Brewster Place. Her mother comes to visit her unexpectedly. The mother clearly wants her to "do something" with her life—to be upwardly mobile like the family she has come from. Kiswana resists this and proclaims her revolutionary identity in the face of what she perceives to be her mother's acquiescence to the dominant white culture.

They argue, Kiswana defending her life-style and the mother saying that she could make more use of herself if she continued her education and became a lawyer or politician for black rights. In many ways, this scene recreates a classic debate over the relative virtues of working within the system and outside of it and mirrors New Left anger at liberal parents (Kiswana's parents are in the NAACP, which she thinks is a sellout organization). When Kiswana insults her mother by referring to her as a "whiteman's nigger," mom blows up and gives her a fiery lecture about her ancestry and her proud heritage that gets around to the question of the name: "It broke my heart when you changed your name. I gave you my grandmother's name, a woman who bore nine children and educated them all, who held off six white men with a shotgun when they tried to drag off one of her sons to jail for 'not knowing his place.' Yet you needed to reach into an African dictionary to find a name to make you proud." This is very reminiscent of Walker's story, where the mother named Dee for a beloved female relative. Kiswana is devastated by this tirade and recognizes her naivete and arrogance, but she can say nothing until her mother rescues her: "Mrs. Browne lifted Kiswana's face gently. 'And the one lesson I wanted you to learn is not to be afraid to face anyone, not even a crafty old lady like me who can outtalk you.' And she smiled and winked."[21]

The story ends with them coming together around typical "women's things"—fashion, sexuality, and such. After an unusual conversation about men and sex, Kiswana is amazed at the recognition that they "inhabit the same world": "I'll be damned, the young woman thought, feeling her whole face tingle. Daddy's into feet! And she looked at the blushing woman on her couch and suddenly realized that her mother had trod through the same universe that she herself was now traveling. Kiswana was breaking no new trails and would eventually end up just two feet away on that couch. She stared at the woman she had been and was to become."[22] The uncertain mother/daughter reconciliation is thus arrived at through a historical and political history that locates their "sameness" in a shared world of struggle *and* femaleness. Their shared identity as women is always placed within a context of their shared reality as black in a white culture, however they may differ in interpreting both those contexts, both those identities.

*Meridian,* a 1976 novel by Alice Walker, also examines the mother/daughter relationship through the lens of political struggle. This story of a woman living through and past the civil rights movement is relevant here even though it is not a "mother/daughter" story in any explicit sense. The main character, Meridian, does reject her mother, as occurs in many white feminist novels, but she expresses it in such a different way as to render that rejection both more complex and more poignant. The fact that the daughter's remembrance of the mother is referenced through the civil rights movement renders this emotional turmoil differently:

Meridian found, when she was not preoccupied with the Movement, that her thoughts turned with regularity and intensity to her mother, on whose account she endured wave after wave of an almost primeval guilt. She imagined her mother in church, in which she had invested all that was still energetic in her life, praying for her daughter's soul, and yet, having no concern, no understanding of her daughter's *life* whatsoever; but Meridian did not condemn her for this. Away from her mother, Meridian thought of her as Black Motherhood personified, and of that great institution she was in terrible awe, comprehending as she did the horror, the narrowing of perspective, for mother and for child, it had invariably meant. Meridian felt as if her body, growing frailer every day under the stress of her daily life, stood in the way of a reconciliation between her mother and that part of her own soul her mother could, perhaps, love.[23]

Here Walker speaks to the institutionalization of motherhood in a way that recognizes both the ossifying nature of the cultural stereotype of "black motherhood" and the harsh realities embedded within it. Her mother doesn't understand her rejection of reli-

gion, doesn't understand her politics, but Meridian's feelings about
the ever widening gap between them are expressed in almost neutral and matter-of-fact tones, as when Meridian has rejected the
church that remains so fundamental to her mother's identity: "Her
mother's love was gone, withdrawn, and there were conditions to
be met before it could be returned. Conditions Meridian was never
able to meet."[24]

Throughout the story, as Meridian thinks back through the
mother, she parallels her own grief at her mother's unlovingness
with a neutral yet detailed account of her mother's sacrifices and
the price they both paid for the inescapability of motherhood. Here
Walker states the realization of her mother's own loss within the
confines of motherhood and marriage, but she says it matter of
factly, never referring back to herself as the one who suffered because her mother shouldn't have had kids: "Her mother was not a
woman who should have had children. She was capable of thought
and growth and action only if unfettered by the needs of depen-
dents, or the demands, requirements, of a husband." Here again
she comprehends with simple clarity the demise of her mother's
independence as a teacher once submerged into the myth of family
life: "She could never forgive her community, her family, his family,
the whole world, for not warning her against children."[25]

This sense of the mother's life as circumscribed by the dictates of
family and husband is a familiar one to feminist fiction, both white
and black. But the difference here is that the daughter is *chroni-
cling* her mother's sorrow; and although the effect on the daughter
is implicit, this chronicler is also able to move away from blame and
toward a politicized understanding: "When her mother asked,
without glancing at her, 'Have you stolen anything?' a stillness fell
over Meridian and for seconds she could not move. The question
literally stopped her in her tracks." Here we see the classic feminist
daughter's dilemma of having, by her very existence, cut short her
mother's possibilities. Yet Meridian never questions the reality of
her mother's "serenity" being "stolen" and thus validates both that
reality and her own in her knowledge that it was not her fault: "It
was for stealing her mother's serenity, for shattering her mother's
emerging self, that Meridian felt guilty from the very first, though
she was unable to understand how this could possibly be her
fault."[26]

It is also important that Meridian recounts her mother's history:

how Meridian's grandmother went without and struggled to make sure her mother got educated and how she rewarded her mother's endurance by becoming a schoolteacher.[27] The sense of endurance is passed on to Meridian:

When her mother talked about her childhood Meridian wept and clung to her hands, wishing with all her heart she had not been born to this already overburdened woman. . . . It seemed to Meridian that her legacy from her mother's endurance, her unerring knowledge of rightness and her pursuit of it through all distractions, was one she would never be able to match. It never occurred to her that her mother's and her grandmother's extreme purity of life was compelled by necessity. They had not lived in an age of choice.[28]

Finally, Meridian comes to realize the importance of simple endurance in the face of racism and poverty and is able beautifully to reverse the theme of "surpassing the mother" that is so prevalent in both white fiction and white theory: "To Meridian, her mother *was* a giant. She had never perceived her in any other way. . . . Besides, she had already forgiven her mother for anything she had ever done to her or might do, because to her, Mrs. Hill had persisted in bringing them all (the children, the husband, the family, the race) to a point far beyond where she, in her mother's place, her grandmother's place, her great-grandmother's place, would have stopped."[29]

Walker's consistent locatedness is mirrored in the work of other women writers of color. Even Paule Marshall's classic 1959 novel *Brown Girls, Brownstones,* in which mother/daughter discord is visceral and central, never lapses into the psychological whining that has marked so many similar tales of struggle. As Gloria Wade-Gayles writes:

The cold, harsh world of racism beyond the community of brownstones gives Selina a larger view of her mother. She does not accept Silla's materialistic values, but she understands the mother's desire for control and power. Silla held the reins tightly because she knew first-hand the vulnerability of being Black, female and Barbadian in white America. She had been suffocatingly overprotective and domineering because she wanted a different reality for Selina.[30]

Toni Morrison's *Beloved,* of course, offers up a reading of the mother/daughter relationship that is precisely so horrifying to the extent it deconstructs typical renderings by its radical "located-

ness." Morrison's own words speak most accurately of the implications of this kind of story telling:

I'm just interested in showing what is hazardous to us and what happens
to women when things are carried to an extreme. I want to present the
dangers so that we as women can find the balance. For Sethe for instance
the condition under which she has lived ie. slavery is such that when her
children are threatened with re-enslavement, murder becomes an act of
mother love. "I took my babies and put them somewhere they'd be safe."
Motherhood was her identity. She lived in a world that tried to deny her
responsibility for her children. So she protected them with the ferocity of
a lioness. That is the dilemma of the novel.[31]

And Morrison's earlier work speaks to the impossibility of representing mothers and daughters along lines that adopt a mainstream
dichotomous approach of "bonding" versus "separation." Morrison's
mothers and daughters are often characterized by what appears to
be maternal "abandonment" and coldness; yet (particularly in the
case of *Beloved*) this seeming rejection often signals the depth of
the mother's love. The exigencies of oppression help construct a
multitude of survival mechanisms, often manifesting themselves in
a toughness that less aware daughters might read as a repudiation
of maternal love but that these writers interpret as a sign of womanly struggle in a world that has repudiated their very existence.

## "*Shou* So Deep": Mah Jong Mothers and Walkman Daughters

Amy Tan's 1989 bestseller, *The Joy Luck Club*, exemplifies with
particular force the rich possibilities for mother/daughter representations that these earlier texts have already indicated. This novel
recounts the stories of four Chinese mothers and their assimilated
Chinese-American daughters. The mothers, immigrants to San
Francisco, have for forty years maintained a regular meeting where
they play mah jong, eat elaborate meals, and share their lives with
each other. The telling of the stories is inaugurated at the death of
one of the mothers.

The book is divided into four sections, each beginning with a
Chinese parable concerning mothers and daughters. Each section
contains four stories. In the first section, the daughter of the dead
Suyuan Woo recounts her entry into Joy Luck (the mahjong club),

and the three remaining mothers tell their stories. The second two sections contain daughters' tales, each one ending with the story of Jing-mei, daughter of the missing member. The final section returns to the mothers, with Jing-mei at the end.

The structure of *The Joy Luck Club* is important because it moves away from the linear chronological model that has lent itself so easily to the dual tropes of "surpassing the mother" and the daughter as repository. It substitutes a much more dialogic mode in which the often suppressed voices of the mothers emerge with full force: they tell their own stories, their own bitterness. This dialogic mode also allows for the full and various experiences of both mothers and daughters to emerge in ways that implicitly argue against any simple construction of blame.

This is not to say that these stories are without pain and anger; on the contrary, they are often full of bitterness and misunderstanding on both sides. But simply allowing the mothers' voices to speak of their lives and their understanding of their daughters places the reader in different emotional territory. In Waverly Jong's story, we feel the huge chasm that so typifies the experience of first- and second-generation immigrants, but we also see the attempt to know the other, her world, her life, her options, her ways of living in the world that both mother and daughter inhabit. After a long and confusing battle with her mother, Waverly is able to express her own desire for selfhood without simultaneously negating her mother's:

I saw what I had been fighting for: It was for me, a scared child, who had run away a long time ago to what I had imagined was a safer place. And hiding in this place, behind my invisible barriers, I knew what lay on the other side: Her side attacks. Her secret weapons. Her uncanny ability to find my weakest spots. But in the brief instant that I had peered over the barriers I could finally see what was really there: an old woman, a wok for her armor, a knitting needle for her sword, getting a little crabby as she waited patiently for her daughter to invite her in.[32]

In the story of An-mei Hsu (one of the mothers), we get a vision of generational rebirth as she recounts an event from her life in China that involves the death of her beloved grandmother, Popo. An-mei's own mother had left her, and she had been raised by this grandmother. But her mother has now come home to take care of the dying Popo, and what ensues creates in An-mei an appreciation of her mother that is far removed from the idealized images she had

kept alive in her fantasy. As the child An-mei watches her stranger/
mother minister to her dying grandmother, she comes to know of a
daughter's love:

I saw my mother on the other side of the room. Quiet and sad. She was
cooking a soup, pouring herbs and medicines into the steaming pot. And
then I saw her pull up her sleeve and pull out a sharp knife. She put this
knife on the softest part of her arm. I tried to close my eyes but could not.

And then my mother cut a piece of meat from her arm. Tears poured
from her face and blood spilled to the floor.

My mother took her flesh and put it in the soup. She cooked magic in
the ancient tradition to try to cure her mother this one last time.

. . . Even though I was young, I could see the pain of the flesh and the
worth of the pain.

This is how a daughter honors her mother. It is *shou* so deep it is in
your bones. The pain of the flesh is nothing. The pain you must forget.
Because sometimes that is the only way to forget what is in your bones.
You must peel off your skin, and that of your mother, and her mother
before her. Until there is nothing. No scar, no skin, no flesh.[33]

In a later story, Ying-ying St. Clair, another mother, details from
the mother's position the gap that separates mother and daughter:

For all these years I kept my mouth closed so selfish desires would not fall
out. And because I remained quiet for so long now my daughter does not
hear me. She sits by her fancy swimming pool and hears only her Sony
Walkman, her cordless phone, her big, important husband asking her why
they have charcoal and no lighter fluid.

All these years I kept my true nature hidden, running along like a small
shadow so nobody could catch me. And because I moved so secretly now
my daughter does not see me. She sees a list of things to buy, her check-
book out of balance, her ashtray sitting crooked on a straight table.

And I want to tell her this: We are lost, she and I, unseen and not
seeing, unheard and not hearing, unknown by others.[34]

This piece poignantly encapsulates the experience of so many
mothers, afraid to speak, to give voice to their self, lest their "selfish
desires fall out." The daughter, now unable to see or hear the
mother who has kept herself so tightly wrapped in, sees and hears
only the sad detritus of an assimilated suburban marriage. Ying-
ying goes on to tell of how she lost herself, thus giving depth and
history to the mother's hiding and absence and giving voice to her
own desire to be found—by her own daughter as well as by her-

self—echoing here Waverly's moment of understanding of her own mother's desire to be "invited in" by the daughter.

This sense of mothers and daughters finding each other is treated in Tan's book in a deeply antiromantic vein, implicitly challenging traditional (Western, patriarchal) notions of the autonomous self who struggles for her independence. The story of Lindo Jong, Waverly's mother, exemplifies this beautifully. Waverly wants to go to China for her second honeymoon, and her mother has been questioning her ability to fit into Chinese society. Lindo muses on the incommensurability of "American circumstances and Chinese character" and wishes for her daughter the knowledge that "Chinese thinking is best":

No, this kind of thinking didn't stick to her. She was too busy chewing gum, blowing bubbles bigger than her cheeks. Only that kind of thinking stuck.

"Finish your coffee," I told her yesterday. "Don't throw your blessings away."

"Don't be so old-fashioned, Ma," she told me, finishing her coffee down the sink. "I'm my own person."

And I think, How can she be her own person? When did I give her up?[35]

This next scene, where Waverly has taken her mother to "Mr. Rory" to get her hair done before the wedding, points out again the mother's sadness at the implications of the daughter's vehement assimilation: her denial of the mother's reality and presence. When Waverly treats her like a "dumb foreigner" in the hairdresser's, translating for her, speaking for her, Lindo is deeply saddened: "I smile. I use my American face. That's the face Americans think is Chinese, the one they cannot understand. But inside I am becoming ashamed. I am ashamed she is ashamed. Because she is my daughter and I am proud of her, and I am her mother but she is not proud of me."[36] What a reversal this scene is! Typically, we hear the beleaguered daughters bemoaning the fact that they will never be able to please their disapproving mothers, never be able to make them proud. Here, instead, we have a mother expressing the simple desire to be known and admired by her daughter.

In all these stories, and in so many more, the difference emerges both from the novelists' cultural choices and from their personal/political location. One of the issues that arises here has to do with the question of address and narrative in various mother/daughter discourses. For example, what are the implications of a narrative that tells of the mother's life through the eyes of the daughter? First, are these daughter-narrated tales more prevalent than mother-narrated ones? Second, if the mother *is* narrating, are the same issues and themes apparent (e.g., blame, judgment on value of life, etc.)? In other words, it is important to distinguish exactly who is telling the story of a mother and daughter. Is it the mother or daughter, or is it from another (perhaps male) point of view? How does this shape the narrative itself? Are there ever narratives that don't speak from either the mother's or the daughter's position?

This raises the important question of whether feminism has allowed the voices of both mothers and daughters to emerge. It has clearly allowed the daughter's (mostly negative and complaining) voice to emerge; yet it is not clear if the mother's voice is still being submerged under various ideologies of motherhood and the overpowering figure of psychological explanation.

In film, too, this question of narrative address is central. In *Mildred Pierce*, Mildred narrates the story to the detective, but whose point of view is really shown? In *Now, Voyager,* the doctor clearly is the one who pronounces the sentence on the relationship. Charlotte's mother's point of view is hardly acknowledged. In a contemporary film such as *Terms of Endearment,* with its alternating and paralleled scenes, are we at last getting to see, in some sense, both sides of the story?

The differences between these two discursive movements should by now be apparent. The work of these women writers of color should point to the possibilities of feminist representations that construct a dialectic of mother and daughter within the context of a social and political world in which both of their lives have been circumscribed to a certain degree. It is this rootedness in a world, in a history, that allows for these more complex and empowering representations to emerge, a rootedness that is perhaps an imperative for minority writers in a way that it is not for white writers:

According to white female interpretations of motherhood . . . The "good" mother in a sexist society teaches her daughter to conform "to female stereotypes such as passivity, spirituality, or irrationality." These interpretations do not apply to the mother-daughter relationships in the Black women's novels we have examined. Because Black women have not stood as fragile figurines on pedestals white feminists seek to dismantle, they have a decidedly different approach to rearing daughters. Quite the contrary, they socialize their daughters to be independent, strong and self-confident. . . . we want the truth of our mothers' lives, even if those truths are sometimes "cruel enough to stop the blood." . . . We dare today to search for sisterhood because our mothers, our "sister warrior(s)" taught us the beauty of struggle.[37]

But this does not imply that similar choices could not be made with equal vigor by white feminists eager to relinquish the power of being the repository of their mothers' lives for the much more complex—and mutually empowering—location of fellow-traveling chronicler.

## Chapter Seven

# Whose Life Is It Anyway?

## *Fatal Retractions in the Backlash Eighties*

> Mother: "When Reenie grows up she's going to have a profes-
> sion if I have to grind myself into dust in that dime
> store."
>
> Daughter: "I don't want a profession! I want to get married and
> have babies like Aunt Marie."
>
> Mother: "You'll do what I say. . . . A woman has to have a
> profession!"
>
> —"Mother and Daughter: The Loving War," 1980

In July 1989, the Supreme Court handed down the most regressive decision regarding women's lives in decades. Although *Roe v. Wade*, the historic 1973 decision legalizing abortion, was not completely struck down, it was dealt a blow from which it may never recover. Predictions are that, in these next terms of court, *Roe* will actually be overturned. Two additional Supreme Court decisions have added to the crisis and effectively limited access, "gagged" publicly funded doctors, and created a climate of fear and hostility. Falling as the 1989 decision did on the day before America's great annual hurrah of freedom and equality, it rendered July 4 more than a little ironic.

The eighties were indeed a strange decade. We undoubtedly were and still are in the midst of a tremendous backlash against the women's movement and civil and human rights of all shades. The 1989 Supreme Court decision was the final chapter in a decade-long right-wing agenda that whittled away at the already dwindling welfare state and sent the message to many Americans that if you aren't a middle-class white male, you don't matter. Homelessness, rampant ghetto drug use, destruction of the environment, de-unionization of industry, and feminization of poverty are all the watchwords of a society increasingly defined by its harsh assertion of the rights of so few over those of so many. Yet feminist cultural practice has exploded, with women's writing taking its place within the established lists of best-sellers and Pulitzer Prize winners.

Perhaps this very disjuncture best describes what contemporary social critics have chosen to call the "postmodern condition." Perhaps this very lack of continuity, this absence of a sense of some wholeness and coherency to an "epoch" or even a decade, describes so palpably what it means to live in the ruins of modernism, in this strangely confusing fin de siècle. If "Father Knows Best" made sense in the world of 1950s domesticity and the politics of containment, then what does "Cagney and Lacey" mean in the age of clinic bombings and the erosion of the Civil Rights Act? Perhaps the defining feature of our era is that there is no defining feature.

One's sense of the movement of history is thrown up for grabs when faced with this: my mother's generation grew up without the right to abortion, felt the special terror of sex that accompanies that reality, knew what it meant to make furtive phone calls, drive women to dark anonymous buildings, hope for the best. And my mother and her generation fought to change that bleak reality, to provide women with at least some control over their bodies, over their sex.

My generation and I have grown up with this hard-won right, accepting it as a right, much as we knew we had a right to vote, even if we didn't exercise it all the time. We came to our sexual maturity without that particular and potent fear of sex. Now, like our mothers, we have witnessed a reversal in our lifetimes: this time not toward freedom, but a sharp turn toward domination. Are we destined to repeat our mothers' labor, to engage once more in a battle we thought they had already won for us? And what of our daughters? Is this miserable retrenchment our final resting place after twenty years of feminism? Is this frustrating "holding the line" what some call "postfeminism"?

As the latest Court decision assures us, our political era is hardly feminist, much less "postfeminist," as some contemporary critics would have it. If one of the cornerstones of feminist practice and thought has been the pro-choice movement and the concomitant knowledge that the heart of patriarchy is the control over women's bodies and reproduction, then we are most assuredly moving back into a "prefeminist" era. There are other indicators of this as well.

A Washington woman named Elizabeth Morgan, for example, sat in a jail cell for two years for refusing to obey the (male) judge and reveal the whereabouts of her young daughter, whom she claimed, with strong evidence, had been repeatedly abused by her ex-husband. For protecting her daughter, she was incarcerated. A parade was held in honor of her ex-husband, her daughter's father, a rapist. But another woman in New York (Hedda Nussbaum) was condemned by the public and feminist writers alike for *not* protecting her child, for "allowing" the abuse to escalate until death released both mother and daughter from their father/captor. *People* magazine printed both stories, defending both women.

What, then, to say of mothers and daughters in the 1980s and early 1990s? First, the representations of the mother/daughter relationship have not escaped this overwhelming sense of imploding contradictions. There has never been so much material on mothers and daughters. Although sitcom and series television, except for that glorious interlude in the mid-1970s, maintains a benign indifference to the subject, mothers and daughters have positively exploded as a media subject. Talk show superhosts Phil Donahue and Oprah Winfrey do regular specials on mothers and daughters, dragging out dirty linen, amusing anecdotes, and glib truisms. Cable stations HBO and Lifetime produce their own movies on mothers and daughters, replay network movies of the week, and air smarmy Mother's Day specials urging viewers to write in with their "mom of the week." Prime-time television annually airs the "Mother-Daughter Beauty Pageant," thus firmly ensconcing mothers and daughters in the popular rituals of our time.[1] Mothers and daughters become a trusty topic for women's magazines and pop psychology, and film treatments emerge again after the long hiatus of the 1960s and 1970s. The problem now, as opposed to in earlier periods of history, cannot be so simply characterized by absence and lack: the women's movement has irrevocably pushed this long shadowed relationship into the cultural and ideological spotlight.

Although this new presence is heartening, it needs to be examined carefully. As we have seen in Chapters 5 and 6, the specifically feminist discussion of this relationship has been deeply problematic, often relying on narrowly psychological ways of understanding and knowing. Looking now at more mainstream images of mothers and daughters, one is struck by the contiguous nature of these popular images and the feminist images. They are not "worlds apart," but indeed often apply quite similar frameworks to this particular relationship. This points to the real and substantial effect the women's movement and feminist thought have had on our culture. The impact of the women's movement becomes apparent in the women's magazines of the 1970s, TV sitcoms like "Maude," and films like *An Unmarried Woman.* This intersection between feminism and mainstream culture—often involving cooptation and vulgarization as well as celebration and popularization—is apparent in every one of the media analyzed here.

Because of this significant overlap and the difficulty in defining what is specifically "feminist," troublesome research questions plagued this chapter. Do I include here (or in Chapters 5 and 6) women writers whose work is popular, assuredly mainstream, yet who clearly address questions and issues raised originally by feminists? There is no simple delineation of what is "feminist theory." However, I have chosen to include here work by writers such as Colette Dowling, Evelyn Bassoff, Ann Grizzle, and Paula Caplan and *Ms.* magazine articles with the rest of the women's magazines because I believe these popular texts are directed toward the "general public" and not toward any specifically feminist readership (with the possible exception of *Ms.*). Therefore, my choice here is largely based on the imputed readership, a readership that marks these texts out as significantly different from those discussed in the previous two chapters.

Indeed, content is less the issue than is availability and style, for I argue that many of these popular texts written by women end up at the same psychological resting place as do the more sophisticated and "academic" works of explicitly feminist writers like Chernin and Chodorow. The exception is the work of Paula Caplan, which constitutes a valiant attempt to counteract the mother-blame so prevalent in our culture.[2]

This resting place is not a completely unified one, although it is dominated by the object relations school of psychology made newly respectable by Nancy Chodorow and popularized by any number of writers. I previously claimed that the defining feature of our postmodern era is the lack of any single defining feature. To a great extent, I think this is true. But the representations of mothers and daughters in the 1980s and early 1990s do present some striking themes that differ sharply from both their early feminist 1970s predecessors and the more class based discourses of the 1930s and the psychological and domestic discourses of the 1940s and 1950s.

The historical movement has been toward the increasing definition of this relationship in solely psychological terms. Yet the women's movement of the 1970s provoked a break from this overwhelming restrictiveness, and there emerged representations and discourses that had as their referent not eternal psychological "truths" but rather the newfound specificity of male domination and the various configurations of women's oppression and struggle. Mothers and daughters can never again be completely relegated to the psychological closet. Nevertheless, this backlash decade has generated a new set of (all too familiar) discourses that continues to construct and imagine the relationship of mothers and daughters as a fundamentally psychological one.

## Loving, Hating, Letting Go: Eternal Truths and Inevitable Conflicts

A 1983 article in *Cosmopolitan* states in its title what I take to be the new discursive structure of the mother/daughter relationship: "Mothers & Daughters: The Eternal Love-Hate Relationship." The author claims, "Women spend their most valiant moments breaking away from their mothers in order to survive." Although the idea of mothers and daughters in a contentious relationship is hardly new, the discourse of the 1980s that structures it in terms of an inevitability helps produce a relationship constructed in conflict, where the mother and her daughter are depicted as eternal combatants in a bloody and unavoidable battle. The issues in this battle repeat the psychological litany: independence, autonomy, individuation, separation. As Madeline Pober notes: "Women *do* sever the maternal connection, and the process can be violent—for rebellion, if it is to result in true autonomy, often entails watching the mother you love suffer pain and confusion because you choose to live a life alien to her."[3] Although we have seen these themes in earlier periods, they have never been so strong or so all-encompassing as in the late 1980s and early 1990s. The infamous Wylie years were equally nasty; then, however, the concern was rarely with the effect of mother on daughter, but rather with what was understood to be the much more significant effect of smothering moms on weakened and passive boys and men.

These contemporary phrases, and the psychological theories they reflect, are left to explain the totality of the mother/daughter relationship. Except for the rare feminist exceptions, discussed in Chapters 5 and 6, this thematic of antinomies (love/hate, bond/separate, enmeshment/autonomy) runs through almost all the cultural material on mothers and daughters in the 1980s. Just a glance at the titles of several magazine articles illustrates this theme: "You and Your Problem Mother," "Mothers and Daughters Who Can't Get Along," "Your Mother, Your First Love—Can You Ever Get Over Her?" "Are You Still Trying to Please Your Mother?" "Should You Divorce Your Mother?" "Daughters and Mothers: Making Peace, Making Friends," "Are You a Better Mother Than Your Mother?" Popular books are no exception, with titles such as *Mothers and Daughters: Loving and Letting Go; Mother Love, Mother Hate: Breaking Dependent Love Patterns in Family Relationships; Mothermania: A Psychological Study of Mother/Daughter Conflict;* and Colette Dowling's *Perfect Women,* whose first chapter is entitled "Mothers and Daughters: A Shared Disorder." The list goes on. If the books and articles don't explicitly explore the inevitable conflict paradigm, they offer homilies of togetherness based on overcoming the inevitable conflict and becoming "friends."

The theme of mothers and daughters as friends is prominent. Almost all happy and healthy mother/daughter relationships are described in terms of friendship (e.g., "She's not just my mother, she's my friend"). As Jean Marzollo writes in the May 1983 edition of *Mademoiselle,* adult mother/daughter relationships can be urged along by these two practical hints: "Whenever it might be helpful, try to forget that the two of you are related [and] don't say anything to your mother that you wouldn't say to a friend."[4] In other words, in order to be "friends" with your mother, you must disassociate yourself from the reality of your "relatedness" to her. In addition, it implies that the mother/daughter relationship is not "naturally" mutual but rather "naturally" conflictual. The discourse of friendship is mobilized precisely because we have so much difficulty conceptualizing mother/daughter mutuality and reciprocity within the terms of their own relationship, within the terms of familial relating.

Even articles that set out as critical of the inevitable conflict paradigm end up repeating many of its terms. For example, an article by Grace Baruch, Rosalind Barnett, and Caryl Rivers attempts to provide alternative data to counter the new wave of mother bashing that Nancy Friday made acceptable (especially to women) in *My Mother/My Self*. The authors acknowledge, "The American mother has not had an easy time of it over the last few generations. In the 1940s she was roundly charged with 'Momism'—of being overprotective and too indulgent towards her children. . . . Then, when she looked to her own life, bending over backward not to 'smother,' new experts appeared to tell her she might be causing 'alienation' by too *little* mothering." Nancy Friday herself is taken to task for seeing mothers "as being locked in mortal combat with her daughters." They report, on the contrary, "that the majority of relationships between adult women and their mothers are characterized by warmth, companionship and compassion."[5]

What Baruch, Barnett, and Rivers give with one hand, they take away with the other, for this alternative testimony is placed within a developmental framework that allows for the positive interpretation while conceding the "truth" of the opposing position that stresses separation, struggle, and the quest for autonomy. Lest anyone worry that this data indicate "that all the mother-daughter *angst* we have been hearing about is nonexistent" or that it is all "a tempest in a teapot," the authors are quick to stress that they are speaking primarily of adult mothers and daughters, where the inevitable battle has already been waged. By using a simplified framework borrowed from Chodorow, they are able to argue that, on the contrary, "it is not surprising that many younger women seem locked in ego-conflict with their mothers" because they are not yet able to see them as less than "giants." In claiming that the adult relationship is different, they thus rely on the inherent conflict model: "But by age 35 . . . most women have completed this process. The inherent conflict in many mother-daughter relationships need not signify a permanent, ongoing battle; it may simply be a part of that difficult process of growing up."[6] Although the framework has been modified to portray the battle in time-limited and developmental terms, the fact remains that the battle metaphor, and the idea of inherency itself, remains unaltered.

This idea of inherent struggle is almost always connected with its developmental result: separation. The "loving and letting go" motif emerges in 1980s popular culture with a vengeance, cropping up in practically my entire sample. Evelyn Bassoff's 1988 *Mothers and Daughters: Loving and Letting Go* states this explicitly in her first sentence: "Although most love relationships are a coming together, the love relationship between a mother and her adolescent daughter requires that each take leave of the other." As much as possible, this "loving and letting go" theme is naturalized so as to appear as the eternal psychological truth: "Maternity has two seemingly opposite aspects: A mother's tasks are to create a unity with her child and then . . . to dissolve it. Yet, as psychoanalyst Helen Deutsch wrote, most mothers suffer as they cut the psychic umbilical cord that ties them to their children; the wish to preserve this tie is inherent in motherliness and its renunciation is one of the major challenges of motherhood."[7]

Here we get a hint of a very powerful theme in both feminist and nonfeminist writing of recent years: the "natural" move of mothers toward "symbiotic unity" with their daughters. In order to maintain the separation battle motif, mother must be understood as inherently reluctant to "let go": she naturally yearns to keep the daughter her "little girl," or, as Pober puts it, "Mothers strive for fusion, while their offspring seek disengagement."[8]

Not only must mothers separate from their adolescent daughters, but they must cut the "ties that bind" from their own mothers: "In order to realize the full possibilities of her individual life . . . the middle-aged mother must not only separate from her adolescent daughter, she must also complete her separation from her aging mother. It is, after all, only as mothers and daughters *grow* apart, that each becomes a full woman." This final line speaks volumes: a woman's selfhood is here defined as her ability to "grow apart" from another woman. Not only does this define feminine selfhood negatively, but the only positive affirmation of selfhood comes through an identification with men. Bassoff again reiterates explicitly what is implicit in so much of the ideological framework of separation: that the end result of separation from mother is not only "autonomy" or "maturity" but, more exactly, identification with men: "As the little girl grows into young womanhood, her awakening sexuality threatens the exclusive mother/daughter bond. . . . As a young girl passes into womanhood, she leaves the open sunlit world of childhood and moves into the mysterious dark world of love and passion. She leaves her mother behind to meet her lovers."[9] This was, after all, Nancy Friday's bottom line: that ties to mother retard, distort, and inhibit the full realization of male-centered femininity.

Writing in *Woman's Day* in 1981, Janet Chase spells this out clearly and adds to the traditional separation motif a dimension of mother's lost opportunities that is clearly ideological runoff from the feminist critique of domesticity: "One of the hardest things a mother must do . . . is to allow her daughter to grow up. . . . And that brings up an important issue: The woman who has ignored other-than-mother dimensions of her self-image may well have a much tougher time letting her daughter separate and grow up."[10] The double bind here is extraordinary: mother cannot "let go" properly if she is too domestic (only a mother); yet that very ideology of woman as wife/mother was precisely the one she was reared on. The difference here between the Wyliesque version of "momism" and this 1980s version is that here mother's culpability lies not in her attempt to be too "masculine" (e.g., not in her position as worker) but rather the opposite: Mother is now made into "mom" because of her *lack* of a more engaged and social life. In either scenario, maternal culpability and neurosis are unquestioned.

This theme of the mother/daughter relationship as a "love/hate" one is typified in a 1988 work by family therapist Ann Grizzle. As with many other texts and articles, much is said in the title itself: *Mother Love, Mother Hate: Breaking Dependent Love Patterns in Family Relationships.* The move here, as in so much of the literature, is from a more inclusive discussion of "family relationships" (which could include fathers, for example) to a specific and definite location: mother. Grizzle's book, relying on her own experience as a family therapist and using clinical anecdotes, describes "loved and loving people" who have "real and even crippling problems" caused by a family pattern "in which necessary, caring love isn't balanced by the encouragement of independence." In other words, she is speaking here of "overprotectiveness." Grizzle then goes on to describe the basic ingredients of the dependent love pattern, which includes a mother who is overinvolved and a father who is underinvolved. Although Grizzle, like so many of her colleagues, is quick to point out that no one person is to blame for this unhealthy family pattern, all her examples are of "overinvolved" mothers and their correspondingly infantilized daughters or sons. Even the test she gives to ascertain if the reader is an overdependent child contains explicit references to actions relating only to the mother, such as "You secretly worry about what Mom would do if she didn't have you to fuss over" or "Your mother-in-law, or your mother, is more in charge of your life than you are." The so-called underinvolved father only signifies a mild "lack," but the overinvolved mother is the creator of the dysfunction itself. The cure, as usual, is more father and less mother: "The greatest challenge for adult children who have grown up in loving but over-caring homes is to break free of the Dependent Love Pattern. . . . To achieve this goal, you first must learn to 'leave' home. Most likely, you're too closely tied to your mother; you lack a deep relationship with your father."[11]

Victoria Secunda (whose book, *When You and Your Mother Can't Be Friends: Resolving the Most Complicated Relationship in Your Life*, comes replete with appreciative jacket blurbs by none other than Dr. Spock) continues down the love/hate road by telling us, "What we know of love we learned from our mothers [and] what we know of hate we learned from her as well. Love and hate are the tandem cadences of the mother-daughter connection."[12]

Along with this "love-hate" relationship theme is the ever present ideology of separation and the need for the daughter to claim herself as an "independent person." This is often placed in the context of a scenario that depicts mother as clinging to daughter as little girl and daughter as struggling to be free of the weight of maternal overinvolvement. Almost all "friction" between mothers and daughters is explained using this one narrative strategy. Theodore Rubin, writing in *Ladies Home Journal*, responds to a daughter who complains that she and her mother have been fighting a lot lately and her mother has not been as supportive as she used to be. Working only from that small bit of information about the two women, the doctor makes this pronouncement: "It's no coincidence that suddenly there's friction between you and your mother. The reasons are complex. For one, your mother is obviously having trouble seeing you as a separate person. Like many mothers, she's made you into an idealized version of herself—and then feels compelled to compete with you."[13] He goes on to invoke the daughter's need to "cut the umbilical cord" that ties her to a mother who, he claims, is motivated by overidentification as well as envy of the daughter's success.

A 1986 article in *McCall's* called "How To Get Over Your Mother" visualizes this idea perfectly. The picture introducing the article is of a "dress for success" young woman with a rope around her waist, trying to cut it with a pair of scissors. At the other end of the rope—holding on with all her might—is an older woman dressed stereotypically like a housewife. Mother is not only demonized in this 1980s version, but made pathetic as well: we are to pity these mothers whose own lives have been so paltry, so lacking, and who thus feel the need to drain us of our young, vibrant life, suck from us not only the juices of our youth but the excitement of our careers: "Besides, when your mother undermines your confidence . . . your intelligence . . . and your diet . . . you know it has more to do with her than you. Emotionally, you lurch into a fetal position, but intellectually you understand she's just competing, compensating and trying to maintain her control." [14]

Author Mary McHugh echoes this statement when she notes, "Pulling away can be painful, but not until we break old parent-child patterns can we get *free* of Mom's judgement and control . . . then find the way to a new and better understanding." She goes on to clue us in on mom's failed life and remind us of her more halcyon days: "You may see your mother as a slightly overweight lady wearing Love That Pink lipstick, but she was once like you—sharp and smart and ready to conquer the world. Then came marriage and a family. . . . Somewhere along the way, she began to let life happen to her instead of grabbing at experiences. Rediscover the young woman she once was. You'll probably like her." [15]

How far is this from the work discussed in Chapter 5? Is this really that different from the explicitly feminist work of writers like Eichenbaum and Orbach and Chernin? The popular discourses are now borrowing from feminism to put a new spin on maternal culpability. Many women's magazine articles and popular nonfiction of the eighties hide their retro sentiments under the guise of a glib feminism. Indeed, numerous authors, such as Evelyn Bassoff in her new book, *Mothering Ourselves: Help and Healing for Adult Daughters*, are quick to name and condemn the mother-blame that permeated so much prefeminist literature. Yet the motif of mother as inherently damaging to daughter's psyche is (perhaps more obliquely) still invoked, even if we are now urged (in the name of feminism?) to "forgive her." Popular pundit Colette Dowling, no feminist, to be sure, locates her tired separation theme within a vaguely defined milieu of feminism that sounds suspiciously like Chernin's theme of the "oppressed mother/liberated daughter": "Girls today are confused by the contradictions in their mothers' lives, and by the discrepancy between what mother *says* and what she *does*. Mothers still give double messages, and the daughters perceive very early that for all her bows to feminism, mother is far from free. Rather, she is anxious, self-absorbed, and often intimidated by daddy."[16]

Many of these books and articles are quick to point out their aversion to "mother bashing" and to note the role of the daughter in constructing a more positive relationship with her mother. Nevertheless, one such article by Elizabeth Tener still frames the relationship in terms of a timeless and primordial bond ("the tie to mother is primitive and profound") and thus sets the narrative stage for the (necessary) "process of cutting this emotional cord."[17] In the true tradition of self-help literature, the author lists the different types of problem mothers (including all the usual suspects of dominating, infantilizing, dependent, etc., but with the added attraction of the "unliberated" mother) and then offers a seven-step "Blueprint for Improving Mother/Daughter Relationships."

A more concise version of this can be found in Barbara Creaturo's article, where she proposes a neat two-step approach to "making friends with Mom." The first step is "Liberation from Mother's Power," and the second is "Forgiveness of her Mistakes."[18] *Mademoiselle* author Annie Gottlieb wonders about "Two women . . . bonded forever by blood and love, rivalry and rage. She gave you life, taught you how to be a woman. Can you ever forgive her?" Never fear, that primordial bond will win out: "No matter whether you overidentify with your mother, reject her ways or strike a happy balance, one fact remains: Your womanhood is a unique, complex answer to your mother's—a lifelong argument full of love and anger, the last word of which is 'Yes.'"[19]

Mothers are now seen to be "poignant" in their inability to "love and let go," their inability to follow the scripts written for them. Aimee Ball, writing in *Mademoiselle,* describes this poignancy, and her language—that of violence and death—is telling here: "There is a poignancy that comes from the recognition of how desperately our mothers still need us to be their children. We forge our emotional distance early on, killing them with small stab wounds, and then we make the job complete with physical distance—a distance they are constantly trying to close up."[20]

## The Perils of Enmeshment and the Rapture of Separation

The metaphor of separation as a violence, a wounding to mother, is no accident. Indeed, it is a defining feature of contemporary images, from the lighthearted "Rhoda" episodes in which the daughters consistently employ battle metaphors to describe their negotiations with their interfering mother to 1980s magazines where this metaphor reveals its ugly underside. Once again authors are telling us, "There is something about the mother-daughter connection that has far more potential for harm than the tie between mother and son."[21]

If this separation is depicted as a violent and inevitable battle, then what are the consequences for a daughter who does not win this particular war or for a mother who refuses to engage in it? *Enmeshment* here emerges as the new pathology of female psychology. In this narrative, separation and struggle are not problematic and are rarely questioned, but are rather necessary parts of this teleological move toward mature adulthood: "'If there were such sameness,' says Donald S. Williamson, Ph.D., director of the Houston Family Institute, 'we would be looking at a very immature daughter, a person in whom no developmental process had taken place. The more extensively a woman reflects her mother, the less likely it is that she possesses an authentic self.'"[22] There it is, no minced words. The carrot on the end of the stick of separation is maturity and adulthood. What is this saying, too, about mothers? If to reflect mother is to be inauthentic, then mother herself is necessarily demeaned and inauthentic. If it is "immature" to be like someone, to resemble her, then mustn't one assume that that person is not worth being like, is not worth resembling?

More pointed attacks on the perils of resembling mother can be seen in many of the TV specials on mothers and daughters. As Ella

Taylor notes, this seems to be a recurring feature of eighties television:

The theme of the disillusioned career woman returning home to her suburban family has been featured in more than one late-1980s made-for-TV movie. Thus the celebration of the opening up of women's roles in the 1970s shows becomes, in the 1980s, at best a rehearsal of the costs of careerism for women, at worst an outright reproof for women who seek challenging work. In this way the genuine difficulties women face in reconciling home and work are often casually translated into a backlash against feminism itself.[23]

One of these shows stands out dramatically, as it seems on first viewing to resonate with many of the ideas of the feminist movement. "Supermom's Daughter" borrows from feminism very selectively and, in doing so, presents an ideological orientation that is infinitely more subtle in its sexism than, say, "Father Knows Best." In this HBO special, star TV news reporter mom is horrified to learn that her teenage daughter has swerved off the academic fast track and is instead intent on achieving an early marriage, producing lots of children, and working in early childhood education. This is every feminist mother's worst nightmare: her daughter wants nothing of the life she has struggled to make available to her. Mother's horror is here treated with gentle humor. In one scene, her guilt ("I haven't been a good mother. . . . I didn't bake cookies for you.") is playfully negated by the daughter's insistence that her choice has nothing to do with her mother's life-style. Yet, as in *'night, Mother,* we find that a bit hard to believe because all our cultural signposts point ineluctably to mother's responsibility.

A television show like this locates itself firmly within the ideological framework of the 1980s, which presents an image of beset womanhood, of striving career women suddenly faced with the deep truth of their bottomless need for hearth and home, hubby and the kids. In this age of *Fatal Attractions* and *Baby Booms,* feminist struggles and gains are reduced to the issue of personal choices, which, we are now informed, have created a no-win situation: we can't have it all. The messages of many 1980s films, TV shows, and other forms of popular culture are precisely this: to further dichotomize mother and woman, this time adding a sort of postfeminist gloss by identifying "woman" not only as sexual, but as climbing-to-the-top "superwoman." The "you can't have it all" issue emerges specifically as a response to real and substantive feminist changes in the workplace and in social and personal life. Thus the super-mom of the TV show confides to her housewife friend (and her daughter's idol) that she often envies her domestic life, and the friend appropriately follows suit, thus reinforcing the work/family dichotomy that has come to be defined as the crucial "postfeminist" issue.

Another 1980 HBO Special, "Mother and Daughter: The Loving War," reinforces this framework even more dramatically by making the mother a single parent who is clearly coded as "overinvolved" and has very little life beyond taking care of her daughter. This working-class mother scrimps and saves so the daughter can go to college and do more with her life than she was able to do with hers. True to form, this 1980s daughter rejects her mother's values to opt for the glories of wifedom.

But, of course, the point here is a woman doesn't have to opt for anything other than domesticity. Feminism, as a positive and constructive theory and political practice, is here circumscribed around the issue of choice (e.g., feminism means having a choice to be a worker or a housewife) and then denigrated by a discourse that declares that too much choice has ruined American women and de-prived them of the joys of family and motherhood.

Yet another TV movie not only focuses on mothers and daughters, but raises the stake by introducing a (wiser than thou) grandmother as well. "Family Secrets" stars Stephanie Powers as the overworked "career mother" Jessie, Maureen Stapleton as her stalwart mother Maggie, and Melissa Gilbert as Jessie's precocious, "parentified" daughter Sarah. In the midst of getting her second divorce, ad exec mom returns to her family homestead to help her mother pack up and move after dad's recent death. The first family secret is revealed rather quickly, as we learn of bitter Sarah's illegitimacy. In the first of many confrontation scenes between several mother/daughter pairs, Sarah confronts her mother around her illegitimacy and "abandonment." The grandmother raised her until she was nine:

*Daughter:*    "You raised me? That's a laugh."
*Mother:*    "I worked my butt off to give you what you wanted."

*Daughter:*     "I wanted *you*. And you weren't there. I was stuck in an apartment with a nanny while you were at your damn office!"

*Mother:*     "Don't lay that guilt trip on me Sarah. My mother was home all day, and it didn't keep me from being neurotic."

The daughter's speech here is eerily reminiscent of the daughter's speech in the 1959 version of *Imitation of Life,* albeit more explicitly savvy about the guilt placed on mothers who work outside the home. But the new motif of life cycle kicks in to stir the pot of daughterly angst, as Jessie next relays to *her* mother: "I just realized how much alike the two of you are! I spent the first part of my life worrying about your approval, now I'm going to spend the rest of my life worrying about hers?" The grandmother replies with the telling truth of inevitable conflict: "Now Jessie, hold on! If Sarah's taking you on for working, it's normal. A girl's got to pick on her mother for *something.*"

The final confrontation scene occurs during the last big dinner at the old family home, where, among other things, Jessie reveals her knowledge of her father's infidelity, a secret the all-knowing grandmother was already privy to. After yet another nasty fight between Jessie and Maggie, Sarah (screaming at the mother, "Are you satisfied?") runs out of the house into the arms of a rather unscrupulous young man. But Jessie's "mistake" is not to be repeated. Instead, the daughter returns home to announce her independence from her mother. This independence includes her decision not to go to college ("That's your dream, not mine") and to stay with her grandmother until she figures out her life.

The next morning, as Jessie prepares to leave, she gets a phone call from her office (which, incidentally, interrupts a poignant confession from her mother) informing her that she has lost the big account she has been working on. Jessie slips into maudlin and drunken despair ("I obviously cannot be a mother and manage a big account at the same time") and is temporarily cheered up by a chorus line dancing mother. The scene ends with Jessie in tears, claiming, "It's not that I've lost the account, it's that I've lost everything." But never fear, the newly vulnerable and chastened mom is now acceptable to the demanding teen. Having already admitted to Maggie that "Sarah's a woman. I have to let go," Jessie is surprised to see Sarah show up on the morning of her departure, suitcase in hand, assuring mom that she still needs her (read: Broken mom needs strong daughter) but will not change her mind about college. Daughter confidently jumps into the driver's seat and they ride into the proverbial sunset. Daughter can now be "an adult" once mom has been made vulnerable and has "given her up."

A Crawford-like evil mom emerges in a 1987 HBO after-school special called "Terrible Things My Mother Told Me." A nasty, harried working mom gets saved not by a man or by death (which would have been the typical response years ago), but by the discovery that the origins of her "illness" are in *her* mother's "emotional abuse" of her. After calling a hotline number, the young teen daughter informs her mother (with all the weight of current psychology behind her), "Mom, I think we're both victims. Your mom yelled at you, you yell at me, now I yell at Katie [her younger sister]." Daughter now doesn't go off into the sunset with the male savior, but rather takes a weeping and penitent mother off into the brilliant light cast by psychotherapy.[24]

Popular writers such as Secunda reinforce this ideology of mother as pitied victim of her own mother's pathology: "The process of healing includes seeing one's mother as *other* than oneself; recognizing that she is the legatee of *her* mother's behavior; acknowledging how terribly limited her choices may have been; realizing that such mothers are more to be pitied." The "child within" rears its (popular) head when the same author declares, "Most unloving mothers don't set out to destroy their daughters. But within them often resides a child who also felt unloved by her mother and who, because she is emotionally wounded, cannot help repeating with her daughter the patterns of her past."[25] As we have seen with many of the psychoanalytic writers in Chapter 5, this idea of the endless reproduction of pathology (from mother to daughter ad nauseam) is a catchy one: "I needed to examine the legacy of self-doubt passed on to me by my mother, and her mother before her. I also had to face how I had passed my self problems along to my daughter."[26]

In all these representations—both the TV specials and the popular treatises—mother's work/career is not denigrated or depicted (as in *Mildred Pierce*) as damaging to her daughter's psyche. Indeed, the ideological discourse has shifted to new ground, implicitly challenging the meaning and substance of feminist gains by portraying these "daughters of feminism" as finding fulfillment as barefoot and pregnant teenagers. In the TV special, the daughter becomes the psychological agent to rescue her mother from the inevitable cycle of abuse and victimization (at the hands of women!) by marching bravely off to therapy and the recovery of the "child within."

Films of the 1980s similarly incorporate feminism while framing the mother/daughter relationship within the (implicitly) antifeminist theme of inevitable conflict. *Terms of Endearment* (1983) is most assuredly the (contemporary) "classic" mother/daughter film, one whose very title brings instantaneous recognition. It was immensely popular, winning Academy Awards for Shirley MacLaine, Jack Nicholson, and director James Brooks.

*Terms of Endearment* has been heralded as a "breakthrough" film about mothers and daughters and about women in general. In large part, this reading is based on the fact that an older woman—a mother—is shown to be sexually active while still retaining her maternal orientation. *Terms of Endearment* presents itself as a work responsive to the women's movement—a film that moves decisively away from the demonized and desexualized mothers that typified films of an earlier era. Although we cannot overlook the significance of this shift, *Terms* reinforces the "love/hate" and "loving and letting go" themes that have dominated both the women's magazines and much of the more explicitly feminist work.

*Terms* was presented as a timeless tale of the enduring and loving bond between mother and daughter. There *is* a certain rapprochement at the end when the daughter dies. But the daughter does, after all, die, and the mother is left to redo her mothering: she now takes her daughter's children, settles in with the astronaut next door, and returns to mothering. By film's end, she is brought back into the nuclear family, as Ellen Seiter notes: "In *Terms of Endearment* Aurora Greenway, Emma's mother, presents a problematic figure because she is unmarried. Throughout the film, Aurora creates disruptions. The film's narrative can be seen as the process of recuperating Aurora into a 'normal' relationship with a man within a family. The story redeems Aurora as a mother at precisely the same time that it redeems her as a woman, by finally replacing her within the family as the one who cares for children."[27]

In *Terms of Endearment,* Aurora is a bad mother because she is not in a relationship with a man. It is only after her affair with Garrett Breedlove, the astronaut, that she stops nagging and endlessly phoning her daughter. Aurora's affair "cures" her of her overmothering, her selfishness, and her hysterical behavior. She becomes a truly sympathetic character only after she relinquishes control to the man. As the contrast between the sexually repressed, almost sterile mother and the sexually aggressive, eminently fecund daughter begins to fade with the mother's rebirth through her affair with Breedlove, the narrative firmly moves to focus on the intimacy and love between these two women. Indeed, after mother is "liberated" through her newfound sexuality, she is able to be both confidante and advocate for her daughter.

In two repetitious scenes, Aurora and Emma are in bed together in the family home. In the first, following the father's funeral, we see a needy Aurora imposing her vulnerability on her young (and thus "parentified") daughter Emma. As Aurora crawls into Emma's bed the night following the funeral, we are immediately struck by Aurora's inability to be an "appropriate" mother (she should be comforting her daughter, not vice versa). The opening shot of the film shows an obsessive young mother, Aurora, pinching baby Emma in her crib until she cries to make sure she is alive. After mom finds freedom (and loosens up) in the arms of the raunchy astronaut, she repeats the bedroom scene. But this time, deliriously giggly mom, legs intertwined with slightly wary daughter, speaks of the joy of sexual love, asserting her ability to befriend her daughter now that she has found liberation in male identification. In that sense, the classic narrative strategy of recuperating the wayward woman is reproduced.

In addition, this film introduces the "love-hate" theme that has been so popular in recent years. As the film moves through the life cycles of these two women, one gets the sense of this endless and almost timeless push-me-pull-you pendulum, exemplified in the popular literature as well: "Mother and daughter, daughter and mother; it is as if we are part of some prepackaged, seamless unit whose characteristics have all been decided ahead of time, by someone else. An unconscious bondage develops in which mothers and daughters rely too heavily on each other for identity. We don't know how to get free to be ourselves."[28] The notion of life cycle is

Fig. 24. Now that repressed mom Aurora (Shirley MacLaine) has found sexual liberation with a lewd astronaut, she can warmly engage in girl talk with her rather bemused daughter Emma (Debra Winger) in the Oscar-sweeping *Terms of Endearment*. (Paramount Pictures, 1983; photo courtesy of Photofest)

important here. Many popular representations of the 1980s construct the mother/daughter narrative around this notion of life cycle, itself increasingly popular in the late 1970s and 1980s within the social sciences. The demarcations of a woman's life are set in stone here as moving from childhood intimacy ("bonding") through adolescence ("separating") and then to marriage and children, which supposedly brings a new form of bonding based on the daughter's new role as mother. These narratives often include the "role reversal" scenario where daughter now "mothers" an old and infirm mother.

## Mommie Meanest: Narcissistic Moms and Neurotic Daughters

In a darker vein, the evil mother theme reemerges with a vengeance that much surpasses Charlotte Vale's almost quaintly Victorian misguided mother. No film typifies this image of the demon-

Fig. 25. Evil mother Joan Crawford (played by Faye Dunaway) faces off against persecuted daughter Christina in the grotesque vamp *Mommie Dearest*. (Paramount Pictures, 1981; photo courtesy of Museum of Modern Art Film Stills Archive)

ized mother better than *Mommie Dearest* (1981). Indeed, the wire hanger scene (in which the Crawford character brandishes a hanger in fury at her cowed daughter's neglect of her cleaning duties) has come to signify to daughters everywhere the violence behind the facade of maternal nurturance.

This film also points to what Nietzsche might have called eternal recurrence or Freud might have called the return of the repressed. For, in *Mommie Dearest*, Faye Dunaway portrays Joan Crawford as the evil mother incarnate, Crawford herself having played a less virulent version of this in one of the most famous (fictional) mother/ daughter narratives of all time, *Mildred Pierce*. The star and the story, the person and the myth here merge to collapse both representational and historical distinctions. There are even scenes when Dunaway as Crawford rehearses lines from *Mildred Pierce* with her victim/daughter. All this is within the cinematic context of a film taken from an account written by Crawford's own daughter, Christina. This trope (tell-all biographies of evil star mothers written by angry daughters) seemed to become very popular in the 1980s. Crawford's daughter wrote the most famous one, but Bette Davis's daughter B. D. Hyman also wrote one (*My Mother's Keeper*), as did Cheryl Crane, daughter of Lana Turner. The irony that all three of these real-life mothers played in famous mother/daughter films

Fig. 26. Even after death, mommie meanest looms ominously behind her newly liberated daughter. (Paramount Pictures, 1981; photo courtesy of Museum of Modern Art Film Stills Archive)

sorely tests any theory of the media that sees images as soundly set off from what we call "real life." [29]

The etiology of Joan's neurotic behavior is spelled out in the early moments of *Mommie Dearest:* her mother was bad, she had too many husbands, they were poor, she never had a father, so now she thinks she can "do it all" ("I never had a father. . . . I can be a father *and* a mother."). So Joan's evil is here, in true psychoanalytic fashion, referred back to her own slovenly mother and the lack of a father figure. This constant referring back (the "mommy did it to me" school of thought) is unique to, or at least much more pronounced in, the present period. Although the mother in *Now, Voyager* was depicted as responsible for her daughter's illness, it was not presented as so inevitable as it appears in contemporary narratives. Nowadays the unhealthy dyad has expanded to encompass a seemingly endless trail of abusive mothers. Although Charlotte's mother was surely awful to the core, we never learn the reason for her nastiness, and it was definitely not referenced back to her own mother's behavior.

In contrast, even Joan's obsessive cleaning is portrayed as a response to her mother's uncleanliness. The desire to have a child is again seen as shaped by her own miserable childhood and the desire to "do it differently." As Joan says, "I'm going to give you all the things I never had." The echo of *Mildred Pierce* renders Joan's motivations for adopting a daughter immediately suspect: she wants to "give her everything," which we all know is not good for a child. Like Mildred, she is punished for wanting and desiring too much.

She is also punished for what can only be described as her narcissism. The daughter is made to be an object for the cameras at all times. This presents an interesting aspect of the male gaze question: Joan is placed as the person who offers up her girl-child as a spectacle for the publicity men, and the blame for this seems to be placed firmly on the head of the mother, who is, after all, herself a "victim" of the male gaze.

*'night, Mother*, made in 1986, deserves brief mention, although the poor quality of the film doesn't do justice to what was a significant and thoughtful stage play about mothers and daughters. Anne Bancroft chose to play the mother as a stupid and slightly hysterical "Southern white trash" woman. Sissy Spacek's anemic portrayal of a daughter who decides to take her own life never gets at the anger and venom directed at the mother in the stage version.

To a great extent, *'night, Mother* is a film version of the "too much mother/not enough father" trope that pervades current discourses on mothers and daughters, feminist and nonfeminist alike. The specter of the dead father haunts this film: his picture is moved around the house, his gun is the one she uses, he is the subject of their fights, a specifically father-centered discussion is the catalyst for their battle throughout the film. In some ways, this film is about a "daddy's girl" whose one link to any depth and vitality was through her father. In one scene, in which the mother accuses her daughter of caring more for the father than for her, the daughter

Fig. 27. Escaping the mother was never represented so literally as in *'night, Mother,* starring Sissy Spacek as a daughter driven to suicide as her mother helplessly looks on. (Universal, 1986; photo courtesy of Museum of Modern Art Film Stills Archive)

belittles her mother's allegation by claiming, "you were just jealous because I'd rather talk to him than wash the dishes with you." The mother's painfully honest reply ("I was jealous because you'd rather talk to him than anything") typifies her dilemma: she is the one faced with her daughter's suicide threats and daily life with her daughter (symbolized by the "washing dishes"); the father represents the escape from that life, from "reality" in a sense. *Of course* the mother is jealous. Who wouldn't be?

The climactic guilt scene follows, in which the mother pleads for her daughter to stop the talk of suicide and says the classic lines:

| Mother: | "It has to be something I did. . . . I don't know what I did, but I did it. I know. This is all my fault Jessie but I don't know what to do about it now." |
| Daughter: | "It doesn't have anything to do with you." |
| Mother: | "Everything you do has to do with me, Jessie. You can't do anything . . . wash your face or cut your finger." |

The double bind is again vividly expressed here: the whole film leads us to believe that it is the mother's fault. Although the daughter explicitly opposes that interpretation ("It doesn't have anything to do with you"), she also implicitly supports it through her insistence on making her mother witness the nightmare of her own daughter's suicide: she is killing herself to escape her mother. The mother doesn't know what to do, how to reverse the "damage" she has unwittingly wrought on her daughter.

Woody Allen's 1987 Bergmanesque film *September* presents a very 1980s twist on the evil mother/victim daughter theme that is similar to both *Mommie Dearest* and earlier films such as *Mildred Pierce*. Allen has never been known to be a filmmaker sympathetic to the situations of women; quite the contrary, in fact. Indeed, women in Allen's films typically play the role of beautiful Gentile foils to his nebbishy neurotic Jewish prince. *September* is something of an exception to his usual setting because it moves out of urban Manhattan and into Allen's American equivalent of the Bergman petit bourgeois suburb. The entire film takes place over a weekend in the rambling Vermont country home of Lane (Mia Farrow). Lane's postbreakdown angst is complicated by the presence of her good friend Stephanie (Diane Wiest), who has come to stay for a bit, a young tenant and would-be writer Peter (Sam Waterston), with whom Lane has carried on an affair over the summer, an elderly neighbor (Denholm Elliott) who loves Lane, and Lane's visiting mother Diane (Elaine Strich) and stepfather (Jack Warden).

The central theme is the tension between mousy, insecure Lane and her vibrant, loud, egocentric mother, a former movie queen. The family secret, revealed in a climactic confrontation scene, is that when Lane was fourteen, she killed her mother's gangster lover (à la Lana Turner's daughter, Cheryl Crane). But the real secret, which we find out almost at the end of the film, is that mom actually pulled the trigger, and Lane was forced to take the rap for her.

The bossy mother's visit taxes the patience of an already flustered Lane, trying desperately to sell the house so she can move to New York and get on with her life (after a recent suicide attempt). The writer with whom she is in love is in love with Lane's friend Stephanie. Lane's mother thwarts her well-laid plans by announcing that she wants to keep the house, but Lane's anger (this is when the family secret is revealed) causes mother eventually to give in, leaving Lane the house at the end of the film.

The film is difficult to categorize because in many ways it represents a very modern perspective on mothers and daughters. This is mother-blame of a new strain, concerned not with simple neglect or with elementary overinvolvement, but with a sort of malicious narcissism born of a too independent mother and an overshadowed daughter. If this seems familiar, it might be because the ideologies of mother-blame have taken on a new edge in the age of the "working woman," the "latchkey child," and the "mommy track." Now mother is too sexual, too lively, too engaged with her own life. The plea of the daughter is now "Hey Mom, what about me? How dare you get on with your life? Getting on with your life has cost me mine!"

Numerous scenes throughout *September* establish Lane's exasperation with her mother and strongly hint at maternal responsibility for Lane's inability to move on with her life. In fact, Lane is quite explicit in blaming her mother (and her mother's active life) for her own stagnation; as Lane says to Peter about the shooting, "Yeah, she went on with her life. I got stuck with the nightmares." This is the heart of the double bind message: Mother is condemned for leaving the past behind, for not remaining forever guilty and miserable about the family tragedy, for living a happy life. She is a bad mother because she goes on and because her refusal of paralyzing guilt means the daughter cannot go on. Yet if she were to remain forever guilty, forever in penance, she would inevitably oppress the daughter with that guilt; she would pass it on to her as a legacy of pain to carry with her throughout her life. She cannot win.

Right from the beginning, we know that Lane is not at all pleased with her mother's presence in the country home. She enters the house a few minutes into the film, leans against the door, and says (with exasperation): "God, I can't believe my mother. She's out there, she's made friends with Peter and she's trying to get him to write her biography. Her stupid life, as told to." So the sexual competition is set up right away: mother is taking her man away. Indeed, in a later scene with Lane and Peter, just about five minutes into the film, Peter is complaining about his frustration with his work, and Lane blames it on the time spent with her mother: "Well, if you wouldn't let my mother seduce you. . . ." Mother is thus both more sexual than daughter and more interesting, and this "problem" is referenced through the desired man: he finds mother more engaging than daughter. This exchange is immediately followed by Lane's devastating line ("Yeah, she went on with her life. I got stuck with the nightmares"), thus narratively linking the mother's seductiveness and vibrancy with the daughter's depression and suicide attempt.

In an early, revealing scene, the mother enters from outside with her husband and Peter, the writer. She comes in like a hurricane, graphically epitomizing the difference between her and the daughter, who has previously entered the house with slumped shoulders and an air of sad resignation. The choppy dialogue that follows perfectly sets up the mother as narcissistic and self-serving and the daughter as withdrawn victim of maternal egomania:

| Mother: | "Lane, I asked the Richmonds over for dinner tonight—I thought we could all have a little party." |
| Daughter: | "What did you do that for? Peter and I were going to drive into town tonight. We were supposed to see the new Kurosawa film." |
| Mother: | "Oh god, I'm sorry. Why didn't you say something?" |
| Daughter: | "I did." |
| Peter: | "That's OK Lane. We can catch it another night." |
| Daughter: | "OK. But it's only there tonight." |
| Mother: | "Where was I?" |

As the mother talks to her, Lane is almost completely off-screen, deep in the background, almost telescoped at the end of the full images of the mother and her male attendees. When she utters the line, "Where was I?" the mother turns away from an already retreating, small Lane and, putting her arm around Peter, walks away. Thus the mother both physically and linguistically ignores the last line and recognizes only the resigned "OK." The daughter's reality, her wishes, are thus completely blotted out by the mother.

The pivotal scene occurs about ten minutes into the film. It is shot in the mother's bedroom, where she is getting ready for the little party with her husband. She says to him, "Lane's changed towards me. She used to get such a kick out of me." At that point, the daughter enters the room when mother and hubby are kissing; she hides behind the door during the entire scene and barely edges her way out. Mother takes up most of the screen and is often shot from below to make her appear even more formidable; the daughter seems small, afraid, and childlike compared to her mother. As they argue about Lane's refusal to move on with her life, the mother's breeziness is again made manifest, "If your life hasn't worked out, stop blaming me for it. It's up to you to take the bull by the horns." The scene shifts from touchy argument to bittersweet poignancy, with the mother gazing into her mirror, musing on her advanced years, and urging her daughter to "make something of herself" while she's still "got the chance." The scene ends with the return of the narcissistic mother as she switches abruptly from this expression of concern to a brisk attention to her evening attire.

Again, this scene reinforces the idea of mother as self-involved, domineering, unconcerned with daughter's problems, yet at the same time intrusive and judgmental, commenting with unmistaken glee on the daughter's failures in love ("The one thing you shouldn't do is let your desperation show. . . . I always felt there was a fatal element of *hunger* in your last affair."). She is sensitive only when it concerns her; then she moves blithely off to breezy trivialities.

This scene could be read a different way. One could understand the mother as powerful, refusing to take responsibility for the daughter's life but taking full responsibility for her own, concerned about the daughter and supportive of her romantic adventures, energetic and full of life, wanting her daughter to live fully, as she had, wanting to pass on her own youth to her. Strangely enough, upon first viewing, I read it completely "against the grain," contrary to the "preferred reading" offered up by the text. In that particular scene, I perceived Lane as insipid, whining, complaining: blaming her mother for whatever befell her. I completely identified with the mother's exasperation ("stop blaming me . . . get on with your life") and felt annoyed at Lane's continual attempts to squelch her mother's exuberance. Clearly, I read it this way at least in part from having done this research on mothers and daughters, for everyone I questioned informally about this film, although not exactly thrilled with Lane's excessive whininess, nevertheless saw it as resulting from this narcissistic and overblown mother.

The only moment when the mother is portrayed sympathetically is qualified by her obvious drunkenness, rendering her apparent love for her daughter more than a little pathetic. She is sitting drunk over a Ouija board and talking to her dead husband, father of Lane: "Your daughter hates me. Our daughter hates me, and I love her. She's my one child and I want her to be happy. . . . I want her to forgive me." But even this sympathetic display could be seen as yet one more instance of her selfishness: she wants the daughter to forgive *her* so *she* can rest easier.

This film perfectly points out some of the double binds mothers and daughters are placed in. If a mother is too aggressive, too sexual (Lane is jealous that Peter is spending so much time with her mother), has her own life, and is self-determined and independent, she has denied her daughter the proper maternal care she needs to flourish; she is a bad mother who is selfish and narcissistic. (Mother here is endlessly talking about how she looks, how others look.) If she is self-sacrificing, solely domestic, and selfless, the daughter wants to escape from her, to leave that boring and depressing domestic/maternal world. If she does much for her daughter, is engaged and involved, she is intrusive, controlling, and "overinvolved." Many women blame their mothers for being boring, not engaged enough with the outside world, not "worldly" enough; yet if they are those things, they are neglectful and selfish mothers, capable of producing "maternal deprivation."

In this contemporary film where a mother is actually allowed to be sexual and alive, she is shown to be predatory, competitive with her daughter's lover, and, by extension, a neglectful parent. The daughter in this case is consequently desexualized, desensualized, and made out to be pathetic and a failure with men. No daughter ever wanted to grow up actually to be June Cleaver or the nearly anonymous mother in "Father Knows Best." Those domestic icons of the fifties are just that, icons, and almost never an image modern women actually strive to emulate. In this film, mother has dared to be "not just a mother," and daughter will inevitably suffer the results of her independence.

The most recent films on mothers and daughters do not bode

well for the future. The terribly miscast and woefully misbegotten remake of *Stella Dallas* (called simply *Stella* this time) starring Bette Midler as a swinging 1960s working-class barmaid (with a heart of gold and a truckload of working-girl integrity) only confirms the impossibility of the maternal sacrifice theme in an era of increasing (and increasingly sophisticated) mother-blame. Hewing very close to the original scenario, this *Stella* just can't tear at our heartstrings anymore. The narratives of sacrifice and class conflict have both been occluded by the onslaught of 1940s "momism," 1980s antifeminism, and the demise of popular representations of working-class life. Although the early Stella's martyrdom was so poignant in its exposure of the double binds of class and motherhood, this updated Stella is a retro narrative in search of a context, which no longer exists.

In *Postcards from the Edge*, Meryl Streep plays Suzanne Vale, the thinly disguised Carrie Fisher—author of the book and screenplay and daughter of Debbie Reynolds. An updated version of the bad Hollywood mother and her benighted daughter, the film traverses the terrain of *September* and *Terms of Endearment* all at once. Starting out as a bright and witty tell-all account of life in the Hollywood fast lane, it quickly slips into maternal melodrama overdrive. Once again, the brassy (but cracking inside) mother victimizes her hapless daughter, only to reunite in the requisite cataclysmic scene where mom's true vulnerability emerges, and daughter can now take care of the newly exposed mom.

Meryl Streep's Suzanne Vale is a young actor locked in a cycle of "B" movies and drug abuse. When an overdose lands her in a rehab hospital, the themes of maternal neglect and maternal narcissism (shades of *September*) emerge. Mother misses the "family thing" at the hospital and instead breezes in late only to ignore her recovering daughter and play beloved movie star to a gay male couple who "do her" in their drag show.

This theme of maternal narcissism—of mother overshadowing the daughter and thereby "causing" her suicide attempt (*September*) or drug overdose (*Postcards from the Edge*)—pervades this film. In a telling scene, mother has thrown daughter a welcome home party after her release from the hospital and forces her to sing for the crowd. Suzanne sings a melancholy song while mom mouths the words, coaching her from the sidelines as daughter stands in front of a framed portrait of mom from her showgirl days. When mother Doris gets up to sing after requests from the assembled throngs, the contrast couldn't be more stark. The daughter's mournful, bluesy "You Don't Know Me" is replaced by mom's brassy, high-kicking showtune, "I'm Still Here." Even the cutaways are different: when mom watches daughter's performance, she is intrusive, anxious, and coaching; when daughter watches mom, she is obviously admiring, breaking into spontaneous shouts of energetic applause.

As in *September*, mom is sexually competitive with daughter. When a man comes to pick Suzanne up and Doris flirts with him, Suzanne says to her, "I would just like to have some people of my own is all, without them having to like you so much . . . why do you have to completely overshadow me?" Mom's response to Suzanne's attempts to challenge her "narcissism" are almost identical to those of the mother in *September:* "I think you should just get over what happened to you in your adolescence. It is time to *move on.*"

But daughter cannot move on until mom is shown to be the weak and vulnerable figure we know her to be. The cataclysmic scene begins with mom dumping vodka in her health shake after having informed her daughter that her agent has run off with all Suzanne's money. As Suzanne sits stricken on the stairs, Doris comes up to stand on the other side of the banister, informing her that "it's no good feeling sorry for yourself." When Suzanne says that she wants to get out of the business, her mother is only able to respond with yet another self-involved story:

Doris: "Let's take this one thing at a time. First, everyone is always getting out of the business and b: you are just like me. Somedays, I wake up and. . . ."

Suzanne (talking over her): "Will you *please* stop telling me how to run my life for a couple of minutes. Isn't it enough that you were right?"

As the battle heats up, mother directly addresses the question of blame ("You feel sorry for yourself half the time for having a monster of a mother like me"). Although daughter denies it ("I never said you were a monster!") and denies her mother's responsibility for her drug taking ("I took the drugs, nobody made me!"), the rest

Fig. 28. Old movie queen Doris Mann (Shirley MacLaine) flirts shamelessly with daughter Suzanne's (Meryl Streep) boyfriend (played by Dennis Quaid) in *Postcards from the Edge.* (Columbia Pictures, 1990; photo courtesy of Photofest)

of the scene (as in *September* and *'night, Mother*) gives us ample evidence of mother's culpability:

| | |
|---|---|
| *Doris:* | "Go ahead and say it. You think I'm an alcoholic." |
| *Suzanne:* | "OK. I think you're an alcoholic." |
| *Doris:* | "Well, maybe I was an alcoholic when you were a teenager. But I had a nervous breakdown when my marriage failed and I lost all my money." |
| *Suzanne:* | "That's when I started taking drugs." |

So maternal culpability is clearly established here, or at least a causal relationship is set up between mother's drinking and daughter's drug abuse. But mother still resists:

Doris:    "Well, I got over it! And now I just drink like an Irishper-
          son. . . ."

Suzanne   (talking over her): "Yeah, I know, you just drink to relax. You
          just enjoy your *wine*, I know, you've told me mother. You
          don't want me to be a singer. *You're* the singer. *You're* the
          performer. I can't possibly compete with *you*. What if some-
          body won? You want me to do well, just not better . . . than
          you."

Mother now stomps haughtily up the stairs past the daughter, turning around to look down at her from the top. As the camera looks
up at her, from the daughter's angle, the imposing and threatening
mother screams at the daughter that she can "handle it" (unlike the
daughter) and then puts the question to her: "Will you please tell
me what is the awful thing I did to you when you were a child?"
Suzanne finally answers: "From the time I was nine years old you
gave me sleeping pills!" As mom pathetically defends herself ("They
were over-the-counter drugs, they were safe!"), she further implicates herself in a pattern of drug abuse and seductiveness toward
the daughter's friends that clearly gives the lie to the daughter's
earlier assertion of her own responsibility for her behavior. As the
camera leaves the imposing maternal figure and moves alongside
the daughter as she walks out the door, we hear off-camera (no
longer the powerful image at the top of the stairs) the mother's desperate plea: "Don't blame me, I did it all out of love for you."

The next scene brings in the all-knowing father figure cum film
director, played by Gene Hackman. He dispenses the wisdom
of the women's magazines and popular psychologists discussed
throughout this chapter: "Look, your mother did it to you and her
mother did it to her and back and back and back all the way to Eve.
At some point you just stop it and say fuck it: I start with me."
Armed with that tidbit of fatherly insight, Suzanne can care for her
(truly, deeply) vulnerable mom after she has a car accident while
driving under the influence. As tender daughter applies makeup to
the (denuded, unmasked, dewigged) mother, she is able to release
her anger as mother is able to admit her jealousy. Both mother and
daughter bounce back: mom goes out bravely to confront the press,
and daughter closes the film with a music video production scene
directed by the benign father figure previously seen granting solace
and advice to a distraught daughter.

Another recent film, *Mermaids*, starring Cher and Winona Ryder as a mother and daughter locked in adolescent angst, helps construct a similar genre of "isn't mom wacky but really pathological underneath it all?" After getting over the initial stretch of imagining Cher as a Jewish mother, we are treated to a narrative that is much more effective as a coming of age drama than as a story about mothers and daughters. The adolescent alienation of mother from daughter is highlighted by the daughter's persistent reference to her as "Mrs. Flax" during her omniscient narration. Cher plays Rachel Flax, a rebellious refugee from a family of kosher bakers who traipses around the country with two young daughters in tow. The theme of movement is a crucial one because daughter Charlotte's rebellion is often signified by anger at her mother's easy mobility and refusal to stay "in place." The mother's constant movement, although momentarily amusing (as is her inability to feed her children anything but hors d'oeuvres: "Anything more," says her daughter, "is too big a commitment"), becomes understood quickly as signifying a more problematic refusal to grow up and a concomitant fear of responsibility. As Charlotte tells us again and again, mom moves on when the going gets tough.

This lighthearted yet melodramatic treatise on wacky moms comes complete with the Kennedy family as the recurring televisual reminder of the wholesome domesticity Charlotte yearns for. As the daughter retreats from mom's irreverence with fervent prayer, fantasies of eternal salvation, and desire for the never-seen absent father, she also begins to experience the sexual desires that seem to rule her mother's life and that will, inevitably, produce the final confrontation scene between mother and daughter. True to melodramatic form, an "event" occurs that brings mother and daughter to angry explosion and tearful reunion. Daughter's budding sexuality eventually provides the terrain for the reunion, which rings false precisely because it is based solely on the sharing of like bodies, not the sharing of values and beliefs.

The opening scene sets the stage, with teenage daughter Charlotte providing a wiser than her years voice-over detailing the nuances of her wacky family and particularly wacky and sexually active "Mrs. Flax." Mom's dereliction as a Kennedy-esque mother is treated with the humor that will eventually turn bittersweet and melodramatic (as in *Terms of Endearment*):

| | |
|---|---|
| *Charlotte:* | "You never came to Parent-Teacher night before. I don't see what's so special about this one." |
| *Mother:* | "Charlotte, you read the invitation: Community begins in the classroom. I *am* your mother, it is my job to watch over your education." |
| *Charlotte:* | "There's so little of it left. What took you so long." |
| *Mother:* | "Ohh, we're going to play my favorite game: who's the *worst* mother in the world? Oh now don't tell me, let me guess, who could it be? Could it be . . . ME?" |

Although the scene is humorous and highlights the mother's awareness of "mother bashing" and refusal of guilt, the knowing humor is undercut by the mother's obvious "lack" in the realm of maternal commitment and responsibility. As funny as the hors d'oeuvres are, they are not what you feed two growing girls. As amusing as the premise of eternal mobility is, we know that it is disruptive to a developing child's sense of identity and continuity; it inspires terror in a child, not humor.

Even though other kids may envy Charlotte her rebellious mom, as we see in the comment a student makes to Charlotte at the PTA meeting ("See that woman there? That's my mom. And when I grow up I want to be just like yours"), we realize all too well that mom's obvious immaturity creates a daughter unable to revel in her own childhood. In one scene, the family has spent the night at the house of Lou Lansky, mom's shoe salesman boyfriend. When a storm wakes her up, Charlotte goes up to the attic, where mom has fallen asleep, having sat earlier for amateur painter Lou. As Charlotte kneels by the couch, she covers her mother up and gazes sadly on this woman dressed like a garish Cleopatra. Her melancholy voice-over utters the telling lines: "Sometimes I feel like you're the child, and I'm the grownup. I can't ever imagine being inside you. I can't imagine being anywhere you'd let me hang around for nine straight months." Again, while this bittersweet moment remains humorous, it also conveys the real sadness of a daughter who is both "parentified" and deeply unsure of her mother's love and concern.

As in so many films, the wise male savior points out to the mother the errors of her ways. In *Mermaids,* Lou repeatedly points out mother's failings and provides analysis and explanation for her bizarre behavior. When the family is at Lou's for dinner, the contrast between his rich and warm family meals and Rachel's haphazard domesticity (where the kids eat standing or sitting on counter-tops) could not be more pronounced. When Charlotte runs away to construct a fictional "Cleaver" family after a painful scene in which she is unable to talk to her mother about her fears of pregnancy, Lou is quick to lecture Rachel on her dangerously aggressive mothering style:

| | |
|---|---|
| *Mother:* | "You know, I know that she's doing this to turn my hair white." |
| *Lou:* | "She's doing this because she has a problem! And she's probably too frightened to talk to you about it!" |
| *Mother:* | "Why would she be frightened?" |
| *Lou:* | "Rachel, you can be a little abrasive! Shit, even I'm scared to talk to you sometimes. She's a kid, lighten up, don't ride her too hard!" |
| *Mother:* | "I don't need a lecture on parenting from *you*! OK, that's it, when she comes, I'm leaving." |
| *Lou:* | "And you wonder why she runs away from problems. Will you listen to yourself?" |

When Charlotte returns, after being fetched by Lou, her mother is furious: "Go to your room. I can't talk to you right now. If I talk to you right now, I'll kill you." After attempts to talk with a resolutely silent Charlotte, who will only speak in cinematic voice-over, Rachel tries to reach her with this matter-of-fact statement of her own ambivalence: "Let me tell you something Charlotte. You know, sometimes being a mother really stinks. I don't always know what I'm doing. It's not like you and your sister came with a book of instructions. You know, if I can help you . . . just tell me. I'll give it my best shot, but I, that's all that I can do." When her daughter doesn't respond, the mother leaves the room.

The denouement occurs when Charlotte, convinced that her mother is trying to steal boyfriend Joe away from her, gets all dressed up and spends an evening getting drunk with her little sister: "OK mom, you want to drive Lou away, that's your business. You want Joe: that's war." As the sisters sit on the front porch, Charlotte's overly parental role in the family is made manifest, a role that will later come back to haunt her by the events that follow:

| | |
|---|---|
| *Katie:* | "Tell me about when I was born." |
| *Charlotte:* | "Aren't you sick of hearing this story?" |

    *Katie:*    "No."

    *Charlotte:*   "OK, you were born in a hospital on a cold winter's day, and when Mrs. Flax brought you home, I pretended you were mine."

Immediately following this scene, Charlotte and Katie go to the convent where Joe (the boyfriend/caretaker) lives. As he and Charlotte make furtive love in the belltower, her inebriated little sister falls into the stream and is saved in the nick of time by the nuns. This event serves as the catalyst for Charlotte's confrontation with her mother. As the furious mother returns from the hospital, the penitent but awakened Charlotte refuses her usual silence in favor of "having it out" with mother:[30]

    *Mother:*   "If you're smart you'll just stay away from me."

    *Charlotte:*  "Don't walk away from me, mom, you're not going to walk away from me! I am not invisible! Talk to me! Now! Yes, I made a mistake. Yes, I am really, really sorry. It was a big mistake. I know that. You make mistakes. You're always screwing up and we're always paying for it. Everytime you get dumped, everytime you dump on somebody. And it's just, it's not fair mommy, it's not fair."

    *Mother:*   "I am sick and tired of being judged by you. You're a kid. OK, when you become an adult you can live your life anyway you want to. But until then, we'll live *my* life *my* way. Start packing."

    *Charlotte:*  "No!"

    *Mother:*   "I said pack. This move is on you and if loverboy doesn't like it, that's too goddamn bad."

    *Charlotte:*  "This is not about him, this is about me, OK? That's over, he is gone, he has left. . . ."

    *Mother:*   "Surprise, surprise. . . ."

    *Charlotte:*  "No, it's not like that. Look, maybe your life works for you but it doesn't work for me. And I want to stay."

    *Mother:*   "And do what?"

    *Charlotte:*  "Finish high school."

    *Mother:*   "Great start, what's your major? Town tramp?"

    *Charlotte:*  "No, Mom. The town already has one."

They do, of course, end up staying, after mother and daughter have bonded over their relationships with men:

| | |
|---|---|
| *Mother:* | "You know, you're just one year younger than I was when I had you. If you hate my life so much, why are you doing your damnedest to make the same mistakes? . . . How do you feel about this guy?" |
| *Charlotte:* | "I thought I loved him." |
| *Mother:* | "Sounds familiar." |

The reunion ends with a teary daughter questioning mother on her relationship with the absent father ("Did you love my father?"), and an epilogue follows that maintains mother's bantering relationship with Lou without completely altering her persona of "wacky mom."

Both *Postcards* and *Mermaids* thus replicate the mode seen in films of the fifties, where mother is not wholly killed off but rather "fixed" within the confines of the nuclear family, as it internally cleanses itself of its own deviations. In keeping with the madcap generic conventions, mom is "fixed" while still retaining her wackiness and idiosyncratic style. Daughter's point has been made: mom is now forced to face up to her responsibilities and finds with the daughter a new intimacy based on a recognition of their mutual enmeshment in the world of (male-defined) sexuality.

These 1980s paradigms have been challenged here and there by the lone book, film, or TV show. A number of books and articles shift significantly away from the simple themes of "loving and letting go," although they are few and far between and generally don't have the same popular appeal as, say, a piece by Colette Dowling. Terri Apter's *Altered Loves* argues explicitly against the ideologies of separation and for a more nuanced and complex understanding of the changing affiliations daughters and mothers negotiate. Apter strongly urges us to distinguish different meanings of "separation":

First, there is separation as individuation—the development of a distinct self, a sense of self-boundary, enabling one to distinguish one's own wishes, hopes, and needs from those of one's parents. . . . The second sense of separation is like a divorce. It is breaking the bonds of affection with the parent. . . . We must distinguish between individuation as self-identity, and some sense of self-determination or self-agency, and between individuation as a means of separating from others, cutting bonds of affection.[31]

Apter's interviews with sixty-five British and American mother/ daughter pairs reveal not the "truth" of inherent separation and struggle, but rather the much more complex negotiation of new patterns of closeness built out of a sense of reciprocal effect and care. Apter eloquently critiques both mainstream and feminist theories for their commitment to the "myth of separation" and their endless perpetuation of mother-blame.

Emily Hancock's *The Girl Within: Recapture the Childhood Self, the Key to Female Identity,* although unfortunately mired in the contemporary obsession with "the child within," nevertheless manages to critique soundly the ideology of separation that is revealed to be more problematic when put to the test of actual interviews: "They did not want to break the mother-daughter bond; they wanted to transform it. Given the cultural ethos that urges separation on adults, the burden fell on each individual daughter to rework the attachment without forfeiting it. In a culture hellbent on separation, this activity took on an almost subversive character."[32]

Paula Caplan challenges mother-blame head on in her passionate treatise, *Don't Blame Mother,* where she urges us to critique both the myth of the "perfect mother" (who must inevitably fail us) and the myth of the "evil mother" (who must also fail us): "Mothers are either idealized or blamed for everything that goes wrong. Both mother and daughter learn to think of women in general, and mothers in particular, as angels or witches or some of each. . . . As daughters and mothers, we have for generations been trapped in a dark web we did not spin. But once we are aware of the myth-threads that form the web, as we tell our mothers' stories and our own, we can begin to sort them out and pick apart the web."[33]

These texts, all using extensive interview material and all written by psychologists, struggle to forge a new conceptualization of mothers and daughters that avoids the dominant patterns of dichotomizing mother-blame while remaining critical of the feminist tendency to replicate these selfsame patterns. However, all three texts remain within a solidly psychological framework and place their revisions within an interpersonal, rather than a more broadly social, context. Although many of these writers point to a culture of mother-blame and woman hate as the culprits in creating a climate of expected hostility between mother and daughter, they often leave these insights as mere asides to the more central topic of psychic reconstruction. Nevertheless, the presence of these alternative frameworks can only help in the project of reimagining the mother/daughter relationship.

The backlash of the eighties and early nineties has thus added a sad twist to the question: Whose life is it, anyway? As all women's lives (daughters and mothers) become more and more out of their own control, popular culture still insists on making this question of social control subordinate to the putative timelessness of maternal control and domination. For Adrienne Popper of *Parents' Magazine*, the question is addressed from daughter to mother: "The division between mothers and daughters here, as always, is one of control, a question of 'whose life is it anyway?' Undoubtedly, daughters can derive enormous benefits from mothers who allow them to live their own lives with maximal maternal support and minimal interference."[34] This question needs rather to be addressed by all women (daughters *and* mothers) to the institutions and persons of male power and authority. The difference is not simply one of enunciation (who speaks what question to whom); it is instead a radically political difference: the difference between turning inward to locate oppression or turning outward to challenge it.

## Chapter Eight

# Beyond Separation

### Located Lives and Situated Tales

*It will be necessary for us somehow to mourn an all-powerful maternal presence (the last refuge) and to establish with our mothers a relationship of reciprocity woman to woman, where they could also eventually feel themselves to be our daughters. In sum, to liberate ourselves with our mothers. That is an indispensable condition for our emancipation from the authority of our fathers. The mother/daughter, daughter/ mother relation constitutes an extremely explosive core in our societies. To think it, to change it, leads to shaking up the patriarchal order.*

—Luce Irigaray

To a great extent, the messages of so many of these cultural images are directed to the daughters, not the mothers. Whenever we see a period of growth in women's rights and agitation by women for equality—for expanded definitions of their own lives—we unfortunately also see a concomitant backlash against women: warnings and threats. Those threats and warnings are largely raised in the familial context (e.g., a working mother will make a bad parent). Applied specifically to mothers and daughters, this message becomes even more pointed. We have moved from a film like *Stella Dallas*, which at least presents the world from both the mother's and the daughter's perspectives—both "points of view" were expressed—to a film like *September* or *Mommie Dearest* or a book like *My Mother/My Self*, in which only the daughter's (or the male culture's) point of view is expressed.

Similarly, we have moved from a golden age of television in the 1970s when shows like "Rhoda," "Maude," and "Mary Tyler Moore" explored sensitively and with great warmth the complex relations between mother and daughter—particularly in the context of changing role expectations—to a culture in which any serious depiction of this relationship is almost absent from the television screen.

In both film and television in the late eighties, mothers and daughters again seem to be disappearing, and fathers and sons appear to be reclaiming center stage. In recent years, we have been inundated with sitcoms depicting valiant fireman dads trying to take care of the kids when mom has precipitously been killed off: "Uncle Buck," "Who's the Boss," "Major Dad," "Coach," "Hunter," "Matlock," "Wonder Years," "Dear John," "The Fanelli Boys," "Jake and the Fatman," "The Young Riders." Moms are, once again, conspicuously absent from the television mediascape. "Make Room for Daddy" has returned with an almost vindictive authenticity. Is our model of modern mother/daughter relating to be Fallon and Alexis on "Dynasty"—forever competing for men, forever vying for the attention of dear old Blake? It is no accident that it is Alexis's sons who work for her, not her daughter.

In so many of these representations, mothers and daughters are inevitably lost to each other, through sacrifice (*Stella Dallas, Mildred Pierce*), conflict and death (*Now, Voyager, 'night, Mother*), or narcissism and neglect (*September, Imitation of Life, Mommie Dearest*). In most of these popular images, there is a clear and present victor, the daughter; in the rest, we are left with a promise of future struggle and conflict. If resolution is reached, mother and daughter are torn asunder. If no narrative conclusion exists, such as in *September*, mother and daughter seem locked in a repetitive cycle of confrontation and angst. In more recent years, the "maternal sacrifice" genre, which at least put a "good face" on motherhood, has given way to a more visceral depiction of a clearly evil mother (*Mommie Dearest*) and a victimized daughter or, more generally, of a mother/daughter relationship structured in terms of conflict.

The double bind in representations reflects an experienced double bind, or contradiction, inherent in the mother/daughter relationship within patriarchal culture, which is precisely why the

themes in popular culture are both so consistent and so seemingly
in contradiction. The daughter is represented as needing to separate from the mother in order to enter the world of adulthood and,
more specifically, the world of male identification. She is asked to
repudiate the maternal in order to discover her own femininity.

Yet, paradoxically, we live in a culture in which the very definition of femininity is intimately connected with motherhood. For as
long as I can remember, motherhood has been seen both as the
natural destiny of all women and as the act that most symbolizes
their achievement of maturity and adulthood. Yet motherhood is
simultaneously denigrated and devalued (witness the appalling lack
of maternal leave policies and adequate child care programs in the
United States). In addition, Western culture has so incorporated
the dichotomization of "mother" and "woman" that identification
with the mother will always imply for the daughter a denial of her
own sexuality.

Tellingly, in films where there is a line of continuity between
mother and daughter, like *I Remember Mama, Little Women,* or *A
World Apart,* both women are generally desexualized. The possibility of mother/daughter continuity that doesn't deny their autonomy, sexuality, or adulthood—that sees them in a relationship
where neither one is "all-powerful" or "all-victimized"—is an option rarely explored in popular culture.

Television has provided a few glimpses into what this could be
with such ground-breaking shows as "Maude" and "Rhoda," depicting adult mothers and daughters where both (in "Maude") are
clearly sexual, adult, and independent. Not coincidentally, these
shows were working within the sitcom format, itself a type of entertainment viewers were not supposed to treat very seriously. It is
surely no accident that these sitcoms were produced at the height
of the contemporary women's movement—the mid-1970s—and
that there was no quality counterpart in the moral majority 1980s.

It should not be surprising that the writings of women of color
help point to alternative ways of representing this relationship. It
is most certainly a privilege to be able to understand the world as
solely circumscribed by the free-floating psyche of individual mothers and daughters. Women who do not have that leisure, who are
required by the force of social and cultural circumstance to write
in and through the contextualized world, have created images of

mothers and daughters that, although not necessarily more "positive" (which is not the goal here in any case), are certainly more complex in their representation of the always contradictory location of mothers and daughters in a culture that remains so resolutely sexist and racist.

In the case of more popular cultural images, we find a similar phenomenon. Representations that treat the familial as configured by the social, images that ground their narratives in the vagaries of class, race, and ethnicity, narratives that break out of the psychological straitjackets and focus on the broader canvas of social relations are the images that give us pleasurable respite from the tedious tales of maternal martyrdom and malice. This broader canvas is evident when the working-class mother in *A Tree Grows in Brooklyn* speaks to her own complicated location as mother and woman, when Maude and her daughter Carol become the shared signifiers for a changing generation of feminist and socially conscious women, when the daughter of the antiapartheid activist in *A World Apart* voices the complex emotions of political awakening and adolescent need, refusing the easy condemnation of the publicly involved mother.

Indeed, a film like *A World Apart* stands out in its adamant refutation of the "preferred reading" of its title. In this beautiful film about a white South African antiapartheid activist seen through the eyes of her young daughter (and actually written by her as well), the "world apart" is most assuredly the racial separatism of the country rather than some tedious generational struggle of mother and daughter. As the mother suffers abuse and imprisonment for her political convictions (abuse that repeatedly attempts to indict her for being a "bad mother"), the daughter's consciousness grows simultaneously with the painful reality of her mother's absence.

This film is almost wholly set apart from the traditional blame motif. Its explicit social and political embeddedness is part of constructing this different narrative. It's not that we don't feel the daughter's real grief at the loss of a more available "mother"; we do, very strongly. But we just as strongly respect and admire the mother's important political choices and see the daughter respect them as well. This dual loyalty is poignantly exemplified in the "big scene" between them, when the daughter reveals to the mother that she is aware of her suicide attempt in prison: "You tried to leave

us! You don't care about us! You should never even have had us!"
As the mother pulls her back into the room, insisting that they talk,
the camera moves to capture the two side by side as the mother
tries to explain:

> *Mother:*   "Please listen to me! I was breaking apart. What good
> would I have been to you in pieces? I was afraid, I was
> afraid I would have put other people in danger."
>
> *Daughter:*   "What people?"
>
> *Mother:*   "Our friends, people like Harold."
>
> *Daughter:*   "*Your* friends, your friends, *your* work. That's all you ever
> care about!"
>
> *Mother:*   "All right, my friends, my work, yes. But what we care
> about is the whole country!"

Mother here refuses the "truth" of the voice of the guilt-inducing
child and instead insists on the visceral truth of the overwhelming
social reality. As daughter continues ("But what about *me*?"),
mother refuses to place their relationship in solely psychological
terms:

> *Mother:*   "You live here. You eat here. I'm down the passage. But
> what about Elsie's [the black housekeeper] child?"
>
> *Daughter:*   "I'm not Elsie's child! I'm your child!"
>
> *Mother:*   "Listen to me! Elsie can't live with her children. Why?
> Because she's black. At Sharpville people were shot down,
> shot in the backs, shot running away. Solomon—he's been
> murdered because he's black. . . ."
>
> *Daughter*   (interrupting her and shouting): "I *know* that! Stop treating
> me like a child!"
>
> *Mother:*   "All right, all right. You do know. I know you know. But I
> also know how much you'd understand if only you'd let
> yourself."
>
> *Daughter*   (crying): "You never tell me anything! I don't know what's
> going on . . . it's not fair!"
>
> *Mother:*   "You're right, it's not fair. It's not fair. And I'm sorry it's not
> fair. You deserve to have a mother. Well, you do have one.
> Just not the way you want her. . . . Molly, I love you."

This scene has bravely shifted the ground from one of maternal
guilt and neglect to one in which the daughter struggles to know

Fig. 29. A rare glimpse of mother/daughter solidarity in the beautiful antiapartheid drama *A World Apart*, starring Barbara Hershey and Jodhi May. (Atlantic, 1987; photo courtesy of Photofest)

the mother and to know fully the politics that her mother has lived so passionately. Yet this scene is not the final moment between mother and daughter. As Molly accompanies her mother to the funeral of black activist Solomon ("I want to go to the funeral. He was my friend."), the camera sweeps the barren landscape to light on mother and daughter. As the mother raises her arm in a clenched fist during a song, her daughter looks at her, slowly raises her fist next to her mother's, and joins in the song as mother puts her arm around daughter. But the camera does not rest on these two, for the story here is so much larger. As the mother and daughter disappear in the upward sweep of the camera, we are left with final images of the funeral mourners—the preacher, grieving family members, brothers and sisters in the struggle. The last shot of the film is a freeze-frame of a man throwing something back at the firing police and the single (anonymous) shout: "Amandla!" These are glimpses, few to be sure, of the limitless possibilities available to us if we will only let go of the easy narratives of bonding and separation, guilt and glory, martyrdom and malevolence.

How can we move beyond these limiting frames and toward a renegotiation, a reconstruction, of both these representations and the experiences they both express and provoke? Most important, we need to tear down these naturalized psychological narratives, expose them as narratives, and construct in their stead not a new truth but rather a multiplicity of possibilities centered on the feminist commitment to woman identification.

This will mean the daughter giving up the grand old antinomous tales in which she plays beleaguered dupe to the nefarious maternal machinations. It will mean developing and elaborating conceptions of *daughtering* that deconstruct the dominant discourses that provide no context for that practice as well as actively constructing feminist modes.

We would do well to take Mary Helen Washington's words to heart:

The educated daughters need to open the "sealed letter" their mothers "could not plainly read," to have their mothers' signatures made clear in their work, to preserve their language, their memories, their myths. . . . Before these signatures can be read clearly, we will have to free the mother from the domination of the daughter, representing her more honestly as a separate, individuated being whose daughters cannot even begin to imagine the mysteries of her life.[1]

But at what point does the mother stop being a daughter? At what point does she switch from the resentful to the resented, from the guilt inspiring to the guilt experiencing? These questions symbolize the intractable dilemmas of the mother of a daughter: to be a mother, she must deny and suppress the daughter in herself or at least split herself in two (a sexual, active daughter still struggling to separate from her denying, asexual mother and that very same character to her own daughter). To be a mother in our culture is to be desexualized, an object of either veneration or scorn, but an object nonetheless. To take on this role, to adopt its version of reality, is to deny one's own experience of daughterhood: to become the other within yourself.

Part of the problem is this assumed split between the identity of "mother" and "daughter." But this split is not a simple parallel. "Mother" is promoted and produced as a unitary and total identity; it contains a vast and complex place in our cultural mythology.

"Daughter" is more of a generational location, almost valueless and without active qualities of volition and control. This disparity in the cultural resonances of the two terms is significant. The terms are immediately split between active and passive; between the doer and the done to. Yet the contradiction here is so apparent: ascribing a unitary and total identity to mother makes her powerfulness become immediately illusory. Unfortunately, many feminists have also bought into this split, identifying as the "daughter" overturning the oppressive mother. As feminist peace activist Ynestra King puts it:

The feminist movement has spoken in the voice of angry rebel daughters. Even when mothers join the movement it is often the wronged daughter in them who speaks. Each of us is familiar as daughters with maternal practice, but most of us in becoming feminists have rejected the self-sacrificing, altruistic, infinitely forgiving, martyred unconditionally loving mother—for this is how I saw my mother—have rejected the mother *in ourselves* as the part of ourselves which is complicitous in our own oppression.[2]

Too often feminist writers—both fiction writers and theorists—have succumbed to the easy answers from psychology. How much easier to struggle against one's mother than against a sexist culture that feels overwhelmingly intractable. Feminists are caught in a dilemma: how to pay attention to this relationship that is clearly so central to so many women's lives without at the same time falling into the dichotomous formations of "bond or blame," how to validate that particular intimacy without turning it into something transcendent, essential, and timeless, how to recognize the ways in which both mothers and daughters have been constructed by a sexist society without at the same time seeing all women simply as victims of male dominance?

If our relationships have been constructed, they can be deconstructed. Mothers and daughters can, and indeed do, resist the discourses that confine them to either bloody battles or merging bliss. But both mother and daughter know that moving beyond these tidy narratives involves great risk, for in toppling Oedipus, we do not intend to put a maternal Electra in his place. It may be scary, but to refuse to do battle, to reject all the old stories, and to resist the temptation of a new grand signifier is to free us up to construct each other anew, this time in our own images. In daughtering our mothers and constructing ourselves dialogically, perhaps we will find the space to be women: As Toni Morrison so beautifully puts it: "If a girl never learns how to be a daughter, she can't never know how to be a woman. . . . You don't need your own natural mother to be a daughter. All you need is to feel a certain . . . careful way about people older than you are. . . . A daughter is a woman that cares about where she came from and takes care of them that took care of her."[3]

But is there another story to tell, another drama to unfold? Are feminist discourses limited to the generic conventions of epic battle or family melodrama? Must our dramas be played out in the alternating scenes of spiritual timelessness or infancy? Are we destined to blame or reclaim, or can a mode of storytelling, a mode of analysis, transcend these limited dichotomies? Is there a way to return to our focus on male dominance without ignoring the real differences but also, very importantly, without ignoring and brushing aside our commonality as women?

We cannot tell *one* story of mothers and daughters. No single narrative, no unified discourse, can possibly flesh out the complexities and contradictions in mother/daughter relationships. The variations of class, race, ethnicity, national identity, sexual preference, and historical location all help create a multitude of possible narratives. So I will not construct another discourse here, for to create any single narrative would be to squeeze out real differences and impose a coherent and deceptive order on a vastly disordered and changing reality. To tell one master narrative, be it the radical feminist or the psychoanalytic one, would be to foreclose possibilities and edge out alternative discourses and explanations.

But there are some ways to begin, some remarks to be made that can at least set the stage for possible new feminist discourses on mothers and daughters. At the outset, we must ask ourselves why—why this rethinking, why the necessity for reevaluating the mother/daughter relationship and constructing oppositional discourses around it? Here a correction can be made to both previous discourses. It is not that we must understand our mother to understand our own inculcation into femininity, that we must reclaim her in order to wrest her—and us—from male control, or that we must denounce her as a weighted chain around our emerging feminist necks. Feminists must analyze the relationship of mother and daughter because it exists as a relationship, a central nexus, *between women*. Now this may seem commonplace, yet it seems necessary to say again. That male scholarship has continuously mystified and obscured relationships between women is by now axiomatic in feminist circles, as is that this mystification has kept women apart and allied to men. If it is also true that the family is a central arena in which people are organized into gender-specific behaviors—where we learn femininity and masculinity—then it would also seem axiomatic that the mother/daughter relationship constitutes a powerful location in that contested terrain of male domination and our resistance to it.

To rethink the mother/daughter relationship is to take the meaning of "woman identification" to heart. This is not to "reclaim" our mothers, for in that reclaiming we imply a lack of agency, a total victimization, that does us all a disservice. It is to say that we cannot be woman identified across all barriers (race, class, sexuality) and stop short at the generational barrier as if to say, "Here, ahh, here I cannot go: here it is too tough, too painful, too filled with mixed emotions and frayed edges." On the long march to a feminist world, we must not leave our mothers behind as remnants of a past we regret but would rather forget. For these mothers are *women* too, and daughters as well. Like it or not, they are part of our shared history *as women,* not only in the specific location of wife, mother, sister, and daughter. We would do better to surpass patriarchy than to surpass our mothers.

# Notes

## 1. The Sacrament of Separation/
## The Penance of Affiliation

1. Adrienne Rich, *Of Woman Born* (New York: W. W. Norton, 1986), 225.

2. Betty Friedan, *The Feminine Mystique* (New York: Dell Publishing, 1963).

3. Betty Friedan, *The Second Stage* (New York: Summit Books, 1981).

4. Nancy Friday, *My Mother/My Self* (New York: Delacorte Press, 1977); Colette Dowling, *Perfect Women: Hidden Fears of Inadequacy and the Drive to Perform* (New York: Simon & Schuster, 1988), and *The Cinderella Complex: Women's Hidden Fear of Independence* (New York: Simon & Schuster, 1981); Robin Norwood, *Women Who Love Too Much* (New York: Pocket Books, 1989).

5. Evelyn Bassoff, *Mothers and Daughters: Loving and Letting Go* (New York: New American Library, 1988), 215.

6. Carroll Smith-Rosenberg, "The Female World of Love and Ritual: Relations Between Women in Nineteenth-Century America," *Signs*, vol. 1, no. 1 (1975), 1–29, esp. 15. See also Elizabeth Ewen, *Immigrant Women in the Land of Dollars: Life and Culture on the Lower East Side 1890–1925* (New York: Monthly Review Press, 1985).

7. Ewen, *Immigrant Women*.

8. This book is not the place to examine these historical changes. To do so completely, I would need to look at a number of social phenomena, including the new consumerism of the 1920s and its re-elaboration in the 1950s, when both mothers and daughters were identified with the realm of the domestic and targeted as potential consumers of domestic products. I would also need to stress the popularization of Freudian psychology—indeed, of psychology in general—and how the psychological framework

came to define certain social and familial relations, such as the mother/
daughter relation; the growth of women's participation in the wage economy; the removal of the home as a site of production; and the growth and
consolidation of industrial capitalism.

9. The early and mid-1970s really mark the beginning of a literature
on women and representation coterminous with the growth of the wom-
en's movement.

10. This brief discussion is limited to theories of visual representation
and culture generally and thus avoids dealing with the enormous literature that makes up the field of feminist literary criticism. Feminist literary
criticism has, to some extent, stood separate from the more general work
on women and culture and women and representation. The relationship
between this field of literary criticism and feminist theories of visual representation awaits further analysis.

11. Annette Kuhn, *Women's Pictures: Feminism and Cinema* (London:
Routledge & Kegan Paul, 1982), 4.

12. See the bibliography for complete references. See also Suzanna
Danuta Walters, "Material Girls: Feminism and Cultural Studies," *Current Perspectives in Social Theory*, in press, which reviews and critically
evaluates feminist cultural theory.

## 2. From Sacrificial *Stella* to Maladjusted *Mildred*

1. There has been an outpouring in recent years of feminist scholarship on the forties and fifties. Particularly helpful to me, with their emphasis on cultural representations of women during these years, has been
the work of Maureen Honey, *Creating Rosie the Riveter* (Amherst: University of Massachusetts Press, 1984), and Elaine Tyler May, *Homeward
Bound: American Families in the Cold War Era* (New York: Basic Books,
1988).

2. *Stella Dallas* was first a 1915 popular novel, which was turned into
a film by Henry King in 1925 and then later by King Vidor in 1937. It was
also one of the longest running radio serials, playing on NBC from 1937
to 1955. The early twentieth century origins may have a great deal to do
with the film's sympathetic rendering of maternal love, insofar as its reference is to a sort of preindustrial "cult of true womanhood" rather than
psychoanalytic angst.

3. Not only were there a great many class-conscious films during the
thirties, but both film and magazine fiction depicted independent, coura-
geous heroines struggling with careers and negotiating the urban jungle.

See Honey, *Creating Rosie the Riveter*, and Betty Friedan, *The Feminine Mystique* (New York: Dell Publishing, 1963). Nevertheless, as both Honey and May, *Homeward Bound*, point out, if these career women ever attempted to maintain their independence after marriage, they were severely vilified.

4. E. Ann Kaplan, "Mothering, Feminism and Representation: The Maternal Melodrama and the Women's Film 1910–1940," in Christine Gledhill, ed., *Home Is Where the Heart Is: Studies in Melodrama and the Women's Film* (London: British Film Institute, 1987), 133.

5. Linda Williams, "Something Else Besides a Mother: *Stella Dallas* and the Maternal Melodrama," in Gledhill, *Home Is Where the Heart Is*, 316.

6. Kaplan, 133.

7. Mary Ann Doane, *The Desire to Desire: The Woman's Film of the 1940's* (Bloomington: Indiana University Press, 1987), 77.

8. Williams, "Something Else Besides a Mother," 312–313.

9. Again, this scene, like many others, sets up the intersection of class and mothering very explicitly. As Stella says, "You're the kind of mother any girl could be proud of. . . ." The entire mise-en-scène agrees with her: compared to the elegant and relaxed Mrs. Morrison, Stella does appear tacky, overdressed, and socially awkward.

10. Williams, "Something Else Besides a Mother," 313.

11. The triumph here is very much like the sacrificial "triumph" of the nineteenth-century "true woman."

12. The mother is here played by Bette Davis, whose character is named Charlotte and whose daughter is named Tina. Several years later, Davis was to play the beleaguered daughter Charlotte whose "adoptive" daughter is named Tina in the film *Now, Voyager.*

13. There is actually a very interesting early silent film called *Dancing Mothers* (1926) in which an actress mother finds her life lonely and curtailed after her marriage to a successful banker. Concerned over her daughter's "wild ways," she plots to steal away her daughter's cad of a boyfriend, only to have him fall in love with her. Her affair causes a break with her daughter and husband, but they try to win her back. The film ends on a highly unusual note in that the wayward mother does not return to the familial nest, but rather indicts both the daughter and the husband for their selfishness and goes off to make her own way.

14. Alice Austin White, "Modern Daughters," *Forum*, January 1932, 62, 64.

15. Helena Lefroy Caperton, "How We Raised Our Six Daughters," *Woman's Home Companion*, December 1930, 38.

16. Mary Ormsbee Whitton, "If I Were That Girl's Mother!" *Parents' Magazine*, August 1932, 17.

17. Marian Castle, "Hard-boiled Mothers: Yesterday's Flapper as Today's Modern Parent," *The Woman's Journal*, April 1931, 35.

18. Estelle Reilly, "Today's Daughters," *Woman's Home Companion*, July 1937, 22.

19. Dorothy Blake, "She Never Tells Me Anything!" *Parents' Magazine*, August 1938, 65.

20. Inez Haynes Irwin, "Insuring Your Daughter's Success," *Woman's Home Companion*, December 1936, 22, 116, 120.

21. Eleanor Boykin, "Should Mothers Be Matchmakers?" *Parents' Magazine*, August 1936, 20, 69.

22. Lovisa C. Wagoner, "This Business of Being a Mother," *Parents' Magazine*, January 1930, 20, 47.

23. Barbara Beattie, "Preparing Your Daughter for Adolescence," *Parents' Magazine*, October 1929, 71.

24. Ruth Hawthorne, "Mothers and Daughters," *Delineator*, vol. 119 (October 1931), 9.

25. Ibid., 38.

26. Michael Renov, quoted in Doane, *The Desire to Desire*, 33.

27. Edward A. Strecker, "What's Wrong with American Mothers?" *Saturday Evening Post*, October 26, 1946, 15.

28. Ibid., 88.

29. Charlotte's most prominent hobby is making what appear to be cloisonne boxes. This film could not be more overladen with Freudian metaphors—boxes, attics, stairways, the fetishizing of legs.

30. Indeed, there was a whole genre of "psychiatrist" films, such as *Spellbound* and *Gaslight*, in which the psychoanalytic motif firmly entrenched itself in the American psyche.

31. Barbara Ehrenreich and Diedre English, *For Her Own Good: 150 Years of the Experts' Advice to Women* (Garden City, NY: Anchor Press/Doubleday, 1979), examine thoroughly and thoughtfully how the reign of the experts developed alongside the rise of popular psychology in the 1940s and 1950s.

32. Maria LaPlace, "Producing and Consuming the Woman's Film: Discursive Struggle in *Now, Voyager*," in Gledhill, *Home Is Where the Heart Is*, 163.

33. Maria LaPlace has convincingly argued that Charlotte is not only an advertisement for a psychologically "correct" motherhood, but that she is an advertisement for a complete "before" and "after" woman, replete with new clothes, hairstyle, and sophisticated demeanor. The relationship

between *Now, Voyager* and both the new psychology and the new consumerism is striking indeed.

34. Karen Anderson, *Wartime Women: Sex Roles, Family Relations, and the Status of Women During World War II* (Westport, CT: Greenwood Press, 1981), 92.

35. Florence Howitt, "Do You Know Everything in Your Daughter's Head?" *Good Housekeeping*, January 1945, 28.

36. In her biography, which includes a running commentary by the star herself, Bette Davis comments that she received a great deal of fan mail after *Now, Voyager* from "children of possessive mothers, whose lives had been ruined as was Charlotte's before meeting Jacquith; also many from mothers admitting their similar mistakes with their children." Whitney Stine, *Mother Goddam* (New York: Berkley Books, 1974), 175. Clearly, the ideology of maternal evil had, and still has, quite a bit of popular appeal.

37. Much has been made of this odd mixture of noir and melodrama. Specifically, it has been argued that the omniscient voice of the male detective in the noir sequences serves to undercut the female narrative of Mildred's own "rags to riches" story. Although I agree with this observation, here I focus on the construction of the mother/daughter relationship within the film, assuming the more general point, already sufficiently argued, about the dominance of the male point of view.

38. Anderson, *Wartime Women*, 91.

39. Linda Williams, "Feminist Film Theory: *Mildred Pierce* and the Second World War," in E. Deidre Pribram, ed., *Female Spectators: Looking at Film and Video* (London: Verso, 1988), 17–18, 25.

40. Kaplan, "Mothering, Feminism and Representation," 134.

41. Anderson, *Wartime Women*, 94–95.

42. J. Edgar Hoover, "Mothers—Our Only Hope," *Woman's Home Companion*, January 1944, 20, 21.

43. Enid A. Niquette, "Daughter's in the Kitchen Now," *Parents' Magazine*, August 1943, 54.

44. Honey, *Creating Rosie the Riveter*, 117.

45. Ibid., 56.

46. Ibid., 124.

47. Josephine Von Miklos, "Girls in Overalls," *Parents' Magazine*, March 1943, 22 +; Stella B. Applebaum, "War Jobs for Mothers?" *Parents' Magazine*, February 1943, 17 +.

48. One assumes the time period is roughly the twenties or perhaps a bit earlier because the film opens with "several decades ago," and it was made in 1945.

49. This is also true of *Stella Dallas*, as well as films such as *I Remember Mama* and *Little Women*.

50. Williams, "Feminist Film Theory: *Mildred Pierce*," 129.

51. Elsie McCormick, "Sometimes Mothers Talk Too Much," *Good Housekeeping*, September 1943, 25.

52. Andrea Walsh, *Women's Film and Female Experience 1940–1950* (New York: Praeger, 1984), 26.

## 3. Father Knows Best about the Woman Question

1. Mary Ann Doane, *The Desire to Desire: The Woman's Film of the 1940s* (Bloomington: Indiana University Press), 28.

2. Donald N. Rothblatt, Daniel C. Garr, and Jo Sprague, *The Suburban Environment and Women* (New York: Praeger, 1979), 50.

3. Cynthia Harrison, *On Account of Sex: The Politics of Women's Issues 1945–1968* (Berkeley: University of California Press, 1988), 4.

4. Rothblatt, Garr, and Sprague, *The Suburban Environment*, 50.

5. Elaine Tyler May, *Homeward Bound: American Families in the Cold War Era* (New York: Basic Books, 1988), 11.

6. Ibid., 8–9, 18–19, 164.

7. Ruth Schwartz Cowan, *More Work for Mother* (New York: Basic Books, 1983), 212.

8. Warren Susman, with Edward Griffin, "Did Success Spoil the United States? Dual Representations in Postwar America," in Lary May, ed., *Recasting America: Culture and Politics in the Age of Cold War* (Chicago: University of Chicago Press, 1989), 22.

9. The number of television sets purchased is a good indication of the enormous expansion of TV as a form of popular entertainment: "Sales of sets jumped from three million during the entire decade of the 1940s to over five million *a year* during the 1950s." George Lipsitz, "The Meaning of Memory: Family, Class, and Ethnicity in Early Network Television Programs," *Camera Obscura*, vol. 16 (January 1988), 83.

10. George Lipsitz, "The Meaning of Memory: Family, Class, and Ethnicity in Early Network Television Programming," in May, *Recasting America*, 93.

11. Harrison, *On Account of Sex*, 6.

12. Bruno Bettelheim, "Fathers Shouldn't Try To Be Mothers," *Parents' Magazine*, October 1956, 125.

13. Mary Beth Haralovich, "Sitcoms and Suburbs: Positioning the 1950s Homemaker," *Quarterly Review of Film & Video*, vol. 2 (1989), 62.

14. E. Ann Kaplan, "Mothering, Feminism and Representation: The

Maternal in Melodrama and the Woman's Film 1910–1940," in Christine Gledhill, ed., *Home Is Where the Heart Is: Studies in Melodrama and the Woman's Film* (London: British Film Institute, 1987), 130.

15. Ferdinand Lundberg and Marynia Farnham, *Modern Woman: The Lost Sex* (New York: Harper & Row, 1947), 363–364.

16. Karen Anderson, *Wartime Women: Sex Roles, Family Relations, and the Status of Women During World War Two* (Westport, CT: Greenwood Press, 1981), 175.

17. Dorothy Lee, "What Does Homemaking Mean To You?" *Parents' Magazine*, January 1947, 89.

18. Serafina Bathrick, "The True Woman and the Family-Film: The Industrial Production of Memory" (Ph.D. dissertation, University of Wisconsin, 1980), 224.

19. George Lipsitz, *Time Passages: Collective Memory and American Popular Culture* (Minneapolis: University of Minnesota Press, 1990), 84–85.

20. Ibid., 88.

21. Ibid., 86.

22. Nina C. Leibman, "Leave Mother Out: The Fifties Family in American Film and Television," *Wide Angle*, vol. 10 (1988), 30–31, 26.

23. Ibid., 31.

24. Haralovich, "Sitcoms and Suburbs," 64.

25. Several writers have examined the manifestations of McCarthyism in popular culture. See especially Nora Sayre, *Running Time: Films of the Cold War* (New York: Dial Press, 1982), and Victor Navasky, *Naming Names* (New York: Viking Press, 1980).

26. May, *Homeward Bound*, 208.

27. The title sequence, with the song in the background, depicts what appear to be diamonds dropping down and forming a pile, representing the falseness of Lora's fame and fortune.

28. Interestingly, in both films, the badness of the daughters is signified by their becoming singer/dancers in sleazy nightclubs for leering men. Both mothers witness the objectification of the daughter as an object of the male gaze. In both cases, the maternal gaze loses out to the male gaze.

29. Elaine Tyler May, "Explosive Issues: Sex, Women, and the Bomb," in May, *Recasting America*, 155–156.

30. Clifford E. Clark, Jr., "Ranch-House Suburbia: Ideals and Realities," in May, *Recasting America*, 173.

31. The doctor as voice of reason, justice, and clarity in a hazy world is a constant in films of the 1940s and 1950s (e.g., *Now, Voyager, Peyton Place, All That Heaven Allows*).

32. Government policies supported the development of the suburban nuclear family, with government supported mortgages, subsidies for roads to the suburbs, the creation of housing acts, support for dependent children, and the encouragement of "buying on time." Susman and Griffin, "Did Success Spoil the United States?" Eugenia Kaledin, *Mothers and More: American Women in the 1950s* (Boston: Twayne Publishers, 1984).

33. Liebman, "Leave Mother Out," 31.

34. Constance J. Foster, "A Mother of Boys Says: Raise Your Girl To Be a Wife," *Parents' Magazine*, September 1956, 44, 43.

35. Ibid., 113, 44, 113.

36. Marjorie Marks, "Be Popular with Your Daughter," *Woman's Home Companion*, June 1950, 105.

37. Jo Martin Wagner, "There Are Only 37 Things Wrong with My Daughter," *Good Housekeeping*, October 1955, 309.

## 4. The Turning Point

1. Sara Evans, *Personal Politics* (New York: Knopf, 1979).

2. Ella Taylor, *Prime Time Families: Television Culture in Postwar America* (Berkeley: University of California Press, 1989), 1.

3. Molly Haskell, *From Reverence to Rape: The Treatment of Women in the Movies*, 2nd ed. (Chicago: University of Chicago Press, 1987), 323.

4. David Considine, *The Cinema of Adolescence* (Jefferson, NC: Mcfarland, 1985), 64–65.

5. Ibid., 67–68.

6. David Marc sees these sixties sitcoms as examples of a sort of "deep escapism": "[D]uring the sixties, faced with more cultural ambiguity than the genre dared handle, the sitcom went into what might be called a period of 'deep escapism.' If the suburbo-realist domesticoms of the fifties had strived to portray a vision of the 'likely,' the next generation of sitcoms . . . seemed utterly indifferent to verisimilitude." David Marc, *Comic Visions: Television Comedy and American Culture* (Winchester, MA: Unwin Hyman, 1989), 128–129.

7. The exceptions include "Petticoat Junction," which didn't exactly concern itself with relationships at all; "Peyton Place," which only "placed" ratings-wise one season; and "Here's Lucy," where the mother and daughter were wholly related via the supposedly humorous playing up of generational differences. Lucy as mother simply did not work, nor was it funny.

8. As TV critic Taylor has noted, the early 1970s witnessed a shift away from a TV schedule designed simply to attract the widest possible audi-

ence and toward the specification of targeted audiences. It is in this marketing context that the new "women's sitcoms" of the 1970s emerged. Ella Taylor, *Prime Time Families: Television Culture in Postwar America* (Berkeley: University of California Press, 1989).

9. Patricia Coffin, "Memo To: The American Woman," *Look*, January 11, 1966, 16, 17.

10. Eunice Kennedy Shriver, "An Answer to the Attacks on Motherhood," *McCall's*, June 1965, 165.

11. Ann Landers, "A Sickness of Our Times," in Forum "Are Girls Getting Too Aggressive?" *The PTA Magazine*, September 1966, 5.

12. David Lester, "Are You Pushing Your Daughter into Too-Early Marriage?" *Good Housekeeping*, October 1961, 217.

13. Ibid., 216.

14. Ibid., 218.

15. "My Problem and How I Solved It: Mother and Daughter," *Good Housekeeping*, June 1962, 17. This section is written by anonymous editors, often with the aid of social service organizations, in this case, the Family Services Association of America.

16. Norman M. Lobsenz, "Are Working Wives Hurting or Helping Their Families?" *Redbook*, July 1961, 31.

17. Elizabeth Schmidt, "The Best Mothers Aren't Martyrs," *Parents' Magazine*, May 1961, 41.

18. Ibid., 78.

19. Ibid.

20. Virgil Damon and Isabella Taves, "The War Between Mother and Daughter," *Look*, January 11, 1966, 30, 34.

21. Janet Kole, "Eight Successful Women Discuss Motherhood," *Harper's Bazaar*, October 1976, 114.

22. Barbara Grizzuti Harrison, "Finding the Way To Be Friends," *McCall's*, October 1975, 94.

23. Teri Schultz, "The Feelings Too Many Daughters Are Afraid To Face," *Redbook*, October 1976, 183.

24. Sabert Basescu, "Why So Many Women Can't Stand Their Own Mothers," *Redbook*, June 1970, 185.

25. Schultz, "The Feelings Too Many Daughters Are Afraid To Face," 108.

26. Myron Brenton, "Mothers and Daughters," *Seventeen*, December 1971, 92.

27. Schultz, "The Feelings Too Many Daughters Are Afraid To Face," 188.

28. Signe Hammer, "Hostility: Why You Hate Your Mother," *Harper's Bazaar*, October 1976, 120.

29. Helen Singer Kaplan, "Can You Ruin Your Daughter's Sex Life?" *Harper's Bazaar,* October 1976, 84.

30. Ann Landers, "What To Tell Your Daughter About Women's Lib," *Today's Health,* October 1971, 53.

31. Benjamin Spock, "Should Girls Expect To Have Careers?" *Redbook,* March 1972, 50, 52.

32. "Maude" was a consistently popular show. It ran from 1972 to 1978, and, except for its final two seasons, it always placed in the top ten of the Nielsen ratings.

33. "Maude" is not alone in this. Many other sitcoms of the 1970s centered on divorced women—with or without children ("Rhoda," post Joe, "Phyllis," "One Day at a Time").

34. I remember avidly watching the series even though I never really thought much of it. I often found it unfunny and rather insipid; yet, as the daughter of a single parent with two teenage sisters of my own, I felt "One Day at a Time" legitimized and validated a family form that was consistently underrepresented in popular culture. My family may not have been as relentlessly cheery and gung-ho as the Romanos (after all, they were Italian, and we were Jewish), but I too knew what it meant to learn how to be responsible to my siblings and to my mother in an entirely different way than before her divorce. I suspect many of my generation felt a similar resonance. It's heartening to be *represented*, even if that representation is lacking aesthetically and politically.

35. Ella Taylor, *Prime Time Families,* 89.

36. "One Day at a Time," about a divorced mother with two teenage daughters, also introduces this new configuration of single parenthood into the popular imaginary. Unfortunately, the series chose to ride on this generic innovation rather than develop and expand on the relationships among these three women. Nevertheless, like *An Unmarried Woman,* this series depicts the struggle to adapt to new family formations and to find skills and competence where previously one had felt the ancillary half of a traditional couple. Even the title suggests a sort of easygoing, teamwork approach to single parenthood. But, like its AA counterpart from which the title is drawn, "One Day at a Time" lacked depth, originality, and the rough and contradictory edges that made sitcoms like "Maude" so interesting and entertaining.

37. The way this posing of *the* issue for young women continues in the popular discourse of the 1980s can be evidenced by the titles of a number of popular best-selling books of recent years: *The Cinderella Complex; Women Who Love Too Much; Perfect Women; Smart Women, Foolish Choices.*

## 5. Terms of Enmeshment

1. E. Ann Kaplan, "Mothering, Feminism and Representation: The Maternal Melodrama and the Women's Film 1910–1940," in Christine Gledhill, ed., *Home Is Where the Heart Is: Studies in Melodrama and the Women's Film* (London: British Film Institute, 1987), 120.

2. Serafina Bathrick, "The Mary Tyler Moore Show: Women at Home and at Work," in Jane Feuer, Paul Kerr, and Tise Vahimagi, eds., *MTM: Quality Television* (London: British Film Institute, 1984), 111–112.

3. There is a pseudofeminist version of this sort of gratuitous "mother bashing" to be found in Nancy Friday's *My Mother/My Self* (New York: Dell Publishing, 1977). Because Friday has been roundly—and rightly— criticized by numerous feminist scholars, I will avoid any discussion of her book here. Suffice it to say that Friday blames mothers for just about everything, but particularly focuses on them as malicious and repressed impediments to their daughters' adult (hetero)sexuality. This tirade would be laughable were it not so popular; sadly, it is the most widely read book on mothers and daughters, a fact that should attest to the deep and lasting resonance of mother-blame.

4. Adrienne Rich, *Of Woman Born: Motherhood as Experience and Institution*, 10th ed. (New York: W. W. Norton, 1986), 226.

5. Carroll Smith-Rosenberg, "The Female World of Love and Ritual: Relations Between Women in Nineteenth-Century America," *Signs*, vol. 1, no. 1 (1975), 17.

6. J. J. Bachofen, *Myth, Religion, and Mother Right*, trans. Ralph Mannheim (Princeton, NJ: Princeton University Press, 1967); Robert Briffault, *The Mothers* (New York: Johnson Reprint, 1969).

7. Rich, *Of Woman Born*, 243.

8. Judith Arcana, *Our Mothers' Daughters* (Berkeley: Shameless Hussy Press, 1979), 1.

9. Rich, *Of Woman Born*, 243.

10. Arcana, *Our Mothers' Daughters*, 150.

11. Rachel Blau DuPlessis, "Washing Blood," *Feminist Studies*, vol. 4, no. 2 (June 1978), 1–12, esp. 3.

12. Rich, *Of Woman Born*, 127, 220.

13. See especially Eleanor H. Kuykendall, "Toward an Ethic of Nurturance: Luce Irigaray on Mothering and Power," in Joyce Treblicot, ed., *Mothering: Essays in Feminist Theory* (Totowa, NJ: Rowman and Allanheld, 1983), 263–274.

14. Rich, *Of Woman Born*, 235.

15. Iris Marion Young, "Is Male Gender Identity the Cause of Male Domination?" in Treblicot, *Mothering*, 129–146, esp. 130.

16. Dorothy Dinnerstein, *The Mermaid and the Minotaur: Sexual Arrangements and the Human Malaise* (New York: Harper & Row, 1976).

17. Jane Flax, "Mother-Daughter Relationships: Psychodynamics, Politics, and Philosophy," in Hester Eisenstein and Alice Jardine, eds., *The Future of Difference* (New Brunswick, NJ: Rutgers University Press, 1985), 20–40, esp. 26, 18, 37.

18. Jane Flax, "The Conflict Between Nurturance and Autonomy in Mother-Daughter Relationships and Within Feminism," *Feminist Studies*, vol. 4, no. 2 (June 1978), 171–189, esp. 175.

19. Kim Chernin, *The Hungry Self: Women, Eating and Identity* (London: Virago, 1986), 43, 54.

20. Flax, "Mother-Daughter Relationships," 37.

21. Jessica Benjamin, *The Bonds of Love: Psychoanalysis, Feminism, and the Problem of Domination* (New York: Pantheon Books, 1988), 7.

22. Ibid., 8, 78.

23. Susie Orbach, "From Mother to Daughter," *New Statesman*, March 29, 1985, 28.

24. Benjamin, 78–79.

25. Ibid., 121, 99.

26. Chernin, *The Hungry Self*, 42–45.

27. Carol Dyhouse, "Mothers and Daughters in the Middle-Class Home, c. 1870–1914," in Jane Lewis, ed., *Labour and Love: Women's Experience of Home and Family 1850–1940* (London: Basil Blackwell, 1986), 44.

28. Gloria Joseph and Jill Lewis, *Common Differences: Conflicts in Black and White Feminist Perspectives* (Boston: South End Press, 1981), 89–90.

29. Carol Stack, *All Our Kin: Strategies for Survival in a Black Community* (New York: Harper & Row, 1974).

30. Jane Flax, "The Conflict Between Nurturance and Autonomy," 180.

## 6. Parting Glances

1. See especially Cathy N. Davidson and E. M. Broner, eds., *The Lost Tradition: Mothers and Daughters in Literature* (New York: Frederick Ungar, 1980), and Mickey Pearlman, ed., *Mother Puzzles: Daughters and Mothers in Contemporary American Literature* (Westport, CT: Greenwood Press, 1989).

2. Several films, such as Michele Citron's *Daughter Rite* and the British film *Bred and Born*, as well as plays and photography books and exhibits, have focused on the mother/daughter relationship. Unfortunately, I could not include them in this book.

3. Mickey Pearlman, "Introduction," in Pearlman, *Mother Puzzles,* 7, 8.

4. Kim Chernin, *In My Mother's House: A Daughter's Story* (New York: Harper & Row, 1983), 12.

5. Ibid., 263.

6. Judith Kegan Gardiner, "A Wake for Mother: The Maternal Deathbed in Women's Fiction," *Feminist Studies,* vol. 4 (June 1978), 146.

7. Chernin, *In My Mother's House,* 122.

8. Mary Helen Washington, "Alice Walker: Her Mother's Gifts," *Ms.,* June 1982, 38.

9. Vivian Gornick, *Fierce Attachments* (New York: Simon & Schuster, 1987).

10. Ibid., 6.

11. Ibid., 9.

12. Robin Morgan, *Dry Your Smile* (Garden City, NY: Doubleday, 1987), 50, 22.

13. Indeed, she even reprises an earlier scene: her own birth through her mother's eyes.

14. Ibid., 20.

15. Madonna M. Miner, "Guaranteed To Please: Twentieth-Century American Women's Bestsellers," in Elizabeth A. Flynn and Patrocinio P. Schweikart, eds., *Gender and Reading* (Baltimore: Johns Hopkins University Press, 1986), 191.

16. Carol Boyce Davies, "Mothering and Healing in Recent Black Women's Fiction," *Sage,* vol. 2, no. 1 (Spring 1985), 41–43.

17. Gloria I. Joseph and Jill Lewis, *Common Differences: Conflicts in Black and White Feminist Perspectives* (Boston: South End Press, 1981), 94.

18. Patricia Hill Collins, "The Meaning of Motherhood in Black Culture and Black Mother/Daughter Relationships," *Sage,* vol. 4, no. 2 (Fall 1987), 7.

19. Gloria Wade-Gayles, "The Truths of Our Mothers' Lives: Mother-Daughter Relationships in Black Women's Fiction," *Sage,* vol. 1, no. 2 (Fall 1984), 8.

20. Alice Walker, "Everyday Use," in *In Love and Trouble* (New York: Harcourt Brace Jovanovich, 1973), pp. 47, 48.

21. Gloria Naylor, *The Women of Brewster Place* (Harmondsworth, Middlesex, England: Penguin Books, 1983), 86, 87.

22. Ibid., 87–88.

23. Alice Walker, *Meridian* (New York: Harcourt Brace Jovanovich, 1976), 92–93.

24. Ibid., 17.

25. Ibid., 39, 40.
26. Ibid., 41.
27. Ibid., 122.
28. Ibid., 123.
29. Ibid., 120–121.
30. Wade-Gayles, "The Truths of Our Mothers' Lives," 10.
31. "Telling Our Story," An interview with Toni Morrison, *Spare Rib* (1988), 12–16.
32. Amy Tan, *The Joy Luck Club* (New York: Putnam's, 1989), 183–184.
33. Ibid., 48.
34. Ibid., 67.
35. Ibid., 254.
36. Ibid., 255.
37. Wade-Gayles, "The Truths of Our Mothers' Lives," 11–12.

## 7. Whose Life Is It Anyway?

1. While watching the 1989 "Mother/Daughter International Contest," I participated in the game they play with the audience: matching up the mothers with the daughters. I was right on all three match-ups and then went on to pick all eight of the semifinalists, thus unambiguously confirming my acumen as a social researcher.

2. Paula Caplan, *Don't Blame Mother: Mending the Mother-Daughter Relationship* (New York: Harper & Row, 1989).

3. Madeline Pober, "Mothers and Daughters—The Eternal Love-Hate Relationship," *Cosmopolitan,* July 1983, 199, 245.

4. Jean Marzollo, "Are You Still Trying To Please Your Mother?" *Mademoiselle,* May 1983, 224.

5. Grace Baruch, Rosalind Barnett, and Caryl Rivers, "How Women and Their Mothers Become Friends," *McCall's,* April 1980, 32.

6. Ibid.

7. Evelyn Bassoff, *Mothers and Daughters: Loving and Letting Go* (New York: NAL Books, 1988), xi, 2.

8. Pober, "Mothers and Daughters," 200.

9. Bassoff, *Mothers and Daughters,* 215, 21.

10. Chase's language here is interesting in its similarity to that of the doctor in *Now, Voyager* condemning the mother for ruining Charlotte. Development as botany seems to transcend historical differences: "The only way you can continue to have a relationship with your daughter that is perennially flowering is to let her go, to help her separate her image from yours, and to see yourself as a separate being. Then a real friendship

can blossom." Janet Chase, "What Mothers and Daughters Can Give Each Other," *Woman's Day*, July 14, 1981, 55, 54.

11. Ann Grizzle, with William Proctor, *Mother Love, Mother Hate: Breaking Dependent Love Patterns in Family Relationships* (New York: Fawcett Columbine, 1988), 4, 7–8, 219.

12. Victoria Secunda, *When You and Your Mother Can't Be Friends* (New York: Delacorte Press, 1990), 310.

13. Theodore Rubin, "Psychiatrist's Notebook: Mothers and Daughters Who Can't Get Along," *Ladies Home Journal*, February 1981, 54.

14. Cynthia Wolfson, "Getting Mad at Mom and Living Happily Ever After," *Glamour*, May 1986, 54.

15. Mary McHugh, "Daughters and Mothers: Making Peace, Making Friends," *Cosmopolitan*, October 1984, 271, 272.

16. Colette Dowling, *Perfect Women: Hidden Fears of Inadequacy and the Drive to Perform* (New York: Simon & Schuster, 1988), 36.

17. Elizabeth Tener, "You and Your Problem Mother," *Cosmopolitan*, June 1981, 228.

18. Barbara Creaturo, "Making Friends with Mom," *Woman's Day*, May 21, 1985, 24+.

19. Annie Gottlieb, "Your Mother, Your First Love," *Mademoiselle*, February 1982, 131, 133.

20. Aimee Ball, "The Secret Life of Mothers and Daughters," *Mademoiselle*, January 1985, 139.

21. Victoria Secunda, "Should You Divorce Your Mother?" *New Woman*, November 1988, 57–58.

22. Creaturo, "Making Friends with Mom," 24.

23. Ella Taylor, *Prime Time Families: Television Culture in Postwar America* (Berkeley: University of California Press, 1989), 159.

24. A maudlin film version of this theme can be found in *Nuts*, starring Barbra Streisand as Claudia, a prostitute brought to court on murder charges. As she tries to prove her sanity and stand trial, the origin of Claudia's "deviation" is revealed: she survived years of incest by her rich and putatively loving stepfather. But, true to form, the mother's inability/refusal to protect her daughter is what really gets raked over. The film ends with the daughter telling her devastated mother, "I still love you," while the mother weeps, "I'm so ashamed." The stepfather's crimes seem to slip by the wayside in favor of this "primal" narrative.

25. Secunda, *When You and Your Mother Can't Be Friends*, xxii; Secunda, "Should You Divorce Your Mother?" 58–60.

26. Dowling, *Perfect Women*, 18.

27. Ellen Seiter, "Feminism and Ideology: The *Terms* of Women's Stereotypes," *Feminist Review*, vol. 22 (February 1986), 70.

28. Dowling, *Perfect Women,* 18.

29. Bette, of course, had the last word. In her own biography (*This 'N That*), she replied with typical Davis sarcasm and wit to her daughter's attacks. She ends her biography with a letter to her daughter, just as her daughter had ended her account with a letter to her mother. Davis claims a confusion was made between real life and the screen ("Many of the scenes in your book I have played on the screen. It could be that you have confused the "me" on the screen with the "me" who is your mother.") and ends her letter with a caustic "p.s": "I hope someday I will understand the title *My Mother's Keeper.* If it refers to money, if my memory serves me right, I've been your keeper all these many years. I am continuing to do so, as my name has made your book about me a success." Bette Davis with Michael Herskowitz, *This 'N That* (New York: Putnam's, 1987), 197–198.

30. As she sits by her daughter's bedside, the mother repeats, almost verbatim, the story of the daughter's birth that Charlotte had earlier told to her sister. This repetition produces a causal effect between the daughter's overly responsible behavior, the mother's overly irresponsible behavior, and Katie's fatal accident.

31. Terri Apter, *Altered Loves: Mothers and Daughters During Adolescence* (New York: St. Martin's Press, 1990), 59.

32. Emily Hancock, *The Girl Within: Recapture the Childhood Self, the Key to Female Identity* (New York: E. P. Dutton, 1989), 147.

33. Caplan, *Don't Blame Mother,* 3.

34. Adrienne Popper, "Mothers and Daughters," *Parents' Magazine,* April 1982, 57.

## 8. Beyond Separation

1. Mary Helen Washington, *Invented Lives* (Garden City, NY: Doubleday, 1987), 352.

2. Ynestra King, talk at Columbia Seminar on Women and Society, Spring 1983, quoted in Sara Ruddick, *Maternal Thinking: Toward a Politics of Peace* (Boston: Beacon Press, 1989), 38–39.

3. Toni Morrison, *Tar Baby* (New York: Knopf, 1981), 281.

# Bibliography

Abel, Elizabeth, Marianne Hirsch, and Elizabeth Langland, eds. *The Voyage In: Fictions of Female Development*. Hanover, NH: University Press of New England, 1983.

Abramson, Jane B. *Mothermania: A Psychological Study of Mother-Daughter Conflict*. Lexington, MA: Lexington Books/D. C. Heath, 1987.

Adams, Parveen. "Mothering." *m/f* 8 (1983): 40–52.

Adorno, Theodor. *Prisms*. London: Neville Spearman, 1967.

Aguilar, Grace. *Home Influences: A Tale for Mothers and Daughters*. New York: Harper and Bros., 1848.

———. *Mother's Recompense: A Sequel to Home Influences*. New York: D. Appelton, 1851.

Allen, Robert C., ed. *Channels of Discourse: Television and Contemporary Criticism*. Chapel Hill: University of North Carolina Press, 1987.

Anderson, Jane McDill. "My Mother, A Stranger." *McCall's*, November 1963, 114.

Anderson, Jerrie Sutfin. "Love—And Let Go!" *Parents' Magazine*, July 1975, 33.

Anderson, Karen. *Wartime Women: Sex Roles, Family Relations, and the Status of Women During World War Two*. Westport, CT: Greenwood Press, 1981.

Ang, Ien. *Watching Dallas: Soap Opera and the Melodramatic Imagination*. New York: Metheun, 1985.

Appelbaum, Stella B. "War Jobs for Mothers?" *Parents' Magazine*, February 1943, 17.

Apter, Terri. *Altered Loves: Mothers and Daughters During Adolescence*. New York: St. Martin's Press, 1990.

Arato, Andrew, and Eike Gebhardt, eds. *The Essential Frankfurt School Reader*. Oxford: Blackwell, 1978.

Arcana, Judith Pildes. *Our Mothers' Daughters*. Berkeley: Shameless Hussy Press, 1979.

Aries, Phillipe. *Centuries of Childhood: A Social History of Family Life*. Translated by Robert Baldick. New York: Knopf, 1962.

Bachofen, J. J. *Myth, Religion, and Mother Right*. Princeton, NJ: Princeton University Press, 1974.

Badinter, Elisabeth. *Mother Love: Myth and Reality*. New York: Macmillan, 1980.

Baehr, Helen, and Gillian Dyer, eds. *Boxed In: Women and Television*. New York: Pandora Press, 1987.

Ball, Aimee Lee. "The Secret Life of Mothers and Daughters." *Mademoiselle*, January 1985, 108.

Barrett, Michele. "Ideology and the Cultural Production of Gender." In *Feminist Criticism and Social Change*, ed. Judith Newton and Deborah Rosenfelt, 65–85. London: Metheun, 1985.

———. *Women's Oppression Today*. London: New Left Books/Verso, 1980.

———, and Mary McIntosh. *The Anti-Social Family*. London: Verso, 1982.

———. "Narcissism and the Family: A Critique of Lasch." *New Left Review* 135 (September/October 1982): 35–48.

Barrett, Michele, et al., eds. *Ideology and Cultural Production*. London: Croom Helm, 1979.

Barthes, Roland. *Elements of Semiology*. London: Jonathan Cape, 1967.

Baruch, Grace, and Rosalind Barnett. "Adult Daughters' Relationships with Their Mothers." *Journal of Marriage and the Family* 45 (1983): 601–606.

———, and Caryl Rivers. "How Women and Their Mothers Become Friends." *McCall's*, April 1980, 32.

Basescu, Sabert. "Why So Many Women Can't Stand Their Own Mothers." *Redbook*, June 1970, 78.

Bassoff, Evelyn. *Mothers and Daughters: Loving and Letting Go*. New York: New American Library, 1988.

Bathrick, Serafina. "The Mary Tyler Moore Show: Women at Home and at Work." In *MTM: Quality Television*, ed. Jane Feuer, Paul Kerr, and Tise Vahimagi, 99–131. London: British Film Institute, 1984.

———. "The True Woman and the Family-Film: The Industrial Production of Memory." Ph.D. dissertation, University of Wisconsin, 1980.

Baudrillard, Jean. *For a Critique of the Political Economy of the Sign*. St. Louis MO: Telos Press, 1981.

Beach, Stewart. "The Tragedy of an Overprotective Mother." *Better Homes and Gardens*, June 1962, 76.

Beasley, Chris. "The Ambiguities of Desire: Patriarchal Subjectivity:

Memories of Motherhood, Marriage, and Sexuality Among Birmingham Working Women and Their Daughters Between the Wars." M.A. thesis, Centre for Contemporary Cultural Studies, 1985.

Beattie, Barbara. "Preparing Your Daughter for Adolescence." *Parents' Magazine*, October 1929, 71.

Benjamin, Jessica. "Authority and the Family Revisited: or, A World Without Fathers?" *New German Critique* 13 (Winter 1978): 35–58.

———. *The Bonds of Love: Psychoanalysis, Feminism, and the Problem of Domination.* New York: Pantheon Books, 1988.

Benjamin, Walter. *Illuminations.* London: Fontana, 1973.

Bennett, Tony, Susan Boyd-Bowman, Colin Mercer, and Janet Woolacott, eds. *Popular Television and Film.* London: British Film Institute, 1981.

Berger, John. *Ways of Seeing.* Harmondsworth, Middlesex, England: Penguin Books, 1972.

Bernard, Jessie. *The Future of Motherhood.* New York: Dial Press, 1974.

Bettelheim, Bruno. "Fathers Shouldn't Try To Be Mothers." *Parents' Magazine*, October 1956, 40.

Betterton, Rosemary. "How Do Women Look? The Female Nude in the Work of Suzanne Valadon." In *Looking On: Images of Femininity in the Visual Arts and Media,* ed. Rosemary Betterton, 217–234. New York: Pandora Press, 1987.

———, ed. *Looking On: Images of Feminity in the Visual Arts and Media.* New York: Pandora Press, 1987.

Biskind, Peter. *Seeing Is Believing: How Hollywood Taught Us To Stop Worrying and Love the Fifties.* New York: Pantheon Books, 1983.

Bittle, Camilla. "Between Mother and Daughter." *Good Housekeeping,* March 1980, 134.

Blake, Dorothy. "She Never Tells Me Anything!" *Parents' Magazine,* August 1938, 65.

Bloom, Lynn Z. "Heritages: Dimensions of Mother-Daughter Relationship in Women's Autobiographies." In *The Lost Tradition: Mothers and Daughters in Literature,* ed. Cathy N. Davidson and E. M. Broner, 291–305. New York: Frederick Ungar, 1980.

Bordwell, David, and Kristin Thompson. *Film Art.* Reading, MA: Addison-Wesley, 1979.

Bowlby, John. *Child Care and the Growth of Love.* Harmondsworth, Middlesex, England: Penguin Books, 1953.

Boykin, Eleanor. "Should Mothers Be Matchmakers?" *Parents' Magazine,* August 1936, 20.

Brenton, Myron. "Mothers and Daughters." *Seventeen,* December 1971, 92.

Briffault, Robert. *The Mothers.* New York: Grosset & Dunlop, 1963.

Brinson, Claudia S. "Becoming a Daughter." *McCall's*, July 1982, 67.

Brothers, Joyce. "Bill of Rights for Wives and Mothers." *Good Housekeeping*, April 1965, 48–56.

Brown, Dorothy. *Setting a Course: American Women in the 1920s*. Boston: Twayne/G. K. Hall, 1987.

Brunsdon, Charlotte, ed. *Films for Women*. London: British Film Institute, 1986.

Burger, Peter. *Theory of the Avante-Garde*. Manchester: Manchester University Press, 1984.

Busby, Linda J. "Sex-Role Research on the Mass Media." *Journal of Communication* 25 (Autumn 1975): 107–131.

Cadden, Vivian. "The Myth of the Perfect Mother." *Redbook*, April 1961, 46.

Cahill, Susan, ed. *Mothers: Memories, Dreams and Reflections by Literary Daughters*. New York: New American Library, 1988.

Cambridge Women's Studies Group. *Women in Society*. London: Virago, 1981.

Campbell, D'Ann. *Women at War with America: Private Lives in a Patriotic Era*. Cambridge, MA: Harvard University Press, 1984.

Caperton, Helena Lefroy. "How We Raised Our Six Daughters." *Woman's Home Companion*, December 1930, 37–38.

Caplan, Paula. *Don't Blame Mother: Mending the Mother-Daughter Relationship*. New York: Harper and Row, 1989.

Carter, Paul A. *Another Part of the Fifties*. New York: Columbia University Press, 1983.

Castle, Marian. "Hard-boiled Mothers: Yesterday's Flapper as Today's Modern Parent." *Woman's Journal* 16 (1931): 11 + .

Castleman, Harry, and Walter J. Podrazik. *Watching TV: Four Decades of American Television*. New York: McGraw-Hill, 1982.

Centre for Contemporary Cultural Studies Women's Studies Group. *Women Take Issue*. London: Hutchinson, 1978.

Chafe, William. *The American Woman*. New York: Oxford University Press, 1972.

———. *The Unfinished Journey: America Since World War II*. New York: Oxford University Press, 1986.

Chase, Janet. "What Mothers and Daughters Can Give Each Other." *Woman's Day*, July 14, 1981, 30.

Chernin, Kim. *The Hungry Self: Women, Eating and Identity*. London: Virago Press, 1986.

———. *In My Mother's House*. New York: Harper and Row, 1983.

Chesler, Phyllis. *Women and Madness*. New York: Avon Books, 1972.

Chodorow, Nancy. "Gender, Relation, and Difference in Psychoanalytic Perspective." In *The Future of Difference,* ed. Alice Jardine and Hester Eisenstein, 3–19. New Brunswick, NJ: Rutgers University Press, 1987.

———. *The Reproduction of Mothering.* Berkeley: University of California Press, 1978.

Clark, Clifford. "Ranch-House Suburbia: Ideals and Realities." In *Recasting America: Culture and Politics in the Age of Cold War,* ed. Lary May, 171–191. Chicago: University of Chicago Press, 1989.

Clarke, John, Charles Chricter, and Richard Johnson, eds. *Working-Class Culture: Studies in History and Theory.* London: Hutchinson, 1979.

Coffin, Patricia. "Memo To: The American Woman." *Look,* January 11, 1966, 18–23.

Cohen, Stanley. *Folk Devils and Moral Panics: The Creation of the Mods and Rockers.* London: MacGibbon and Kee, 1972.

Collins, Patricia Hill. "The Meaning of Motherhood in Black Culture and Black Mother/Daughter Relationships." *Sage* 4 (Fall 1987): 3–10.

Considine, David. *The Cinema of Adolescence.* Jefferson, NC: McFarland, 1985.

Coogan, Jeanmarie. "So You're Kate's Girl!" *Reader's Digest,* July 1963, 219–223.

Cook, Pam. "Duplicity in *Mildred Pierce.*" In *Women in Film Noir,* ed. E. Ann Kaplan, 68–82. London: British Film Institute, 1978.

———, ed. *The Cinema Book.* New York: Pantheon Books, 1986.

Coss, Clare, Sondra Segal, and Roberta Sklar. "Daughters." Part I of "The Daughters Cycle." Women's Experimental Theatre, 98 E. 7th St., New York, NY 10009. 1977–81.

Cowan, Ruth Schwartz. *More Work for Mother.* New York: Basic Books, 1983.

Creaturo, Barbara. "Making Friends with Mom." *Woman's Day,* May 21, 1985, 24–29.

Curran, J., M. Gurevitch, and J. Woollacott, eds. *Mass Communication and Society.* London: Edward Arnold, 1977.

Dally, Ann. *Inventing Motherhood.* New York: Schocken Books, 1982.

Damon, Virgil S., and Isabella Jabes. "The War Between Mother and Daughter." *Look,* January 11, 1966, 30–34.

Davidson, Cathy N., and E. M. Broner. *The Lost Tradition: Mothers and Daughters in Literature.* New York: Frederick Ungar, 1980.

Davies, Carol Boyce. "Mothering and Healing in Recent Black Women's Fiction." *Sage* 2(1) (Spring 1985): 41–43.

Davis, Bette, with Michael Herskowitz. *This 'N That*. New York: Putnam's, 1987.

Davitz, Lois Leiderman. "Are You a Better Mother Than Your Mother?" *McCall's*, July 1984, 83.

de Beauvoir, Simone. *Memoirs of a Dutiful Daughter*. Cleveland: World, 1959.

———. *The Second Sex*. New York: Vintage Books, 1974.

de Bord, Guy. *Society of the Spectacle*. Detroit: Black and Red, 1977.

Decter, Midge. "Sex, My Daughter, and Me." *Harper's*, August 1967, 27–32.

de Lauretis, Teresa. *Alice Doesn't: Feminism, Semiotics, Cinema*. Bloomington: Indiana University Press, 1984.

———. *Technologies of Gender: Essays on Theory, Film, and Fiction*. Bloomington: Indiana University Press, 1987.

———, ed. *Feminist Studies/Critical Studies*. Bloomington: Indiana University Press, 1986.

Dickstein, Morris. *The Gates of Eden: American Culture in the Sixties*. New York: Basic Books, 1977.

Dinnerstein, Dorothy. *The Mermaid and the Minotaur: Sexual Arrangements and Human Malaise*. New York: Harper and Row, 1976.

Doane, Mary Ann. *The Desire to Desire: The Women's Film of the 1940s*. Bloomington: Indiana University Press, 1987.

———. "Film and Masquerade: Theorizing the Female Spectator." *Screen* 23 (September/October 1982): 74–87.

———. "The Woman's Film: Possession and Address." In *Re-Vision: Essays in Feminist Film Criticism*, ed. Mary Ann Doane, Patricia Mellencamp, and Linda Williams, 283–298. Los Angeles: American Film Institute, 1984.

———, Patricia Mellencamp, and Linda Williams, eds. *Re-Vision: Essays in Feminist Film Criticism*. Los Angeles: American Film Institute, 1984.

Dominick, J. R. "The Portrayal of Women in Prime-time, 1953–1977." *Sex Roles* 5 (1979): 405–411.

Donzelot, Jacques. *Policing the Family*. London: Hutchinson, 1979.

Dormen, Lesley. "How To Get Over Your Mother." *McCall's*, February 1986, 40.

Dowling, Colette. *The Cinderella Complex: Women's Hidden Fear of Independence*. Glasgow: Fontana Paperbacks, 1982.

———. *Perfect Women: Hidden Fears of Inadequacy and the Drive To Perform*. New York: Simon and Schuster, 1988.

Duerst, Norma. "My Daughter and I." *Redbook*, April 1975, 38–41.

Duffy, Maureen. *That's How It Was*. London: Virago, 1983.

DuPlessis, Rachel Blau. "Washing Blood." *Feminist Studies* 4 (June 1978): 1–12.

Duruz, Jean. "Motherhood, Marriage, and Sexuality: The Glitter or the Gold? Ideologies of Working Class Girls in Birmingham During the Interwar Years." M.A. thesis, Centre for Contemporary Cultural Studies, 1985.

Dyer, Gillian. "Women and Television: An Overview." In *Boxed In: Women and Television*, ed. Helen Baehr and Gillian Dyer, 6–16. New York: Pandora Press, 1987.

Dyer, Richard. *Stars*. London: British Film Institute, 1979.

Dyhouse, Carol. *Girls Growing Up in Late Victorian and Edwardian England*. London: Routledge and Kegan Paul, 1981.

———. "Mothers and Daughters in the Middle-Class Home, c. 1870–1914." In *Labour and Love: Women's Experience of Home and Family 1850–1940*, ed. Jane Lewis, 27–47. London: Basil Blackwell, 1986.

Eagleton, Terry. *Literary Theory*. Minneapolis: University of Minnesota Press, 1983.

Ehrenreich, Barbara, and Deidre English. *For Her Own Good: 150 Years of the Experts' Advice to Women*. Garden City, NY: Anchor Books, 1979.

Eisenstein, Hester. *Contemporary Feminist Thought*. Boston: G. K. Hall, 1983.

Eisenstein, Hester, and Alice Jardine, eds. *The Future of Difference*. Boston: G. K. Hall, 1980.

Eisenstein, Zillah. *Capitalist Patriarchy and the Case for Socialist Feminism*. New York: Monthly Review Press, 1979.

Ellis, John. *Visible Fictions*. London: Routledge and Kegan Paul, 1982.

Elsaesser, Thomas. "Tales of Sound and Fury: Observations on the Family Melodrama." In *Home Is Where the Heart Is: Studies in Melodrama and the Women's Film*, ed. Christine Gledhill, 43–69. London: British Film Institute, 1987.

Engels, F. *The Origins of the Family, Private Property, and the State* (1884). London: Lawrence and Wishart, 1972.

Erens, Patricia, ed. *Sexual Stratagems: The World of Women in Film*. New York: Horizon Press, 1979.

Erikson, Erik. *Identity: Youth and Crisis*. New York: Norton, 1968.

Evans, Sara. *Born for Liberty: A History of Women in America*. New York: Free Press, 1989.

———. *Personal Politics*. New York: Knopf, 1979.

Ewen, Elizabeth. *Immigrant Women in the Land of Dollars: Life and Culture on the Lower East Side 1890–1925*. New York: Monthly Review Press, 1985.

Farnham, Marynia. "How To Handle Your Teenage Daughter." *Cosmopolitan*, September 1955, 112–117.

Farrar, Marcella. "Mother-Daughter Conflicts Extended into Later Life." *Social Casework* 36 (1955): 202–207.

*Feminist Studies* 4(2) (June 1978). "Toward a Feminist Theory of Motherhood" (special issue).

Feuer, Jane. "Daughter-Rite: Living with Our Pain and Love." *Jump Cut* 23 (1980): 12–13.

———. "Melodrama, Serial Form and Television Today." *Screen* 25 (January/February 1984): 4–16.

Firestone, Shulamith. *The Dialectic of Sex* (1970). London: Women's Press, 1979.

Fischer, Lucy Rose. *Linked Lives: Adult Daughters and Their Mothers.* New York: Harper and Row, 1986.

Fiske, John. *Television Culture*. London: Metheun, 1987.

Fiske, J., and J. Hartley. *Reading Television*. London: Metheun, 1978.

Flax, Jane. "The Conflict Between Nurturance and Autonomy in Mother-Daughter Relationships and Within Feminism." *Feminist Studies* 4 (June 1978): 171–189.

———. "Mother-Daughter Relationships: Psychodynamics, Politics, and Philosophy." In *The Future of Difference*, ed. Hester Eisenstein and Alice Jardine, 20–40. New Brunswick, NJ: Rutgers University Press, 1985.

Flynn, Elizabeth A., and Patrocinio P. Schweickart, eds. *Gender and Reading: Essays on Readers, Texts, and Contexts.* Baltimore: Johns Hopkins University Press, 1986.

Foster, Constantine J. "A Mother of Boys Says: Raise Your Girl To Be a Wife." *Parents' Magazine*, September 1956, 143.

Foster, Hal. *Recordings: Art, Spectacle, Cultural Politics.* Port Townsend, WA: Bay Press, 1985.

———, ed. *The Anti-Aesthetic.* Port Townsend, WA: Bay Press, 1983.

Francis, Dorothy. "The Unpopular Daughter." *Good Housekeeping*, November 1949, 43.

French, Brandon. *On the Verge of Revolt: Women in American Films of the Fifties.* New York: Frederick Ungar, 1978.

French, Marilyn. *Her Mother's Daughter.* New York: Ballantine Books, 1988.

———. *The Women's Room.* New York: Summit Books, 1977.

Friday, Nancy. *My Mother/My Self.* New York: Delacorte, 1977.

Friedan, Betty. "Beyond Women's Liberation." *McCall's*, August 1972, 82.

———. *The Feminine Mystique.* New York: Norton, 1963.

———. *The Second Stage.* New York: Summit Books, 1981.

*Frontiers: A Journal of Women's Studies* 3(2) (1978): "Mothers and Daughters" (special issue).

Gallop, Jane. *The Daughter's Seduction*. Ithaca, NY: Cornell University Press, 1982.

Gardiner, Judith Kegan. "A Wake for Mother: The Maternal Deathbed in Women's Fiction." *Feminist Studies* 4 (June 1978): 146–165.

Gerbner, George. "The Dynamics of Cultural Resistance." In *Hearth and Home: Images of Women in the Mass Media*, ed. Gaye Tuchman, Arlene Kaplan Daniels, and James Benet, 46–50. New York: Oxford University Press, 1979.

Gilbert, James. *Another Chance: Postwar America, 1945–1968*. New York: Knopf, 1981.

Gilbert, Lucy, and Paula Webster. *Bound by Love: The Sweet Trap of Daughterhood*. Boston: Beacon Press, 1982.

Gilligan, Carol. *In a Different Voice: Psychological Theory and Women's Development*. Cambridge, MA: Harvard University Press, 1982.

Gitlin, Todd. *Watching Television*. New York: Pantheon, 1986.

Gittings, Diana. *The Family in Question: Changing Households and Familiar Ideologies*. Atlantic Highland, NJ: Humanities Press International, 1982.

Gledhill, Christine, ed. *Home Is Where the Heart Is: Studies in Melodrama and the Women's Film*. London: British Film Institute, 1987.

Glennon, Lynda, and Richard Butsch. "The Family as Portrayed on Television 1946–1978." In U.S. Department of Health and Human Services, *Television and Behavior: Ten Years of Scientific Progress and Implications for the Eighties*, vol 2: Technical Reviews, pp. 264–271. Washington, DC: U.S. Government Printing Office, 1982.

Gluck, Sherna B. *Rosie the Riveter Revisited: Women, the War, and Social Change*. Boston: Twayne, 1987.

Goffman, Erving. *Gender Advertisements*. New York: Harper and Row, 1976.

Goldman, Eric. *The Crucial Decade—and After: America 1945–1960*. New York: Vintage Press, 1960.

Gordon, Michael, ed. *The American Family in Social-Historical Perspective*. New York: St. Martin's Press, 1973.

Gornick, Vivian. *Fierce Attachments*. New York: Simon and Schuster, 1987.

Gottlieb, Annie. "Your Mother, Your First Love—Can You Ever Get Over Each Other?" *Mademoiselle*, February 1982, 131–133.

Gray, Adann. "Reading the Audience." *Screen* 28 (1987): 24–35.

Greene, Gael. "A Vote Against Motherhood." *Saturday Evening Post*, January 26, 1963, 10–12.

Grizzle, Ann F., with William Proctor. *Mother Love, Mother Hate: Breaking Dependent Love Patterns in Family Relationships*. New York: Fawcett Columbine, 1988.

Gross, Amy. "Were You a Daddy's Girl or Mother's Daughter—the Difference It Makes to Your Life." *Mademoiselle*, March 1974, 114.

Gurevitch, Michael, Tony Bennett, James Curran, and Janet Woollacott, eds. *Culture, Society and the Media*. London: Metheun, 1982.

Hagood, Margaret Jarman. *Mothers of the South: Portraiture of the White Tenant Farm Woman*. Chapel Hill: University of North Carolina Press, 1939.

Hall, Ann. "Your Quarrel with Your Daughter." *Good Housekeeping*, December 1949, 44.

Hall, Nor. *Mothers and Daughters: Reflections of the Archetypal Feminine*. Minneapolis, MN: Rusoff Books, 1976.

Hall, Stuart. "Cultural Studies: Two Paradigms." *Media, Culture, and Society* 2 (1980): 57–72.

———, ed. *Culture, Media, Language: Working Papers in Cultural Studies 1972–1979*. London: Hutchinson, 1979.

———. *Resistance Through Rituals*. London: Hutchinson, 1976.

Hall, S., J. Jefferson, J. Clarke, and B. Roberts. *Policing the Crisis*. London: Macmillan, 1978.

Hall, Stuart, and Paddy Whannel. *The Popular Arts*. Boston: Beacon Press, 1964.

Haller, Scott. "The Tough Terms of Motherhood." *People Weekly*, February 6, 1984, 81–87.

Hammer, Signe. *Daughters and Mothers, Mothers and Daughters*. New York: Quadrangle/New York Times, 1975.

———. "Hostility: Why You Hate Your Mother." *Harper's Bazaar*, October 1976, 120.

Hancock, Emily. *The Girl Within: Recapture the Childhood Self, the Key to Female Identity*. New York: E. P. Dutton, 1989.

Haralovich, Mary Beth. "Sitcoms and Suburbs: Positioning the 1950s Homemaker." *Quarterly Review of Film & Video* 2 (1989): 62.

Harrison, Barbara Grizzuti. "Finding the Way To Be Friends." *McCall's*, October 1975, 94.

Harrison, Cynthia. *On Account of Sex: The Politics of Women's Issues 1945–1968*. Berkeley: University of California Press, 1988.

Hartmann, Susan. *The Home Front and Beyond: American Women in the 1940s*. Boston: Twayne, 1982.

———. "Prescriptions for Penelope: Literature on Women's Obligations to Returning World War Two Veterans." *Women's Studies* 5(3) (1978): 223–239.

Hartsock, Nancy C. M. *Money, Sex and Power: Towards Feminist Historical Materialism.* Boston: Northeastern University Press, 1983.

Haskell, Molly. *From Reverence to Rape: The Treatment of Women in the Movies,* 2nd ed. Chicago: University of Chicago Press, 1987.

Hawkes, Terence. *Structuralism and Semiotics.* London: Metheun, 1977.

Hawthorne, Ruth. "Mothers and Daughters." *Delineator* 119 (1931): 9+.

Heath, Stephen. *Questions of Cinema.* Houndsmill, Basingstoke, Hampshire, England: Macmillan, 1981.

Heath, Stephen, and Teresa de Lauretis, eds. *The Cinematic Apparatus.* London: Macmillan, 1980.

Hebdige, Dick. *Subculture: The Meaning of Style.* London: Metheun, 1979.

Heffner, Elaine. *Mothering: The Emotional Experience of Motherhood After Freud and Feminism.* Garden City, NY: Doubleday, 1978.

Herman, Nini. *Too Long a Child: The Mother-Daughter Dyad.* London: Free Association Books, 1989.

Hirsch, Marianne. "Mothers and Daughters." *Signs* 7 (Autumn 1981): 200–222.

———. *The Mother/Daughter Plot: Narrative, Psychoanalysis, Feminism.* Bloomington: Indiana University Press, 1989.

Honey, Maureen. *Creating Rosie the Riveter: Class, Gender, and Propaganda During World War II.* Amherst: University of Massachusetts Press, 1984.

———. "Feminism and Women's Imagination After the Vote: Periodical Fiction of the 1920s." Unpublished manuscript, 1980(?).

Hoover, J. Edgar. "Mothers—Our Only Hope." *Woman's Home Companion,* January 1944, 20–21.

Howell, Mary. "Having a Mother/Being a Mother." *Glamour,* May 1988, 252–253.

Howitt, Florence. "Do You Know Everything in Your Daughter's Head?" *Good Housekeeping,* January 1945, 28.

Humphreys, Nancy K. *American Women's Magazines: An Annotated Historical Guide.* New York: Garland, 1989.

Hyman, B. D. *My Mother's Keeper.* New York: Berkley Books, 1985.

Irigaray, Luce. "Les corps a corps avec la mère." Montreal: Les editions de la pleine lune, 1981. Quoted and translated in Eleanor Kuykendall, "Toward an Ethic of Nurturance: Luce Irigaray on Mothering and Power." In *Mothering: Essays in Feminist Theory,* ed. Joyce Treblicot, 263–274. Totowa, NJ: Rowman & Allanheld, 1983.

Irwin, Inez. "Insuring Your Daughter's Success." *Woman's Home Companion,* December 1936, 22.

Jameson, Fredric. *The Political Unconscious*. Ithaca, NY: Cornell University Press, 1981.

Johnson, Lesley. *The Cultural Critics: From Matthew Arnold to Raymond Williams*. London: Routledge and Kegan Paul, 1979.

Johnston, Claire. "The Subject of Feminist Film Theory/Practice." *Screen* 21/22 (Summer 1980): 27–29.

Johnston, Sheila. "Film Narrative and the Structuralist Controversy." In *The Cinema Book*, ed. Pam Cook, 222–251. New York: Pantheon, 1986.

Joseph, Gloria I., and Jill Lewis. *Common Differences: Conflicts in Black and White Feminist Perspectives*. Garden City, NY: Anchor Books, 1981.

Kaledin, Eugenia. *Mothers and More: American Women in the 1950s*. Boston: Twayne, 1984.

Kaplan, E. Ann. "Feminist Criticism and Television." In *Channels of Discourse: Television and Contemporary Criticism*, ed. Robert C. Allen, 211–253. Chapel Hill: University of North Carolina Press, 1987.

———. "Mothering, Feminism and Representation: The Maternal in Melodrama and the Woman's Film 1910–1940." In *Home Is Where the Heart Is: Studies in Melodrama and the Woman's Film*, ed. Christine Gledhill, 113–137. London: British Film Institute, 1987.

———. *Women and Film: Both Sides of the Camera*. New York: Metheun, 1983.

———, ed. *Regarding Television*. Frederick, MD: University Publications of America, 1983.

Kaplan, Helen Singer. "Can You Ruin Your Daughter's Sex Life?" *Harper's Bazaar*, October 1976, 119.

Kappeler, Susanne. *The Pornography of Representation*. Cambridge, MA: Polity Press, 1986.

Kay, Karyn, and Gerry Peary, eds. *Women in the Cinema: A Critical Anthology*. New York: Dutton, 1977.

Keller, Catherine. *From a Broken Web: Separation, Sexism, and Self*. Boston: Beacon Press, 1986.

Kendrick, Mary Alice. "Forestalling Delinquency." *Parents' Magazine*, July 1943, 28.

Kipnis, Laura. "'Refunctioning' Reconsidered: Towards a Left Popular Culture." In *High Theory/Low Culture: Analysing Popular Television and Film*, ed. Colin MacCabe, 11–36. New York: St. Martin's Press, 1986.

Kole, Janet. "Eight Successful Women Discuss Motherhood." *Harper's Bazaar*, October 1976, 114.

Komaiko, Jean. "My Children Are Bringing Me Up to Date." *Parents' Magazine*, July 1956, 40.

Konner, Linda. "Mothers and Daughters: Secrets They Share, Secrets They Keep." *Seventeen*, January 1979, 100.

Kornblatt, Joyce Reiser. *Nothing To Do with Love*. London: Women's Press, 1982.

Kuhn, Annette. "Women's Genres." *Screen* 25 (January/February 1984): 18–28.

———. *Women's Pictures: Feminism and Cinema*. London: Routledge and Kegan Paul, 1982.

Kuykendall, Eleanor. "Toward an Ethic of Nurturance: Luce Irigaray on Mothering and Power." In *Mothering: Essays in Feminist Theory*, ed. Joyce Treblicot, 263–274. Totowa, NJ: Rowman and Allanheld, 1983.

Landers, Ann. "A Sickness of Our Times." *The PTA Magazine*, September 1966, 4.

———. "What To Tell Your Daughter About Women's Lib." *Today's Health* 49 (October 1971): 52.

Landers, Ann, Mary S. Calderone, Lester Kirkendall, and Robert Mears. "Are Girls Getting Too Aggressive?" *The PTA Magazine*, September 1966, 4–7.

LaPlace, Maria. "Producing and Consuming the Woman's Film: Discursive Struggle in *Now, Voyager*." In *Home Is Where the Heart Is: Studies in Melodrama and the Woman's Film*, ed. Christine Gledhill, 138–166. London: British Film Institute, 1987.

Lasch, Christopher. *Haven in a Heartless World: The Family Besieged*. New York: Basic Books, 1977.

Lazarre, Jane. *The Mother Knot*. New York: Dell, 1976.

Lazere, Donald, ed. *American Media and Mass Culture: Left Perspectives*. Berkeley: University of California Press, 1987.

Lears, Jackson. "A Matter of Taste: Corporate Cultural Hegemony in a Mass-Consumption Society." In *Recasting America: Culture and Politics in the Age of Cold War*, ed. Lary May, 38–57. Chicago: University of Chicago Press, 1989.

Lee, Dorothy. "What Does Homemaking Mean to You?" *Parents' Magazine*, January 1947, 24.

Leibman, Nina C. "Leave Mother Out: The Fifties Family in American Television." *Wide Angle* 10 (1988): 24–41.

Lein, Laura. *Families Without Villains*. Lexington, MA: D. C. Heath, 1984.

Leonard, Eugenie Andruss. *Concerning Our Girls and What They Tell*

*Us.* New York: AMS Press/Columbia University Teachers College, 1930.

Leshan, Eda J. "Good Mothers, Impossible Children." *Redbook*, April 1965, 59.

Lester, David. "Are You Pushing Your Daughter into Too-Early Marriage?" *Good Housekeeping*, October 1961, 80–81, 216–221.

Levy, David. *Maternal Overprotection.* New York: Columbia University Press, 1943.

Lewis, Jane. *The Politics of Motherhood.* London: Croom Helm, 1980.

————, ed. *Labour and Love: Women's Experience of Home and Family 1850–1940.* London: Basil Blackwell, 1986.

Lewis, Jane, and Barbara Meredith. *Daughters Who Care: Daughters Caring for Mothers at Home.* London: Routledge, 1988.

Lipsitz, George. *Class and Culture in Cold War America: "A Rainbow at Midnight."* South Hadley, MA: J. F. Bergin, 1982.

————. "The Meaning of Memory: Family, Class, and Ethnicity in Early Network Television Programming." In *Recasting America: Culture and Politics in the Age of Cold War,* ed. Lary May, 79–116. Chicago: University of Chicago Press, 1989.

————. *Time Passages: Collective Memory and American Popular Culture.* Minneapolis: University of Minnesota Press, 1990.

List, Shelly Steinmann. "When Our Daughters Discover Love and Sex." *McCall's*, September 1973, 65.

Lobsenz, Norman M. "Are Working Wives Hurting or Helping Their Families?" *Redbook*, July 1961, 30.

Lochridge, Patricia. "The Mother Racket." *Woman's Home Companion,* July 1944, 20.

Long, Elizabeth. *The American Dream and the Popular Novel.* Boston: Routledge and Kegan Paul, 1985.

Lopate, Carol. "Daytime Television: You'll Never Want to Leave Home." *Feminist Studies* 4(6) (1976): 69–82.

Lundberg, Ferdinand, and Marynia Farnham. *Modern Woman: The Lost Sex.* New York: Harper and Row, 1947.

Lynn, David. *Daughter and Parents: Past, Present, and Future.* Monterey, CA: Brooks/Cole, 1979.

MacCabe, Colin, ed. *High Theory/Low Culture: Analyzing Popular Television and Film.* New York: St. Martin's Press, 1986.

MacDonald, J. Fred. *Blacks and White TV: Afro-Americans in Television Since 1948.* Chicago: Nelson-Hall, 1983.

Macdonnell, Diane. *Theories of Discourse.* London: Basil Blackwell, 1986.

Maglin, Nan Bauer. "Don't Never Forget the Bridge That You Crossed

Over on: The Literature of Matrilineage." In *The Lost Tradition: Mothers and Daughters in Literature*, ed. Cathy N. Davidson and E. M. Broner, 257–267. New York: Frederick Ungar, 1980.

Marc, David. *Comic Visions: Television Comedy and American Culture*. Winchester, MA: Unwin Hyman, 1989.

March, Judith. "Not a Case History, Not a Statistic: Our Daughter." *McCall's*, August 1967, 76.

Margary, Louise. "Severe Disturbances in Young Women Reflecting Damage to Mother-Daughter Relationship." *Social Casework* 11 (1959): 202–207.

Margolis, Maxine. *Mothers and Such: Views of American Women and Why They Changed*. Berkeley: University of California Press, 1984.

Marks, Marjorie. "Be Popular with Your Daughter." *Woman's Home Companion*, June 1950, 104–105.

Marzollo, Jean. "Are You Still Trying to Please Your Mother?" *Mademoiselle*, May 1983, 176.

Mast, Gerald, and Marshall Cohen, eds. *Film Theory and Criticism*. New York: Oxford University Press, 1979.

May, Elaine Tyler. "Explosive Issues: Sex, Women, and the Bomb." In *Recasting America: Culture and Politics in the Age of Cold War*, ed. Lary May, 19–37. Chicago: University of Chicago Press, 1989.

———. *Homeward Bound: American Families in the Cold War Era*. New York: Basic Books, 1988.

May, Lary, ed. *Recasting America: Culture and Politics in the Age of Cold War*. Chicago: University of Chicago Press, 1989.

Mayne, Judith. "The Woman at the Keyhole: Women's Cinema and Feminist Criticism." *New German Critique* 23 (1981): 27–43.

McBride, Angela. *The Growth and Development of Mothers*. New York: Harper and Row, 1973.

McCormick, Elsie. "Sometimes Mothers Talk Too Much." *Good Housekeeping*, September 1943, 25.

McHugh, Mary. "Daughters and Mothers: Making Peace, Making Friends." *Cosmopolitan*, October 1984, 271.

Meehan, Diana M. *Ladies of the Evening: Women Characters of Primetime Television*. Metuchen, NJ: Scarecrow Press, 1983.

Mellen, Joan. *Women and Their Sexuality in the New Film*. New York: Horizon Press, 1973.

Mellencamp, Patricia, ed. *Logics of Television: Essays in Cultural Criticism*. Bloomington: Indiana University Press, 1990.

Metz, Christian. *Film Language: A Semiotics of the Cinema*. Translated by Michael Taylor. New York: Oxford University Press, 1974.

Miller, Douglas T., and Marion Nowak. *The Fifties: The Way We Really Were*. Garden City, NY: Doubleday, 1975.

Miner, Madonna M. "Guaranteed to Please: Twentieth-Century American Women's Bestsellers." In *Gender and Reading: Essays on Readers, Texts, and Contexts*, ed. Elizabeth A. Flynn and Patrocinio P. Schweickart, 187–214. Baltimore: Johns Hopkins University Press, 1986.

Mintz, Steven, and Susan Kellogg. *Domestic Revolutions: A Social History of American Family Life*. New York: Free Press, 1988.

Mitchell, Juliet. *Psychoanalysis and Feminism*. Harmondsworth, England: Penguin, 1975.

Mitchell, Juliet, and Jacqueline Rose, eds. *Feminine Sexuality: Jacques Lacan and the "école freudienne."* New York: Norton, 1982.

Mitz, Rick. *The Great TV Sitcom Book*. New York: Perigee Books, 1983.

Modleski, Tania. "Femininity as Mas(s)querade: A Feminist Approach to Mass Culture." In *High Theory/Low Culture: Analysing Popular Television and Film*, ed. Colin MacCabe, 37–52. New York: St. Martin's Press, 1986.

———. *Loving with a Vengeance: Mass-produced Fantasies for Women*. New York: Metheun, 1982.

———, ed. *Studies in Entertainment: Critical Approaches to Mass Culture*. Bloomington: Indiana University Press, 1986.

Moi, Toril, ed. *The Kristeva Reader*. New York: Columbia University Press, 1986.

Morgan, Robin. *Dry Your Smile*. Garden City, NY: Doubleday, 1987.

———, ed. *Sisterhood Is Powerful: An Anthology of Writings from the Women's Liberation Movement*. New York: Vintage Books/Random House, 1970.

Morley, David. *Family Television: Cultural Power and Domestic Leisure*. London: Comedia, 1986.

Morrison, Toni. *Beloved*. New York: Knopf, 1987.

———. *Tar Baby*. New York: Knopf, 1981.

"Mothers and Daughters." *Good Housekeeping*, May 1980, 123.

Mulvey, Laura. "Afterthoughts on 'Visual Pleasure and Narrative Cinema' . . . Inspired by 'Duel in the Sun.'" *Framework* 15/16/17 (1981): 12–15.

———. "Melodrama in and out of the Home." In *High Theory, Low Culture*, ed. Colin MacCabe. New York: St. Martin's Press, 1986.

———. "Visual Pleasure and Narrative Cinema." *Screen* 16 (1975): 6–18.

"My Problem: My Daughter Was an Unfit Mother." *Good Housekeeping*, February 1980, 28.

"My Problem: My Daughter Didn't Want Me To Be Her Best Friend." *Good Housekeeping*, November 1983, 38.

"My Problem and How I Solved It: Mother and Daughter." *Good House-keeping*, June 1962, 10–17.

"My Problem and How I Solved It: Teenage Mother." *Good Housekeep-ing*, February 1965, 8.

Myerson, Abraham. "Let's Quit Blaming Mom." *Science Digest*, March 1951, 10–15.

Navasky, Victor. *Naming Names*. New York: Viking Press, 1980.

Naylor, Gloria. *The Women of Brewster Place*. New York: Viking Press, 1982.

Neisser, Edith G. *Mothers and Daughters: A Lifelong Relationship*, rev. ed. New York: Harper and Row, 1967.

———. "The Special World of Mothers and Daughters." *Parents' Maga-zine*, May 1967, 41.

Nelson, Joyce. "*Mildred Pierce* Reconsidered." *Film Reader* 2 (1977): 65–70.

Newton, Judith, and Deborah Rosenfelt, eds. *Feminist Criticism and So-cial Change: Sex, Class and Race in Literature and Culture*. London: Methuen, 1985.

Niquette, Enid A. "Daughter's in the Kitchen Now." *Parents' Magazine*, August 1943, 54.

Oakley, Ann. *Becoming a Mother*. Oxford: Martin Robinson, 1979.

———. *Housewife*. New York: Pantheon, 1974.

———. *Subject Woman*. New York: Pantheon, 1981.

———. *Woman Confined: Towards a Sociology of Childbirth*. New York: Schocken, 1980.

O'Barr, Jean F., Deborah Pope, and Mary Wyer, eds. *Ties That Bind: Essays on Mothering and Patriarchy*. Chicago: University of Chicago Press, 1990.

O'Connor, John. *American History/American Television*. New York: Fred-erick Ungar, 1983.

O'Donnell, Lydia. *The Unheralded Majority: Contemporary Women as Mothers*. Lexington, MA: D. C. Heath, 1985.

Ogden, Annegret S. *The Great American Housewife: From Helpmate to Wage Earner 1976–1986*. Westport, CT: Greenwood Press.

Olsen, Tillie, with Julie Olsen Edwards. *Mothers and Daughters: That Special Quality*. New York: Aperture, 1987.

Orbach, Susie. "From Mother to Daughter." *New Statesman*, March 29, 1985, 28.

Osmond, Marie, with Julie Davis. "What Grown-up Daughters Owe Their Mothers." *Good Housekeeping*, March 1980, 98.

Park, Christine, and Caroline Heaton, eds. *Close Company: Stories of Mothers and Daughters*. London: Virago, 1987.

Parsons, Talcott, and Robert F. Bales. *Family, Socialization and Interaction Process.* Glencoe, IL: Free Press, 1955.

Payne, Karen, ed. *Between Ourselves: Letters Between Mothers and Daughters.* Boston: Houghton Mifflin, 1983.

Pearlman, Mickey, ed. *Mother Puzzles: Daughters and Mothers in Contemporary American Literature.* Westport, CT: Greenwood Press, 1989.

Peck, Ellen. "Good Old Motherhood Can Be an Evil, Too." *Today's Health,* March 1972, 70–71.

Peterson, E. T. "The Impact of Maternal Employment on the Mother-Daughter Relationship and the Daughter's Role Orientation." Ph.D. dissertation, University of Michigan, 1958.

Pilcer, Sonia Hanna. "Are You Just Like Your Mother?" *Seventeen,* February 1976, 44–52.

Pober, Madeline. "Mothers and Daughters—The Eternal Love-Hate Relationship." *Cosmopolitan,* July 1983, 119.

Pollock, Eleanor. "The Children Who Can't Stay Home." *Woman's Home Companion,* September 1954, 30.

Pollock, Griselda. "What's Wrong with Images of Women?" *Screen* 24 (Autumn 1977): 25–33.

Pope, Elizabeth. "Is a Working Mother a Threat to the Home?" *McCall's,* July 1955, 29.

Popper, Adrienne. "Mothers and Daughters." *Parents' Magazine,* April 1982, 53–58.

Poster, Mark. *Critical Theory of the Family.* London: Pluto Press, 1978.

Pribram, Deidre, ed. *Female Spectators: Looking at Film and Television.* London: Verso, 1988.

Radway, Janice. "Identifying Ideological Seams: Mass Culture, Analytic Method, and Political Practice." *Communication* 9 (1986): 93–123.

———. *Reading the Romance: Women, Patriarchy, and Popular Literature.* Chapel Hill: University of North Carolina Press, 1984.

Rafkin, Louise, ed. *Different Daughters: A Book by Mothers of Lesbians.* San Francisco: Cleis Press, 1987.

Raymond, Diane, ed. *Sexual Politics and Popular Culture.* Bowling Green, OH: Bowling Green State University Popular Press, 1990.

Reilly, Estelle. "Today's Daughters." *Woman's Home Companion,* July 1937, 22.

Reisman, David, with Nathan Glazer and Deeny Reuel. *The Lonely Crowd: A Study of the Changing American Character.* New York: Doubleday Anchor Books, 1955.

Rheingold, Joseph C. *The Fear of Being a Woman: A Theory of Maternal Destructiveness.* New York: Grune and Stratton, 1964.

————. *The Mother, Anxiety and Death.* Boston: Little, Brown, 1967.

Rich, Adrienne. *On Lies, Secrets, and Silences: Selected Prose 1966–1978.* New York: Norton, 1979.

————. *Of Woman Born: Motherhood as Experience and Institution.* New York: Norton, 1986.

Riley, Denise. *War in the Nursery: Theories of the Child and Mother.* London: Virago Press, 1983.

Rivers, Caryl, Rosalind Barnett, and Grace Baruch. *Beyond Sugar and Spice: How Women Grow, Learn, and Thrive.* New York: Putnam's, 1979.

Rose, Jacqueline. *Sexuality in the Field of Vision.* London: Verso, 1986.

Rosenman, Ellen Bayuk. *The Invisible Presence: Virginia Woolf and the Mother-Daughter Relationship.* Baton Rouge: Louisiana State University Press, 1986.

Rosinsky, Natalie M. "Mothers and Daughters: Another Minority Group." In *The Lost Tradition: Mothers and Daughters in Literature,* ed. Cathy N. Davidson and E. M. Broner, 280–290. New York: Frederick Ungar, 1980.

Rothblatt, Donald N., Daniel C. Garr, and Jo Sprague. *The Suburban Environment and Women.* New York: Praeger, 1979.

Rubin, Rachel. "Whose Apronstrings?" *American Home,* May 1944, 28.

Rubin, Theodore Isaac. "Psychiatrist's Notebook: Mothers and Daughters Who Can't Get Along." *Ladies Home Journal,* February 1981, 54.

Ruddick, Sara. "Maternal Thinking." *Feminist Studies* 6(2) 342–367.

————. *Maternal Thinking: Toward a Politics of Peace.* Boston: Beacon Press, 1989.

Rupp, Leila, and Verta Taylor. *Survival in the Doldrums: The American Women's Rights Movement 1945 to the 1960s.* New York: Oxford University Press, 1987.

Ryan, Mary. *The Empire of the Mother: American Writing About Domesticity 1830–1860.* New York: Harrington Press, 1985.

Sapirstein, Milton R. "The Paradox Mother." *Vogue,* August 15, 1955, 92–93.

Sayre, Nora. *Running Time: Films of the Cold War.* New York: Dial Press, 1982.

Schmidt, Elizabeth. "The Best Mothers Aren't Martyrs." *Parents' Magazine,* May 1961, 40.

Schultz, Terri. "The Feelings Too Many Daughters Are Afraid To Face." *Redbook,* October 1976, 108.

Sebald, Hans. *Momism: The Silent Disease of America.* Chicago: Nelson-Hall, 1976.

Secunda, Victoria. "Should You Divorce Your Mother?" *New Woman,* November 1988, 57–61.

———. *When You and Your Mother Can't Be Friends.* New York: Delacorte Press, 1990.

Seiter, Ellen. "Feminism and Ideology: The *Terms* of Women's Stereotypes." *Feminist Review* 22 (February 1986): 58–81.

———. "Semiotics and Television." In *Channels of Discourse,* ed. Robert Allen, 17–41. Chapel Hill: University of North Carolina Press, 1987.

Shapiro, Susan. "Between Love and Ambition: A Daughter and Mother Find Each Other." *Cosmopolitan,* November 1986, 64.

Shreve, Anita. *Remaking Motherhood: How Working Mothers Are Shaping Our Children's Future.* New York: Viking Penguin, 1987.

Shriver, Eunice Kennedy. "An Answer to the Attacks on Motherhood." *McCall's,* June 1965, 89.

Silverman, Kaja. *The Acoustic Mirror: The Female Voice in Psychoanalysis and Cinema.* Indianapolis: Indiana University Press, 1988.

Silverman, Sylvia. "Why Girls Are Like That." *Parents' Magazine,* March 1947, 29.

Simpson, Mona. "What My Mother Knew." *Mademoiselle,* October 1982, 106.

Sklar, Robert. *Movie-Made America: A Cultural History of American Movies.* New York: Vintage Books/Random House, 1975.

Smith, Liz. *The Mother Book.* New York: Crown, 1984.

Smith, M. Dwayne, and George D. Self. "The Congruence Between Mothers' and Daughters' Sex-role Attitudes: A Research Note." *Journal of Marriage and the Family* 42 (1980): 105–109.

Smith-Rosenberg, Caroll. "The Female World of Love and Ritual: Relations Between Women in Nineteenth-Century America." *Signs* 1 (1975): 1–29.

Snitow, Ann. "Thinking About *The Mermaid and the Minotaur.*" *Feminist Studies* 4 (June 1978): 190–198.

Sontag, Susan. *A Barthes Reader.* New York: Hill and Wang, 1982.

Spigel, Lynn. "Installing the Television Set: Popular Discourses on Television and Domestic Space, 1948–1955." *Camera Obscura* 16 (January 1988): 11–46.

———. "Television in the Family Circle: The Popular Reception of a New Medium." In *Logics of Television: Essays in Cultural Criticism,* ed. Patricia Mellencamp, 73–97. Bloomington: Indiana University Press, 1990.

Spock, Benjamin. "Should Girls Expect To Have Careers?" *Redbook,* March 1972, 50–54.

Stack, Carol. *All Our Kin: Strategies for Survival in a Black Community.* New York: Harper and Row, 1974.

Steedman, Carolyn. *Landscape for a Good Woman: A Story of Two Lives.* London: Virago, 1986.

Stein, Sara, and Carter Smith. "Return of Mom." *Saturday Review of Education,* April 1973, 37–40.

Stern, Leslie. "Feminism and Cinema: Exchanges." *Screen* 20 (1979–1980): 89–105.

Stinnett, Lon. "My Mother Loves Me! My Mother Loved Me!" *McCall's,* May 1969, 71.

Strecker, Edward A. "What's Wrong with American Mothers?" *Saturday Evening Post,* October 26, 1946, 14.

Suleiman, Susan Rubin. "On Maternal Splitting: A Propos of Mary Gordon's *Men and Angels.*" *Signs* 14 (1988): 25–41.

Susman, Warren. *Culture as History: The Transformation of American Society in the Twentieth Century.* New York: Pantheon, 1973.

Susman, Warren, with Edward Griffin. "Did Success Spoil the United States? Dual Representations in Postwar America." In *Recasting America: Culture and Politics in the Age of Cold War,* ed. Lary May, 19–37. Chicago: University of Chicago press, 1989.

Tan, Amy. *The Joy Luck Club.* New York: Putnam, 1989.

Taylor, Ella. *Prime Time Families: Television Culture in Postwar America.* Berkeley: University of California Press, 1989.

Taylor, Marion A. "What's It Like To Be a Mother?" *Parents' Magazine,* October 1943, 134.

Tener, Elizabeth. "You and Your Problem Mother." *Cosmopolitan,* June 1981, 228.

Thurman, Judith. "Ready to Wear: Are You Still Dressing for Your Mother?" *Mademoiselle,* September 1982, 244.

Tims, Hilton. *Emotion Pictures: The 'Women's Picture,' 1930–55.* London: Columbus Books, 1987.

Tornabene, Lyn. "The Liberation of Betty Friedan." *McCall's,* May 1971, 84.

Treblicot, Joyce, ed. *Mothering: Essays on Feminist Theory.* Totowa, NJ: Rowman and Allanheld, 1983.

Tuchman, Gaye. "Introduction: The Symbolic Annihilation of Women by the Mass Media." In *Hearth and Home: Images of Women in the Mass Media,* ed. Gaye Tuchman, Arlene Kaplan Daniels, and James Benet, 3–38. New York: Oxford University Press, 1978.

———. "The Newspapers as a Social Movement's Resource." In *Hearth and Home: Images of Women in the Mass Media,* ed. Gaye Tuchman, Arlene Kaplan Daniels, and James Benet, 186–215. New York: Oxford University Press, 1978.

Tuchman, Gaye, Arlene Kaplan Daniels, and James Benet, eds. *Hearth and Home: Images of Women in the Mass Media.* New York: Oxford University Press, 1978.

Velie, Lester. "Come Back to the Work Force, Mother!" *Reader's Digest,* September 1965, 201–210.

Von Miklos, Josephine. "Girls in Overall." *Parents' Magazine,* March 1943, 22.

Wade-Gayles, Gloria. "The Truths of Our Mothers' Lives: Mother-Daughter Relationships in Black Women's Fiction," *Sage* 1(2) (Fall 1984): 8.

Wagner, Jo Martin. "There Are Only 37 Things Wrong with My Daughter." *Good Housekeeping,* October 1955, 62.

Wagoner, Louisa C. "This Business of Being a Mother." *Parents' Magazine,* 1930, 18–20.

Walker, Alice. "Everyday Use." In *In Love and Trouble.* New York: Harcourt Brace Jovanovich, 1973.

———. *Meridian.* New York: Harcourt Brace Jovanovich, 1976.

Walker, Janet. "Hollywood, Freud and the Representation of Women: Regulation and Contradiction, 1945–early 60s." In *Home Is Where the Heart Is: Studies in Melodrama and the Woman's Film,* ed. Christine Gledhill, 197–214. London: British Film Institute, 1980.

Walsh, Andrea. *Women's Films and Female Experience, 1940–1950.* New York: Praeger, 1984.

Wandersee, Winifred. *On the Move: American Women in the 1970s.* Boston: Twayne, G. K. Hall, 1988.

———. *Women's Work and Family Values 1920–1940.* Cambridge, MA: Harvard University Press, 1989.

Ware, Susan. *Holding Their Own: American Women in the 1930s.* Boston: Twayne, 1982.

———. *Modern American Women: A Documentary History.* Chicago: Dorsey Press, 1989.

Washington, Mary Helen. "Alice Walker: Her Mother's Gifts." *Ms.,* June 1982, 38.

———. *Invented Lives.* Garden City, NY: Doubleday, 1987.

Wearing, Betsy. *The Ideology of Motherhood.* Sydney, Australia: George Allen and Unwin, 1984.

Weedon, Chris. *Feminist Practice and Post-Structuralist Theory.* Oxford: Basil Blackwell, 1987.

Weibel, Kathryn. *Mirror Mirror: Images of Women Reflected in Popular Culture.* Garden City, NY: Anchor Press/Doubleday, 1977.

Weiner, Lynn Y. *From Working Girl to Working Mother: The Female Labor Force in the United States 1820–1980.* Chapel Hill: University of North Carolina Press, 1985.

Westin, Jeane. *Making Do: How Women Survived the '30s*. Chicago: Follett, 1976.

Westkott, Marcia. "Mothers and Daughters in the World of the Father." *Frontiers* 3(2) (1978): 16–21.

White, Alice Austin. "Modern Daughters." *Forum* 87 (1932): 61–64.

White, Lynn. *Educating Our Daughters*. New York: Harper and Row, 1950.

Whitman, Evelyn Ardis. "Twelve Ways To Be a Friend." *Parents' Magazine*, June 1944, 72.

Whitton, Mary Ormsbee. "If I Were That Girl's Mother!" *Parents' Magazine*, August 1932, 17.

Wiggins, A. *Sex Role Stereotyping: A Content Analysis of Radio and Television Programs and Advertisements*. Vancouver: National Watch on Images of Women in the Media, 1985.

Williams, Linda. "Feminist Film Theory: *Mildred Pierce* and the Second World War." In *Female Spectators: Looking at Film and Television*, ed. E. Deidre Pribram, 12–30. London: Verso, 1988.

———. "Something Else Besides a Mother: *Stella Dallas* and the Maternal Melodrama." In *Home Is Where the Heart Is: Studies in Melodrama and the Woman's Film*, ed. Christine Gledhill, 299–325. London: British Film Institute, 1987.

———, and Ruby Rich. "The Right of Re-vision: Michele Citron's *Daughter-Rite*." *Film Quarterly* 35 (1981): 17–21.

Williams, Raymond. *Communications*, 3rd ed. New York: Penguin, 1976.

———. *Marxism and Literature*. Oxford: Oxford University Press, 1977.

———. *Television: Technology and Cultural Form*. New York: Schocken Books, 1975.

Williamson, Judith. *Decoding Advertisements: Ideology and Meaning in Advertising*. New York: Marion Boyars, 1978.

———. "Woman Is an Island: Femininity and Colonization." In *Studies in Entertainment: Critical Approaches to Mass Culture*, ed. Tania Modleski, 99–118. Bloomington: Indiana University Press, 1986.

Willis, Paul. *Learning to Labour*. Farnborough, England: Saxon House, 1977.

———. *Profane Culture*. London: Routledge and Kegan Paul, 1978.

"Window Dressing on the Set: Women and Minorities in Television." Report of the United States Commission on Civil Rights, August 1977.

Winship, Janice. "Handling Sex." In *Looking On: Images of Femininity in the Visual Arts and Media*, ed. Rosemary Betterton, 25–39. New York: Pandora Press, 1987.

Wodak, Ruth. *The Language of Love and Guilt: Mother-Daughter Rela-*

*tionships from a Cross-Cultural Perspective.* Philadelphia: J. Benjamins, 1986.

Wolfson, Cynthia. "Getting Mad at Mom and Living Happily Ever After." *Glamour,* May 1986, 54.

Wollen, Peter. *Signs and Meaning in the Cinema.* London: Secker and Warburg/BFI, 1972.

"Women in the Wasteland Fight Back." Report on the image of women portrayed in TV programming. Washington, DC, National Organization for Women, National Capitol Area, 1972.

Woolf, Janet. *The Social Production of Art.* New York: New York University Press, 1981.

Wylie, Philip. *Generation of Vipers.* New York: Pocket Books, 1960.

———. *Sons and Daughters of Mom.* Garden City, NY: Doubleday, 1971.

Young, Iris. "Is Male Gender Identity the Cause of Male Domination?" In *Mothering: Essays on Feminist Theory,* ed. Joyce Treblicot, 129–146. Totowa, NJ: Rowman and Allanheld, 1983.

# Selected Film Chronology

*Dancing Mothers*, 1926, directed by Herbert Brenon

*Lady for a Day*, 1933, directed by Frank Capra

*Little Women*, 1933, directed by George Cukor

*Imitation of Life*, 1934, directed by John Stahl

*Stella Dallas*, 1937, directed by King Vidor

*Four Daughters*, 1938, directed by Michael Curtiz

*Four Wives*, 1939, directed by Michael Curtiz

*The Old Maid*, 1939, directed by Edmund Goulding

*Yes, My Darling Daughter*, 1939, directed by William Keighley

*The Little Foxes*, 1941, directed by William Wyler

*Now, Voyager*, 1942, directed by Irving Rapper

*Claudia*, 1943, directed by Edmund Goulding

*Since You Went Away*, 1943, directed by John Cromwell

*A Tree Grows in Brooklyn*, 1943, directed by Elia Kazan

*Watch on the Rhine*, 1943, directed by Herman Shumlin

*Mr. Skeffington*, 1944, directed by Vincent Sherman

*Mildred Pierce*, 1945, directed by Michael Curtiz

*The Best Years of Our Lives*, 1946, directed by William Wyler

*Claudia and David*, 1946, directed by Walter Lang

*Possessed*, 1947, directed by Curtis Bernhardt

*I Remember Mama*, 1948, directed by George Stevens

*Three Daring Daughters*, 1948, directed by Fred Wilcox

*Little Women*, 1949, directed by Mervyn LeRoy

*Cheaper by the Dozen*, 1950, directed by Walter Lang

*Hard, Fast and Beautiful*, 1951, directed by Ida Lupino

*Belles on Their Toes*, 1952, directed by Henry Levin

*I'll Cry Tomorrow*, 1955, directed by Daniel Mann

*Picnic*, 1955, directed by Joshua Logan

*Rebel Without a Cause*, 1955, directed by Nicholas Ray

*All That Heaven Allows*, 1956, directed by Douglas Sirk

*Peyton Place*, 1957, directed by Mark Robson

*The Goddess*, 1958, directed by John Cromwell

*The Restless Years*, 1958, directed by Helmut Kautner

*Imitation of Life*, 1959, directed by Douglas Sirk

*The Parent Trap*, 1961, directed by David Swift

*A Pocketful of Miracles*, 1961, directed by Frank Capra

*Return to Peyton Place*, 1961, directed by Jose Ferrer

*Splendor in the Grass*, 1961, directed by Elia Kazan

*The Pumpkin Eater*, 1964, directed by Jack Clayton

*Where Love Has Gone*, 1964, directed by Edward Dymtryk

*Inside Daisy Clover*, 1965, directed by Robert Mulligan

*Madame X*, 1966, directed by David Lowell Rich

*The Graduate*, 1967, directed by Mike Nichols

*Rachel, Rachel*, 1968, directed by Paul Newman

*The Last Picture Show*, 1971, directed by Peter Bogdanovich

*Carrie*, 1976, directed by Brian de Palma

*The Turning Point*, 1977, directed by Herbert Ross

*Autumn Sonata*, 1978, directed by Ingmar Bergman

*Daughter Rite*, 1978, directed by Michelle Citron

*Interiors*, 1978, directed by Woody Allen

*An Unmarried Woman*, 1978, directed by Paul Mazursky

*Mommie, Dearest*, 1981, directed by Frank Perry

*Only When I Laugh*, 1981, directed by Glenn Jordan

*Frances*, 1982, directed by Graeme Clifford

*Terms of Endearment*, 1983, directed by James Brooks

*Testament*, 1983, directed by Lynne Littman

*'night, Mother*, 1986, directed by Tom Moore

*Bred and Born*, 1987, directed by Joanna Davis and Mary Pat Lee

*The Glass Menagerie*, 1987, directed by Paul Newman

*Nuts*, 1987, directed by Martin Ritt

*September*, 1987, directed by Woody Allen

*The Stepfather*, 1987, directed by Joseph Rubin

*A World Apart*, 1988, directed by Chris Menges

*Mermaids*, 1990, directed by Richard Benjamin

*Postcards from the Edge*, 1990, directed by Mike Nichols

*Stella*, 1990, directed by John Erman

# Selected Television Chronology

## Sitcoms

"Mama," 1949–1957 (CBS)

"Father Knows Best," 1954–1962 (CBS, 1954–1955, NBC, 1955–1958, CBS, 1958–1962)

"The Donna Reed Show," 1958–1966 (ABC)

"The Patty Duke Show," 1963–1966 (ABC)

"The Mary Tyler Moore Show," 1970–1977 (CBS)

"All in the Family," 1971–1983 (CBS)

"Maude," 1972–1974 (CBS)

"Rhoda," 1974–1978 (CBS)

"One Day at a Time," 1975–1980 (CBS)

"Phyllis," 1975–1977 (CBS)

## Made-for-Television Movies and Specials

"Like Mom, Like Me," 1978, CBS

"Mother and Daughter: The Loving War," 1980, HBO

"Family Secrets," 1984, NBC

"Terrible Things My Mother Told Me," 1988, ABC

"Like Mother, Like Daughter," 1989, Lifetime

"Mothers and Daughters," 1989, "Oprah Winfrey Show," CBS

"Supermom's Daughter," 1989, HBO

# Index

Compositor: Graphic Composition
Text: 11/13 Caledonia
Display: Caledonia
Printer and Binder: Haddon Craftsmen